Breathing Out

Also by David Dalton

Piece of My Heart: A Portrait of Janis Joplin

El Sid: Saint Vicious

Been Here and Gone: A Memoir of the Blues

James Dean—The Mutant King

Faithfull: An Autobiography

Living with the Dead

Also by Coco Pekelis Dalton

Everything I Know I Learned on Acid

Breathing Out

Peggy Lipton

with

David and Coco Dalton

St. Martin's Press ⚏ New York

www.stmartins.com

BOOK DESIGN BY JENNIFER ANN DADDIO

Library of Congress Cataloging-in-Publication Data

Lipton, Peggy, 1947–
    Breathing out / Peggy Lipton with David and Coco
Dalton.— 1st ed.
      p. cm.
    ISBN 0-312-32413-8
    EAN 978-0312-32413-1
      I. Lipton, Peggy, 1947– 2. Actors—United States—
    Biography. I. Dalton, David, 1945– II. Dalton, Coco.
    III. Title.

PN2287.L47A3 2005
792.02'8'092—dc22
[B]   2004063289

First Edition: June 2005

1   3   5   7   9   10   8   6   4   2

For all the beauty my eyes have beheld, for the words I have spoken and ultimately written here, for the sacred deities I have encountered, for the sacred poems I have recited and sung, for every time my heart has turned over with excitement and anticipation, for every person I have reached out to and in some way helped, for those who have cherished me in return and for the great love that lives in my heart, I dedicate this book to

Masta Ram Kenneth Joseph Lipton
May 27, 1948–September 1, 1998

Contents

I Was a Hippie Cop

The Story of Q

Being Momma

Childhood

I .

Changeling

*In folklore, a child who is
secretly substituted for
another by fairies.*

As a child I would often make
myself lie absolutely still before
falling asleep. Once there, fantasy would overtake me. It was a world
that I alone owned, a place I had dominion
over. I chose the thoughts and the desires. I
played my own game and always came out
the winner. No one and nothing could
rein me in.

In the way that changelings know, I always sensed I didn't quite belong. I knew I
had to find others like me—the magical
helpers who would show me how to get to
the other side, although I didn't know exactly what it was or how to get there. The
burning desire to be free of the small-town
life never left me for long, and I stoked its
fire by reading poetry and tawdry novels,
going to movies and Broadway plays, and
listening to all kinds of music. These were
my doors to the other side. But I was stuck

on the wrong side of the looking glass, waiting for that *Alice in Wonderland* hatch to suddenly appear. One tumble could, and would, send me into the netherworld of my dreams.

In that enchanted space before falling asleep, I sometimes saw myself as the actress everyone was talking about. Or I was the possessed journalist hunkered down at her typewriter, capturing the latest big news story. At other times I imagined myself a poet like Sylvia Plath, with every nerve in my body alive and aching to tell my strange and haunted tale. I read *The Bell Jar* at fifteen as I was embarking on my career, worried that I had fallen into it, and that if I wasn't careful and vigilant and in some way anchored to the outside world, I could slip over the edge into a dark abyss.

I kissed and hugged my pillow nightly. It became the boy or man I wanted to love me. I imagined all my embraces being returned. Much of it was a blur of longing and I would fall asleep, blissful or sad. When I was a young teen, my sexual fantasies ran rampant. I began having these fantasies during the day at school, or at home watching TV, or spending the afternoon listening to Johnny Mathis or John Coltrane. I had yet to experience love. I still had never touched myself, not even my small, budding breasts. Oh, but the mind was having wild sex all the time: hot visions of prolonged and languorous kissing sessions and pledges of love—to Dion and all the Belmonts, James Dean, and Warren Beatty. I could wrap my long, skinny arms around them all. Spin the bottle, so popular with pre-teens, could send me into a frenzy—if I got lucky enough to get invited to one of "those" parties.

One night I was invited to a thirteen-year-old's basement party. Parents redid the basements of their suburban homes in the 1950s as recreation rooms. Kids had their own friends over to play the forty-fives in their ever-increasing record collections on a jukebox or Victrola, drink Coca-Cola, and have make-out sessions. Moms with their pageboy hairdos, dressed in billowing cocktail dresses, would swirl into the underground adolescent Mecca with a cocktail in hand to check us out. We would dance or huddle in corners, eating Wise potato chips and giggling over which boys we liked.

At one of these spin-the-bottle parties I wore a beautiful blue mohair turtleneck I had painstakingly picked out. I often got hand-me-down clothes from a friend of my mother's—all items her daughter had out-grown: checkered shirtwaist dresses, full skirts, Peter-Pan collared blouses, and sweaters. That night I chose carefully from my newly obtained wardrobe, applying blue eye shadow to match the sweater. Quite uncere-moniously, during Frankie Lymon's "Why Do Fools Fall in Love," I was told by a nasty, nasal little girl from across the street, "You have body odor." Embarrassed, I surreptitiously smelled my armpits all night long.

That year at summer camp I had my first kiss on a hayride with Bobby Leon. It was a romantic, picture-perfect setting. I remember thinking: "This is it! This is what I've waited for: The beginning of life. And I'm do-ing it! I'm actually doing it!" He gave me a sloppy wet kiss, then pulled away. Suddenly I was an observer, oddly outside of the situation, knowing I didn't measure up: my breasts, body odor, and, by now, braces and acne.

At fifteen I fell for Allan the heartbreaker. He was twenty and engaged to a beautiful high school senior. Allan lived on what people in the Five Towns agreed was the wrong side of the tracks. This only added to his al-lure. I went to the Town Diner on Central Avenue looking for him, then to Juniors Diner in Hewlett, in hopes of a sighting. He drove a red Chevy. I sat at the windows of these diners anticipating that any minute he would turn the corner in his convertible—hopefully without his girlfriend. I knew he was too much of a catch for me. After all, I was young and not very popular. I felt at any moment I would be crushed. But my passion ran strong as I plotted for months for a way to get him to notice me.

Finally, I got up the nerve to invite him out under the ruse of a triple date. His two best friends with my two best friends. It was a very good plan. We went to Coney Island and rode the Cyclone rollercoaster to-gether on a summer night in seedy Brooklyn. We picked at sticky pink cotton candy and chased it down with Nathan's hotdogs. Between the food and the ride I got sick to my stomach. I was caught in a valiant struggle: trying to appear grown up and sophisticated, while not revealing that at any moment I might barf. But it wasn't just the junk I had piled in that night. My equilibrium was teetering and panic was setting in by the time he walked me to my door and thanked me.

"Good night, Peg," he whispered and gave me a little kiss on the cheek. It was all over before it even began. My first love, and not even reciprocated. There was absolutely nothing I could do to win his love. I cried and cried and cried and looked in the mirror constantly to see what was wrong with me. Well, for one thing, I wasn't Nancy, his beautiful teen-queen fiancée. In the mirror I saw only my awkwardness.

2.

The Five Towns

grew up in the Five Towns on the south shore of Long Island, New York. I was given the name Peggy Ann at birth. Forty years later, I learned from my father that my mother went back and changed my birth certificate to read Margaret Ann, feeling the name Peggy was either too Irish or too unsophisticated. But it was too late. I was always known as Peggy. The Five Towns were quite infamous in those days, known for being sassy, brassy, and rich. Lawrence, Cedarhurst, Inwood, Hewlett, and Woodmere: each town bordering the other. I lived in Lawrence, having moved there at the tender age of two from the big, bad, beautiful New York City of the late '40s. I might as well have moved to Mars.

The area was originally a WASP enclave, dotted with duck ponds and green marshy swamps. Magnificent old brick estates loomed over huge yards set back from the tree-lined streets. And into this sleepy enclave came a large post-war Jewish population, families by the hundreds, fathers donning yarmulkes and some wearing prayer shawls. Delicatessens featuring a Sunday brunch of lox, bagels, and chopped liver; Reform, Conservative, and Orthodox synagogues springing up across the towns. Pedal-pusher-wearing, bouffant-haired moms with their baby prams and maids in tow walked the avenues with their kids trailing behind on new tricycles.

Jewish families entered the Five Towns as if flung from slingshots—which in a sense they were: They were immigrants or refugees fleeing racism and a hostile world, all combustible nervous energy, humor, and angst. Their children were spoiled. Here they could have everything they wanted. Things their parents and grandparents had only dreamed of. There were the private beach clubs, the expensive shops on Central Avenue, the dances at the Temple and unlimited access to Hebrew schools, tutors, doctors, dentists, and orthodontists.

Not far from this, the town of Inwood rested uneasily on the other side of the Long Island railroad tracks in Lawrence. Here, the black families and most of the Italians had settled. Without my parents knowing, I'd walk the seven or eight blocks from home, cross the tracks and wander around, sometimes going into a candy store or a pizza parlor. I had to see it and experience it in any way I could. Living in such close proximity to a poor neighborhood made me aware that there was more to growing up in the world than hot-rod cars and parties in newly renovated basements.

We lived on a very beautiful street, lined with elm and birch trees that led to a golf course and, ultimately, wound its way to the Rockaway Hunt Club, where I knew of no Jews who belonged. The two sides of our street were like before and after photographs. On one side—ours—were the newly built homes; on the other, exquisite old mansions.

I loved scaring myself when I'd walk home from a friend's house in the late afternoon. In the winter it was dark and there were unpaved streets, with ominous hedges and unlit homes. I'd relish the stillness of the evening, half walking, half running down my block. Here, all around me as a child, was a feast for the senses. There were enormous specimen trees on acres of land, the majestic Atlantic Ocean a short car ride away, and flower-filled gardens, marshes, and rolling lawns. The physical beauty of the Five Towns was extraordinary. It was idyllic and safe, as long as you didn't cross the tracks.

My family was upper-middle-class, but we weren't wealthy. And my mother never did anything that the Five Town ladies did. She was cut from a different cloth and enjoyed being the individualist she truly was. Other parents would send their kids to Florida for school break. My mother never did that. We spent our vacations in "exotic" Atlantic City.

I don't think my Mom was happy on Long Island. I could sense it even though she never voiced it. Whenever she could, she'd drive into the city and visit museums. She could never be a country club person—she made a bold statement just by wearing jeans and smoking a pipe. Nobody behaved like that in the Five Towns in 1953. But these eccentricities were never to draw attention to herself; they were just her natural way of doing things. Rita Lipton was a wonderful painter. Her canvases were filled with vibrant colors and striking subjects: nudes, still-life, and abstracts. She painted in oils and watercolors—she could do it all. She had more than a dozen one-woman shows over the years, received numerous awards, and was listed in *Who's Who in American Art*. As a child I didn't appreciate her talent. She was so high strung, and sitting with her in her studio in the basement of our home, I sometimes felt nothing but dread. She wanted me to paint with her, but I had absolutely no ability. I just wanted her to listen to what was in my heart, but I held back as much as she did. At times, Rita was an excessive and compulsive character. It's amazing and slightly sad that she managed to live in that middle-class community as a brilliant artist with her outbursts and strange unconventional ways, while other mothers were baking apple strudel and holding coffee klatches.

My bedroom was my sanctuary. I could spend hours alone reading or listening to music. I wrote plenty of poetry in that space, poetry that I would later gather and make into my high school thesis. In the spring the backyard became an extension of my cocoon. The branches of a beautiful tree in the center of the lawn touched my second-story windowsill. From that perch I watched the seasons come and go. The glorious tree with its leaves, first green then burnt orange, and finally bare, was like a talisman.

At night when its branches moved with the wind, I listened and let the gentle sound put me to sleep. All my treasures and icons were in my bedroom. A little Geisha doll my father had brought from Japan, a stuffed animal won at Rockaway Playland, and pictures of movie stars, writers, and models pinned to a bulletin board on the wall: images of Warren Beatty, Audrey Hepburn, Joyce Carol Oates, James Dean, and Delores Hawkins—a top model at the time.

On my fourteenth birthday my parents gave me a television. I watched it until all hours of the night, often finding it difficult to get up for school the next day. These were the halcyon days of live theatre on TV—great actors performing weekly dramas written by the brightest new playwrights in America: Tennessee Williams, Gore Vidal, Edward Albee, and Paddy Chayevsky. I was so moved by the plays of William Inge (who had written *Dark at the Top of the Stairs*, *Picnic*, and *Bus Stop*) that, as a freshman in junior college, I interviewed him and wrote my semester thesis on his life and works.

I always had to have a crush on someone. My heart was in a state of perpetual longing. Any object of desire that could take my mind off my teenage angst and insecurities made me feel empowered. My huge crush then was on Paul Burke, the lead in the TV series *Naked City*. "There are eight million stories in the Naked City. This has been one of them," was the tag line. I wanted to *be* one of those stories. A girl who loves so deeply that her universe is transformed. At the center of my bulletin board shrine was a picture of Paul Burke torn from *TV Guide*. He wore a classic fedora and a suit and tie. His smile was enigmatic; he reminded me of my father.

One afternoon while my older brother, Bob, was out, I oh-so-carefully snooped around his room—a true Pandora's box. He was by then a very hip rocker teenager, with his greased-down hair, black leather motorcycle jacket, boots, and extreme good looks. I knew his room was forbidden territory and that I could get into serious trouble, but my curiosity outstripped my fear. Every moment in that room, my heart beat wildly as I discovered paperback books about gangs like the Amboy Dukes and came across a wolf deck—playing cards of naked women smiling and gazing erotically over their creamy white shoulders. I even found a knife. Though I thought I had carefully covered my tracks, when Bob came home he knew that I had entered his domain. While I was eating dinner that night, he went into my room and, in a fit of retribution, inked out Paul Burke's face on my wall. I was furious. I complained to my parents, but they had so little control over my brother. They really couldn't do much except try to enforce the room boundaries a little better.

"Just don't go in there, Peggy," they told me in an admonishing tone of voice. They didn't want any more problems. But I did go back many times after that. What younger sister could resist the temptation of mining the hidden treasures of her older brother's mysterious world, especially when he was the most feared, revered, and charismatic character she had ever known?

3.

Family Secrets

had two brothers: Bob was three and a half years older and Kenny eighteen months younger. Bob told me that his first memory of me was on the night I was born. While Mom was in the hospital giving birth, he waited with the new baby nurse at home. Upon hearing the news that he now had a baby sister, he threw up. He had been brought up by my mother's family, the Irish side. While Dad was in the war, Mom had moved to Atlantic City to be with her parents and her sister. They anointed little Robert "the Prince of Ventnor Avenue" and lavished him with attention and affection. Until, that is, my dad came back from the war. When he saw his father for the first time at age three and a half, it was in a hospital. He encountered a big hairy man who was swallowing gobs of pills to cure the "trench foot" he had contracted on the march across France after the Normandy invasion. Bob had gone from being an only child without a father, to the son of a man with very strict ideas about how to raise him. Now I had arrived. He had a baby sister, and suddenly she was the favorite. His world had altered again.

Dad never hid his profound sense of disappointment with Bob. Whether it was not getting good grades in school, not graduating from Harvard, not becoming a lawyer, or not *doing* something with his life. In Dad's eyes, Bob was always a failure, and it became a self-fulfilling prophecy. He was kicked out of one high school after another and was always getting into trouble with authority: teachers, police, anyone and everyone who might provoke his defiance.

By the time I was seven, Bob and my father had arguments that shook the walls of our tiny house. I cried. I loved them both. My mother would slam the door to her room and not come out. Only after Bob had found a way of channeling all the frustration and anger that had built up over the years did his behavior change. He found an outlet for his energies in acting. Overnight, his antisocial and antagonistic behavior stopped. He had found his calling. Lee Strasberg, founder of the Actor's Studio, recognized Bob's talent, immediately took him in, and became a father figure to him. Over the years, that calling has only grown and deepened. Bob emerged from a difficult childhood to become a very talented actor, director, and teacher.

Kenny was the "lost child." Being the third born was already a strike against him. His needs were often ignored as my parents' energy went in other directions. Kenny had asthma that would get so severe he would be rushed to the hospital in the middle of the night. I never felt as sad for anyone as I did for my baby brother, although these late-night hospital visits were usually hidden from me. I remember being sent to bed without ever knowing if he was all right. Like twins, we were inseparable. We also fought like cats and dogs.

One day when I was fourteen, I realized that I had gotten too strong. After punching Kenny in the eye, I was as shocked as he was to see the area around it turn green. I apologized profusely and cuddled him. Then we laughed and I vowed never to hit him again. Our childhood tiffs were over.

Kenny had difficulties in school with reading and writing because he was severely dyslexic, a disorder undiagnosed at the time. Mom and Dad didn't understand, nor did they have the patience to deal with it, so I always felt responsible. When I finally went off to school in New York, he had to fend for himself. Ironically, he harbored frustration and a temper much like my mother's. Yet he was always a seeker. At seventeen, he went around the world for a semester on a ship with 300 other students. That changed his life and destiny. By eighteen he was making the first of many trips to India. It was there that he found solace and acceptance. I've never known anyone who had a sweeter, kinder, or gentler essence. His faith in the goodness of humanity and his love for God stirred my soul. I always called him "the ecstatic." This was his natural state when he had the freedom to be himself.

4.

Rita's Hidden Past

My mother had astonishing poise, stunning clothes and dazzling taste. Yet she was a dyed-in-the-wool bohemian who could make friends with anyone. She didn't care where or what you came from—high or low, it didn't matter. People were immediately attracted to her. When Rita walked into a room, her energy would shift out of her somewhat agitated state and she'd become radiant. All her insecurities would fall away. Her presence was magnetic, and the whole room would gravitate toward her. She was a buxom natural redhead, an extraordinary beauty with tremendous charisma. I certainly hadn't inherited her looks or acquired any of her social graces.

My parents loved going out at night: dinner, cocktails or card playing. They were always up for an evening out. When they were readying themselves, I would feel my anxiety take over. The sun went down and night seemed to fall with the impact of a sledgehammer. I dreaded them leaving. I didn't want to be home with my two brothers and the babysitter. Things would always go awry. Bob would get frustrated and tease Kenny and me. And Kenny, being so sensitive, would just crumble. Kenny and I shared a bedroom until I was ten. I moved six feet down the hall, and each night for a year he'd beg to come in and sleep with me. I always let him in until one night I finally cut the cord. After pleading with me to let him sleep in my room just one more time, he collapsed outside my door in a heap. My heart broke. I don't know where I got the strength to say no, but I knew we'd never get over our dependency on each other if I let it go on.

Most nights after dinner, I would enter my mother's sanctum to watch her put on her makeup. I was nervous. I wanted to scream. I tried to distract her by hinting at how lonely I would feel and then pleaded with her not to leave at all. She'd smile and tell me I was exaggerating. I would kneel by her vanity table and momentarily find solace watching her immersed in her preparations. She was beautiful and very glamorous. She would get out of her painting overalls, put on a lace corset, and lean toward the mirror. She'd pile on black cake mascara that she'd moisten with saliva, then dust her face and ample cleavage with white powder from a pink down puff. I wanted a normal mother, someone who stayed home with you at night and wore an apron, someone who'd spend the day figuring out recipies and cooking dinner for her family. But that just wasn't my mother. She was an artist. She was volatile. Years went by with me constantly afraid she was going to get angry, scream, turn red, and lock herself in her room. Her fits, though, were never aimed at me. I never posed a problem for her. I was the good little girl.

I just wanted to keep as far away as I could when she got into those states. These were unsettling times. I didn't understand her at all, and she didn't have a clue who I was. The truth is we three kids never understood our parents. There were so many secrets in both my parents' families. Their lives, what they felt—it was all a mystery to us. My brother Bob often would ask me, "Who are they?"

My mother's past was the most mysterious of all. It was as if she'd been an entirely different person before she met my father. There was no "before"; she'd simply wiped it out. When routine goings-on got too much for her, she had to go to bed at midday. She never told me one thing about her past, *ever*. I longed to know who she had been before having us, what she had seen and how she had lived, but I was afraid to ask. Her moods were precarious and her temper uncontrollable. I didn't want to set her off.

Later in my life I would come to know many things about her. Her maiden name was Rita Hetty Benson. She was a fiery red-haired, green-eyed Irish Jew, breathtakingly beautiful once she passed her awkward stage. She didn't hesitate to play on her looks and smart personality to win people over. She was born in Dublin, Ireland, the youngest of three children. Shortly afterward, the family moved to Glasgow, Scotland, and lived for a short time in a beautiful house with servants.

As a child growing up in Scotland, her temper sometimes got the better of her. Her mind was acutely focused and radarlike, and, for the most part, she got what she wanted. Her jaw would clamp down and her determination would emanate right through her pores. At that point, nothing could stop her. She could be mean and accusatory, and even with her great beauty she was profoundly insecure.

This quality, I believe, had something to do with her mother—my grandmother—who was unable to show affection. My mother never showed me the affection and attention I longed for, either—the kissing and cuddling I craved. My grandmother Jennie was a proper English lady from a large, strict family. With a substantial dowry in tow, she married an immigrant tailor named Hymen Benson, from Lithuania. For a while, they lived in an elegantly furnished home in Glasgow, which was foreclosed after my grandfather won and then lost all his money gambling on horses. He was a sweet man with the bluest eyes and palest skin. He was wonderful and loving with his children. In 1928 my grandparents could no longer afford to keep the family together and sent their daughters, Rita and Pearl, off to Nyack, New York, to be with cousins, go to work, and attend school. My mother went to high school for a month and then, at the age of sixteen, she left on a train to New York City and never returned.

Pearl nearly went crazy looking for Rita in the city, and once she found her, begged her to come back. Rita refused—and from that moment on began to reinvent herself. She was highly sophisticated despite her lack of formal education. Running from her rigid European roots and strict upbringing, she became a rebel and a true bohemian, and I most likely got my own rebellious streak from her. From that point on, Rita fended for herself and carved out a life—ready to take on a new identity in the big city.

I only know of these details from Aunt Pearl, whom I took care of when she was in her eighties. She shed some light on their childhood. Rita, she told me, had worked as a photographer's assistant, doctoring negatives, and as an illustrator and a sometime model. She had also studied art and sculpting at the Art Students League. Then she quit school completely. Rita loved to party and socialize. She had also been a dance-hall girl and was kept by a wealthy married man, a fact that slipped out in a fit of tears at my aunt's apartment, years after Rita died. My aunt didn't want me to know any of this, but she felt guilty about harboring these secrets. I extracted the information from her with bribes of chocolate and cigarettes.

There were so many family secrets that I discovered as an adult: the heart attack death or possible suicide of an uncle, which no one would clarify; the death of a baby dropped by a nurse; the loss of great fortunes; the affairs; a young, close relative in a mental hospital on Staten Island; the shunning of the relatives who didn't measure up to my parents' high standards, and many more. This pattern of withholding spanned a lifetime, filtered down into our lives, and came to rest on the children. So all was hidden, and as time went on we learned to hide, too.

Before her marriage, Rita traveled each year back to Europe on the *Queen Mary* with the New York City Ballet. Though she wasn't a ballet dancer she had made friends with the troupe, and she in turn became their mascot. According to my aunt, they loved my mother so much they took her on all their trips. Mother was as chic as they came, with great taste in clothes, food, and art. She would rather freeze her ass off walking the six blocks to the market in the winter than do without her quail eggs for breakfast.

Rita went from New York to Hollywood in the 1930s with some guy on the back of a motorcycle. Once there, she became even more glamorous, wearing her flaming red hair bobbed and close to her face. In a photograph that sits on my desk, she is posing on a wide stretch of sand at Santa Monica Beach, a knit one-piece bathing suit clinging to her voluptuous body.

5.

The Man in the Fedora

My father was the product of mismatched Jewish parents. His father, Max Lipton, had come on the proverbial boat from Russia, another poor immigrant in a sea of many thousands. Grandpa Max was a self-made man. He had studied to be a rabbi, but had left home as a young man and ended up taking care of his parents, who owned a dry-goods store on the Bowery. Grandpa Max learned some English, hustled, and eventually owned and ran a garment factory in North Carolina. Like my other grandfather, he, too, was a gambler. My mother could barely tolerate his presence—not that she told any of us, but as kids that was just the feeling we got. It was always vaguely uncomfortable and disquieting when Max would show up for our Passover seder puffing on his cigar and giving us cash that he pulled from his suit pockets.

Mom's tension around Dad's family was impossible to ignore. Nevertheless, it felt pathetically good when any of our family came together. I craved something that I would never get, a family that loved and understood each other, hugged, and kissed—an open family with the courage to expose the secrets that had shut down their longing and dreams. My dad's mother's family were also Russian Jews but, as my mother would say, an altogether different kettle of fish—a more cultured clan of high-rolling, steel-nerved gamblers. Though I never really knew my paternal grandmother, Alice, I'm told that she was elegant, cold, and fiercely domineering and that my mother was the only one who wasn't afraid of her. They forged a close relationship leading right up to the time Alice died in my mother's arms. Years later, in a strange echo of that relationship, I would form a similar bond with a schizophrenic mother-in-law.

Harold Lipton, my dad, was a New Yorker. He had lived with his mother until he was thirty. He idolized her and was raised to take over his absent father's role. Wearing a Homburg hat, he squired my grandmother around New York at the tender age of six.

My mother met my father on a blind date at a concert in Central Park and wasn't impressed. She later confided that she hadn't wanted to go that night, and was only doing a favor for a friend so they could double date with his brother. She was looking for someone a little flashier, perhaps. My father was incredibly handsome, but he wasn't a flashy guy. His personality was contained and subtle.

Then one day they met again by chance. Just as World War II was declared, they declared their love and married. I'm told the photographs barely capture what a beautiful couple they were. He was madly in love with her, but she knew once married it would be hard for her to contain her wildness and sense of adventure. Knowing my mother, I'm sure she carefully weighed the pros and cons. Just as I would, later, in similar circumstances. Perhaps my parents married to forge a bond, just in case Dad didn't return from the war, for within a month he was off to Europe, a sergeant in the infantry. And there he stayed for the next three and a half years.

My father was everything to me. I idolized him. He graduated from City College at sixteen, going on to Columbia University and Harvard Law School. When he returned from the war, he set up a private law practice in Manhattan on Madison Avenue. He was a typical nine-to-five commuter-train guy, with his hat and folded newspaper. But in other ways he was very different. Self-possessed, elegant, and extremely fastidious. He always had to have his tea served in a teacup—never in a mug. At restaurants he ordered the best wines and always insisted on paying the check. He was color blind, so my mother picked out the ties to go with his suits. Still, he knew how to dress. Dad had superb manners and a way of listening that complemented his skills as a successful lawyer.

My father was my moral role model. While helping me with homework, he would sit and talk to me in my room about what it meant to be a good person. Dad never divulged much about his own feelings, and I in turn was unable to tell him about mine: my insecurities about being teased and being unpopular at school. There was no time or place in our family for sharing thoughts and feelings. Anytime anyone felt they wanted to share something they'd tune out, go to their room and shut the door. And so I turned to my dad in other ways, asking him to explain homework problems and to help me to write essays. I always wanted to be near him— preferably without my mother, but that was quite impossible. Her health and personal demands always took top priority. Although she suffered from migraine headaches, a bout with polio, and a severe thyroid condition, she mesmerized my dad with her artistic gifts, intelligence, beauty, and grace. My mother always came first.

When Dad was eighty years old, the California law firm where he had worked for twenty-five years let him go. Instead of retiring, he again opened a law practice and continued to maintain his cheerful, positive attitude. Dad was as bright during those years as he had been as a young man starting out.

My father was a caring and gentle man and I loved him dearly. I accepted who he was even though he was no longer perfect in my eyes. Both my parents were formidable people. They had looks, intelligence, and so-cial grace. Before he came home on D-Day, my mother had spent almost three years wondering if he'd return at all, not knowing, for much of that time if he was dead or alive. This absence would intensify their need to spend all their free time with each other.

6.

Eggy

My parents loved Europe and usually traveled there in the summer. They sent Kenny and me to camp, which most of the time was a lonely and isolating experience. Before we went to sleep-away camp, we spent a summer going to day camp at Atlantic Beach near our home. In the early morning we would wait for the bus on a curved stone stoop under a pine tree as if we were about to be executed. I was six and my adorable annoying brother was four. He was my responsibility and I had somehow become his dependable guardian. I loved the ocean and always wanted to swim in it even though I wasn't old enough to do so on my own. We'd have access to a pool and make arts and crafts, take a nap, and then get dropped off at our house by three.

That first day at camp we formed a line and I had to give my name. I couldn't do it. I couldn't get the "P" in "Peggy" to come out. I stood there shaking, my lips trying to get themselves around the consonant. My eyes twitched and danced around my head from the enormous effort. I was summoned to the front of the line. "Oh just write your name down on the list," the exasperated counselor finally said. When later in life, as a model I had to initiate phone calls to photographers asking if they would be interested in seeing my book, I had to leave off the first letter of my name. I still couldn't say the letter "P." I'd say, "Eggy." "What?" people would ask, stumbling through the options until they reached "Peggy," at which point I'd enthusiastically agree. Yes, yes. That's it! I was a severe stutterer, which made me reluctant to open my mouth at all.

One year at summer camp I found myself with a crush on a counselor named Danny. I had just gotten my junior life-saving badge, which meant I could swim the lake. I remember seeing him on the raft and swimming out there and thinking this is great, I get to be alone with him, but when I got to the edge of the raft he took my head and held it under water for what seemed like forever. I was thrashing around, swallowing water and trying to press against his hands to get myself up for air. I almost passed out.

"Oooh, are you okay?" he and his friends condescendingly asked. Of course I wasn't okay. I started stuttering, trying to say how I really did not like the way he had treated me. I coughed up lake water and tears and swam breathlessly back to the dock. No one had seen what happened on the raft. All shivering bones in my bathing suit and rubber swimming cap, I dragged myself back to the camp cabin in humiliation. In those days, I never fought back—I was incapable of it. Somewhere in the back of that little ten-year-old head was the idea I had brought this on myself by being a skinny, stuttering, clumsy, ugly duckling.

At sleep-away camp, I felt I might just wither away and die. Being that homesick was eating away at my stomach, as was the terrible camp food. Where did my parents think they were leaving my brother Kenny and me? I'm sure they had checked it out thoroughly but they would've had to actually be in our tennis shoes in order to realize the stress we were under. Maybe some kids were content with being away from home for the summer, but I missed my parents too much to enjoy it. I don't believe in being separated from your parents for such a long time at that age. You're still bonding and not old enough to sort out serious problems. But my parents had their lives and travels, and they wanted that time for each other. Though they cared for us and were always kind, their need for each other came first.

I had terrible nightmares at camp. Girls would sit around the campfire and tell stories about how bats could fly down during the night and become entangled in your hair. On a camping trip when I was nine, my tent mate had a breakdown at three o'clock in the morning. She became hysterical. Her father had been killed in the war and she curled up in a ball screaming. She was frightened and so was I. Neither one of us could move. There was no counselor nearby and we stayed together like that for the rest of the night. I never wanted to go camping again and always found an excuse when we had to sign up for a trip.

The only events I looked forward to were sports and games. I loved competing. It fueled a need in me to excel and be a winner, and I also enjoyed the strategizing. Treasure hunts, capture the flag—the more complex the game, the better. Aside from gymnastics, volleyball, and cheerleading, schools didn't have sports for girls in those days. And I could never be a cheerleader. That was an exclusive club for pretty, coordinated, *popular* girls. My awkwardness alone eliminated that possibility. But I was fair at horseback riding, and my long skinny legs made me good at running relays. I ran the last lap and usually raced the baton home for first place. I returned to camp every summer until I was fourteen, and each year proved to be a little less intimidating.

During the summer of 1959, I suddenly found I could barely drag myself out of bed or to breakfast. I couldn't do any of the chores. As a result I began to be called "Pokey Peggy," a nickname used by all, including the counselors. I hated being teased relentlessly just because I couldn't participate in the usual camp activities. But because I didn't understand what was happening to me, I, too, began to accept my condition as laziness. In order to try and forget my situation I would go off to the lake alone, or run like a crazy person up a small hill until I collapsed in exhaustion. The mystery was solved when I was diagnosed with mononucleosis, but until then I felt like an absolute pariah. Back home, I went to bed for two months. It was a lonely experience, and I watched autumn come and go and shift into winter from my window. Being sick deepened my introvertedness. I dreamed a lot and of course had my ongoing fantasies to keep me company during the very long days and nights.

When I finally went back to school, I was thirteen years old and in eighth grade. While I was sick my mom had trimmed my hair short into a pixie cut and it was slowly growing out. I'd break a sweat every night rolling my hair on very large wire rollers that looked like instruments of Gothic torture. I wanted pretty hair and cute features like the other popular girls at school—not pimples and braces. My hairdo was going all over the place. I wanted to make the bottom of my hair turn under, and each morning I arrived in class frustrated from the night before. My hair still looked awful. One morning before the bell, a girl named Judy Penzer came over to my desk and said, "Why don't you forget about curling your hair? Just let it do what it wants to do." I felt exposed, as if she had looked inside me with a magnifying glass. Given her pointed comments about my looks, I was wary when she asked me to play at her house that afternoon. Judy was an amazing artist, and even though she hung around with the most popular clique in school, she seemed more approachable to me than most of these girls. As I made my way to her house, I was thinking, "Why would she even bother to notice me?"

In her bedroom, she walked me over to the full-length mirror. "Look!" she said. I saw a tall greasy-haired, pimply-faced girl with braces. I wanted to close my eyes.

"One day, Peggy, you will be beautiful," she said. I couldn't imagine, even in my wildest fantasies, what she was talking about, but based on her word and faith in the future, I stopped curling my hair, and by the time I hit junior high school, I had the long straight hair that would become my trademark. As far as I could tell, no one else was lucky enough to get such expert advice from Judy Penzer. The freshmen girls went on styling their teased bouffants and spraying the hell out of them.

7.

Donny

Just when I thought I was destined to live out my adolescence in oblivion, a significant event took place. I was walking with two friends across Central Avenue, where people shopped before there was anything called a mall. Here there was a theater, a Chinese restaurant, a girls' clothing store, a florist, a drugstore, Bea's Tea Room, and a Stride Rite shoe shop where I got my first pair of Buster Brown oxfords. The area was always bustling with school kids, Cadillac and T-bird convertibles, and the occasional group of varsity basketball players sauntering *en masse* to get a hamburger and Coke at the Town Diner.

When I crossed the street at Cedarhurst and Central Avenue, a young guy came up and gently touched my arm. His black hair was slicked back in a ducktail, and he wore a black wool coat, with the collar turned up, and pointy boots.

"Are you Peggy?" he asked. "Yes," I replied, surprised by the fact that I didn't know him. He wasn't in the usual group of boys we were chasing—while pretending we weren't.

"I saw you at a basketball game," he said, adding that his name was Donny. Why would he remember me and approach me on the street? I found that bold and alluring. Right there and then he asked me for a date. I was shocked. I had never been formally asked out. He was nineteen. I was fifteen. I found that enticing, too.

Donny turned out to be quite different from the boys who were terminally uninterested in me. He had graduated high school and worked at a restaurant. He lived on the other side of the tracks and was the only child of a single mother. He was Jewish, but all his friends were Italian. He had his own car and he smelled good—and he had handpicked *me*, although I didn't know why. I let him take me out that night.

He picked me up at my house in a white Buick low-rider sedan. I couldn't believe I had a date with a cute boy who not only wasn't friends with the wimps who we wanted to notice us, but worked and had his own car, too! We went to a pizza place on the second floor of an old brick building and made out for two hours. He thought I was pretty; I thought he was slick in a '50s way, like the bad boys in *Grease*.

Each day after school, he'd be waiting for me in front of Lawrence Junior High. This did not go unnoticed. No one—and I mean *no one*—had a boyfriend who picked them up at school. Without hearing their words, I knew what my classmates were saying: How did *she* get *him?* What can he possibly see in her? I felt their eyes burn holes in me and I liked it.

After a week as an object of gossip, I stopped being affected by it. I was too busy spending time with Donny. When the school bell rang, I wanted to burst through the double doors, run down the steps, throw my books with abandon into the backseat and cover Danny's face with kisses. Instead, I was cool. I'd wait for him to open the door and demurely slip into the passenger seat. We'd hold hands until we arrived at his apartment. His mother worked, so within minutes we'd be on his bed, listening to the radio and making out. Of course, we never went all the way. Unless they planned to marry, "nice girls" didn't.

When summer came, we went to the beach and spent carefree days swimming in the gentle, blue Atlantic. We'd make out for hours in his car under a moonlit sky, listening to Jocko's Rocket Ship and to Murray the K on the radio. We decided one night to hold a kiss for the entire length of "There's a Moon Out Tonight" by the Capris. We did it! And when we came up for air, we did it again for the next song.

Each week, Donny would spend whatever money he'd made at work on movies and dinners with me at the Town Diner. He said he loved me, and within two months he said he wanted to be with me for the rest of his life. Almost overnight, he became ferociously attached to me, which, of course, made me want to call the whole thing off. I fretted about how I would let him know. Finally, in one long tearful phone conversation, I broke up with Donny. I was still fifteen.

Things were beginning to look up. I was starting to get attention at school from boys. And I was getting good marks from my teachers. I was diligent about my schoolwork. I wanted to be a writer and I took it seriously. But when I looked around at everything I had grown up with, I realized I wanted more juice from life. I wanted to have the satisfaction of knowing I could make things happen for myself, instead of life happening to me. I could never envision myself married to a hometown boy who takes over his father's business and settles down, right back where he grew up. That was never going to happen.

8.

Through the Looking Glass

At fifteen I got my first inkling how to escape small-town life. My father ran into an Army buddy who had become successful in advertising. He came to our house for dinner. Something about me—in all my adolescent gawkiness—struck him. He encouraged me to have test photos done and to set up a meeting with the premier modeling maven, Eileen Ford. I went to her offices in Manhattan with my mother by my side. We were both nervous. I knew nothing of this world.

Sitting there in her hectic space, on top of her desk with her long arms folded and her legs dangling below her skirt, Eileen Ford was a force to be to reckoned with. Test photos of the world's most beautiful women were pasted on her office walls.

"Get rid of your pimples," she told me.

"Then if you lose ten pounds and cut your hair, I'll sign you to a contract." I was thin, but evidently, not thin enough. I did what she told me, inwardly quaking at the irony of such a self-conscious, slouching-to-disguise-her-height, hiding-behind-her-hair shrinking violet as myself pursuing the most conspicuous, look-at-me profession. But I was disciplined when it came to getting what I wanted, and for the next month I dieted, cut and colored my hair, and started using Noxema. It was my ticket out of the ordinary, and there was no way I was going to miss the train.

I started modeling and enrolled at the Professional Children's School in Manhattan, where for the first time in my life I met like-minded friends—young dancers, actors, and musicians. I began to study acting and speech at HB Studios with Herbert Berghof, the legendary brilliant and gruff Russian maestro whose passion for the art of acting stoked all our fires. He was tremendously encouraging. After I did my first scene playing Emily in *Our Town* he said, "And you, young lady, are a fine actress." I was flabbergasted. Modeling, on the other hand, I didn't care for. Being accepted in an industry solely based on your looks didn't resonate with me. I was so shy it was hard for me to strike the poses necessary to invoke the sexiness and allure the advertisers demanded. I appeared in women's magazines like *Glamour* and *Seventeen,* and an ad for Chantilley Lace perfume.

It was fairly easy extricating myself from my former life, but as a result of my newfound career I had suddenly become popular back in the Five Towns. This had a very sweet ring to it. I was now seen in a new light: as a cosmopolitan—going to high school in the city and attending nightly acting classes. The fact that I was a model for the Ford Agency was exotic and glamorous, and at times I felt like a wild animal turned loose.

Away from the Five Towns, I enjoyed my life anew. My parents were supportive, and every day I got to go into the deliriously intoxicating city. I'd take the Long Island Rail Road, usually walking to the station carrying my heavy school books. I loved the train ride: cold in winter, unless you sat next to the heater, and sweltering in the summer. Those mornings, I was submerged in a commuter's world in which every office-bound man resembled my father in his gray suit, striped tie, and white shirt. Their collars were never button down—that was Ivy League. These were no longer college kids, but fathers with small families working in the oh-so-get-ahead early 1960s. They were like soldiers in uniform marching off to their own personal battles. You could sense the tang of anticipation that permeated the train cars, a mixture of newsprint, coffee breath, cigar and cigarette smoke. But mostly there was silence, broken only by the clanking of the wheels against the tracks and the perpetual turning of the bi-folded pages of *The New York Times*. Each man had the requisite fedora. Some wore them and others found room on a seat next to them, or on their laps, to lay down their totem. These were young adults and this was their rite of passage—becoming men in a new, strange, and highly competitive world. The fedora, worn as the com-muter's badge, reminded me of my father. And that image, deep and con-soling, carried me through most of my days commuting on the Long Island Rail Road.

In December of that year, on my way to school at Sixty-first Street and Columbus Circle, I came up the subway steps to see a film crew at the entrance to Central Park. There he was: Paul Burke, my crush from the TV show *The Naked City*. This time in the flesh. I nearly "plotzed," as they used to say in my neighborhood. I hung around and missed the first school period worrying whether I should introduce myself or not. I was unbearably shy in most circumstances, but this was different: I felt like I knew him and that—having been my lover in my dreams—he must know that I existed. He was even handsomer in person, standing within inches of me. It was one of those brutally cold mornings when your breath shoots out icy fog. Burke was warming himself by a free-standing heater bundled in his black overcoat and wearing, of all things, my absolute fa-vorite accessory for any older man—a fedora. I was looking at a younger version of my dad. I summoned up the courage and kept my stammer in check. "Hello Mr. Burke, my name is Peggy." *There.* I'd gotten it out. He shook my hand with his cold leathery glove and said, "Very nice to meet you," and off he went to do a scene. Nothing felt the same the whole day. I wasn't aware yet that this was a subtle sign: If I wanted something, I could get it. But at sixteen, I couldn't yet indulge myself in this notion. For now, nothing could equal my fantasies.

9.

The Dark Side
of the Moon

wasn't exactly a sunny child to begin
with. Sometimes I would make myself
very still and try to imagine myself dead.
I tried to invoke the feeling of the very last
breath I would take. If I could stop my
breath permanently, then I would know
what it was like to be dead. My mother
said I was a child who rarely smiled. The
only person who could arouse a giggle in
me when I was an infant was my brother
Bob. In an old home movie Bob is sticking
his hands inside my baby carriage and
I am fitfully laughing, but even then there
was a menacing edge of something out of
control in the air. And, of course, I stuttered. My stutter probably had some basis
in physiology, for both my brothers had
problems with language. Bob had a disorder that made him stammer. Kenny had
dyslexia, the reversing of words, along

with a speech impediment that made it difficult for him to grasp and say many phrases. In my case there was a very specific psychological component to my stutter, for it began around the time I was first sexually abused.

My mother's friends would always say I was a pretty child, but I didn't feel pretty. Feeling pretty as a child is not so much about physical beauty. It's more about your essence, and when I looked at my essence I saw only a deep sadness.

I don't have a clear picture of when it began. When I look at a photograph of myself at seven years old, I feel it must have started around that time. Sometimes I look at pictures when I was even younger and I wonder, "Was it happening then, too?" I hope not.

The abuser was my aunt's husband. Decades later I found out that as a boy he had seen his parents murdered on the steps of the synagogue in their small Russian village. He was clearly demented. His first wife committed suicide by sticking her head in a gas oven. Especially confusing to a child was that his attacks were not violent. I suppose they couldn't have been; we all stayed together each holiday in my aunt and uncle's house in Atlantic City.

My brother Kenny and I slept in the attic, a small dismal cavern right above my parents' room. My abuser could never push me too hard because I might scream. I was compliant, which many victims have to be, especially if it is happening in the family. I didn't understand that I had any choice in the matter. And, of course, I was ashamed and afraid. If I had screamed, my parents, my aunt, my grandparents would come, and then what? It was almost as if I was afraid of getting caught—as if *I* was the one who was doing something wrong. The lack of violence during the act was extremely insidious. It made me feel complicit, that I was somehow acquiescing—as if I had caused it to happen.

So I would simply leave my body; I would close my eyes and pretend it wasn't happening, or I'd look at my brother sleeping. At least I think he was sleeping; God knows he probably didn't sleep through all of it. But he never talked about it. Nobody in our family ever talked about anything. The abuse went on for years, and it left me with real physical as well as psychological symptoms. I began having terrible bladder infections. I was never treated for them, just told to take an aspirin to reduce the fever. I'd go home and writhe in my bed. My mother was worried but didn't know what to do.

Other symptoms soon began to surface. I'd be sitting somewhere like the dinner table or in the dark at a movie matinee and I would have the sudden agonizing sensation of being stripped naked. It was so painful that I wanted to die. It was an unbearable physical sensation that started in my groin and moved up to my chest. I would become flushed with shame and mortification. In front of my parents, I never let on that it ever happened. Even now at odd moments I get this feeling. I just breathe through it and acknowledge that this is a memory lodged in my body. Eventually it passes.

Of course, I never actually *forgot* that I'd been abused, but I avoided acknowledging it most of my adult life. Instead, I'd try to minimize it in my mind. Even some of my closest friends were confused by the fact that I came from such a good home and yet was subject to such fits of melancholy. Why was I struggling on a daily basis with my identity? Why was I subject to sudden panic attacks and debilitating depression? Eventually, I came to understand that a child who has been abused sexually is in every sense robbed of his or her identity.

I never really confronted any of it until 1985 in an acting class I took with Sandra Seacat. It came as a shock and a revelation. We were doing an exercise using sense memory to recreate a moment in time when we were let down or disappointed. In this type of exercise you are encouraged to use all five senses. Lying on the floor relaxed, I remembered a time when I was with my father holding his hand on the boardwalk in Atlantic City. It was a chilly, star-filled night. We had left my aunt and uncle's house and walked the long block to the ocean. I was so happy; I had my daddy all to myself. He was walking with me and only me. There in class, lying very still, I could feel myself in my little body; ethereal and light. I was about seven years old as I watched myself gazing up at him. I felt safe. I went into a deep meditative state.

I was no longer on the floor of the room; I was there beside him.

When I spoke, I heard a tiny voice ask him to explain the stars to me. He was tender and keenly interested and really wanted to give me the world in that moment. Quite suddenly, lying there in the fetal position, I began weeping.

There, through the eyes of a child, I saw him as clearly as if he were in the class with me. I saw myself trying to tell him something. I looked down at the broad wooden slats of the boardwalk beneath my feet as they caught the illumination of the light from the lamppost. I smelled the sand and felt the cold hit my face. My eyes were stinging and burning with tears. My ears were filled with a loud booming noise. My mouth couldn't move as I tried to get the words out. My heart was caught in my throat and I was overwhelmed with love for him and indescribable grief for myself.

"Daddy! Please help me," I said. "When I sleep in this scary house a bad man comes into my room. He sneaks in silently like a cat, and tells me to be quiet. He gets into my bed. He pulls the covers over us. I smell his oily skin and bad breath. He whispers into my ear while he's covering my body with his. His accent is thick and I don't understand what he's saying. I lie rigid. I am wanting it to end, *praying* it will end. He is pinching and licking me on my chest. He's pulling my pajama bottoms down. His bald, sweaty head is moving down my legs. I don't cry, Daddy. I don't open my legs. I just wait for it to be over. Help me. Make him disappear. Hit him. Hard. Make him disappear from the family. While you beat him, hold me high in your arms like I am a princess, your princess. The one you care most for in the world. I'm a good girl, Daddy. I am good."

But my prayer is a silent one. I say nothing to my daddy—not a single word. I look up at him. He is distant, lost in his thoughts, thinking, no doubt, about Mom. Getting back to her. To the delicious food, the card game, the homey banter. He doesn't do anything. He doesn't even hear me because I never say these things aloud. In the cold night my words are caught up in the wind like particles of sand from the beach and blown out to sea.

California Dreamin'

10.

Landing on Mars

When I was seventeen my father had a heart attack while on vacation with my mom in California. He survived, but Mom came home and notified us that the family would be moving there. Dad had been offered a job, finally able to escape the rat race of New York. He still had a long recovery ahead of him, however, and his dream job was going to take a while to yield real income. In the meantime we slipped down into the lower middle class. I felt sorriest for my mother: she had to leave her lovely Long Island home for a tacky little box in Westwood. But as always she was game.

"Let's just go," she said, and within two weeks we'd sold our house, packed, and moved to California, the Golden State. In my fantasy U.S.A., anything was possible. And in California dreams grew on trees, along with grapefruit, oranges, and avocados. I had left my childhood and the gulag of the Five Towns behind me forever.

It was difficult for my parents the first year. Mom had few friends so her usual social life would have to be put on hold. She unpacked boxes, studied art, and actually cooked for us. When money was especially tight I remember her making us some rather unappetizing meals with buffalo meat. Dad was beginning to work long hours again. He was the general counsel to a new company and he was working with some pretty high rollers. Being a gambler at heart, he loved what he was doing. He would once again become immersed in his work.

Mom did her best without him home most days and nights, and I became her constant companion as we explored our new environment together. We listened to the Beatles as they emerged as the next great thing and, devestated, we watched the funeral of John F. Kennedy on our little black-and-white TV. The times were changing, all right, and for me life was just beginning. Somewhere along the way, without my trying and in spite of my initial resistance, I was on my way to becoming the quintessential California girl.

California was the land of *Beach Blanket Bingo,* blond surfer boys hot-rodding in souped-up cars, "Kookie, Kookie lend me your comb," *77 Sunset Strip,* fat juicy hamburgers skated over to your car window, and tennis matches in the backyards of famous people. As a transplanted, unsunny New Yorker, my culture shock was profound.

I started off at University High in Westwood, a huge school that scared me to death. The classes were enormous. My legs would wobble as I headed down the halls, "dazed and confused." Walking into those classes not knowing anyone, listening to the boys with their flat open vowels and their constant referral to the nonexistent "dude," I was sure I was in a foreign country. The boy's bodies were easy and tanned. They had great teeth and sun-streaked hair. They were sincere, they flirted with you; they always smelled of beer and Coppertone. Seventeen years old and in love with themselves, they were hardly models of sophistication. But they were sexy to look at and utterly unlike the guys I knew from Brooklyn, Queens, and Long Island, who, if cast in the California sunlight, would appear as brooding thugs. My career as a Ford model was now over. I was a senior and back in high school.

I tried not to feel like a total outcast at Uni High. After school I got a job at the Village Theatre in Westwood, first as an usherette and then as a candy girl. I'd go down to the basement to put on my uniform, a sodden piece of burgundy fabric and a hat I refused to wear. Those were the days when there were ushers in theaters who showed people to their seats with flashlights. Watching the same movies over and over left untold time in the dark for fantasy and the delicious feeling that the world would open up to me at any moment.

I was jarred by the California way of doing things. I adapted slowly to the daunting super highways, the eternal sunshine, and snow-topped mountains even in summer. I would come to love these elements—they were, in the end, irresistible—but the culture shock persisted for a year.

I looked strange, especially at school. I dressed like an Easterner. Skirts to the knee, kitten heels, cardigans, my hair bobbed and side parted, books carried neatly in my arms like a Vassar coed. I felt incurably odd. In an effort to correct my Long Island accent I took speech classes, but I still stood out, and there was no way—and I mean no way—I would adopt the California twang. Even though I longed to fit in, I resisted everything that was around me, a paradox that would soon drive my rebelliousness even deeper. I begged my parents to get me out of that school. I told them I was having a breakdown. I told them my life was in danger. When I told them I couldn't stand to hear another surfer say "dude" again, they finally agreed.

So I transferred to a new school and life began again. Hollywood Professional School on Hollywood Boulevard was not very strict about attendance. If you came in for a class or two a few days a week and applied yourself, you could still get an A.

Every morning on my way to school I tooled along Sunset Boulevard from Westwood deep into Hollywood. It took twenty minutes. Driving was freedom, and I loved to deftly maneuver my box of a green Ford Falcon through the rushing lanes of traffic.

Hollywood Professional was the kind of school that you could make a movie about because everything about it was slightly off. This was not your normal high school. The teachers, the students—everything was odd. You didn't, for instance, have the usual cliques. There was no time for that. Everyone was busy doing their own thing. It was designed primarily for children who were working as actors, dancers, and singers, plus a sprinkling of dyslexic geniuses who couldn't fit into other schools. We could come and go as we wanted.

The teachers seemed ancient; they doddered and fell asleep at their desks in midclass. There was a geometry test at the end of the final semester, and I hadn't the foggiest idea about geometry. I hadn't a clue what an obtuse angle was. My protractor and triangle were as mystifying to me as Masonic symbols. I stared into space, hoping some ray of inspiration would strike me. Just then I looked at my teacher sitting at her desk and caught her opening her drawer . . . to take a quick swig from her flask. I applied simple math, and putting two and two together, I got up and put my paper next to her trembling hand on the desk and said, "Miss Bell, do you think you could you help me with these questions?" She must have known that I'd seen her drinking. She took her pencil and checked off the right answers, and that's how I passed geometry. I don't know what made me do that, a newly discovered survival instinct perhaps.

I didn't learn too much at Hollywood Professional School. No one, including myself, could concentrate. We were all busy checking the clock to get out and rush to our cars, turn on the radio, and hit the Sunset Strip. I wanted to learn, but not what school could teach me. I was seventeen; it was time to experience life. My partner-in-crime-to-be was a stunning girl named Jill.

II .

The Magic Girl

The minute I saw Jill, I was enchanted. I watched her from afar
for weeks. "You have to get to
know that girl," I kept telling myself.

Jill was my total opposite. I was the
nice little Jewish girl with the good-girl outfits, neatly turned-under pageboy hairdo,
and just the right barrette in place. On Jill
everything was tight and slinky. Shirts,
skirts, and cardigans that strained against
her tiny bosom. Her skin was translucent.
Her hair was black, her eyes cobalt blue. She
was the most enigmatic, strange, mystical,
magical, scary, wonderful person I'd ever
seen, and, no matter what it took, I had to
get to know her.

Jill would slink around like a cat, slith-
ering between the desks or remaining completely still to observe someone making a
complete fool of themselves. She had long
cat fingers and long cat nails and a tiny,

pouty mouth. She "oozed" Brigitte Bardot. She was meticulous about her appearance. No creases or stains ever on her clothes and her thick bangs were combed long and smooth enough to hide the expression in her eyes. She'd only let you see what she wanted you to see. She didn't fidget. Everything about her was in slow motion, which fascinated me. I watched her with awe, wondering how I would ever get to know her.

Finally one day I made the approach. I was unbearably shy in most ways, but if I really wanted something, I could psych myself up to go after it. Outside in the cafeteria area, I saw Jill methodically unwrapping her sandwich so not one morsel of food would soil those impossibly glamorous fingernails. When I got my nerve, I asked her if I could have a bite of her sandwich. She said nothing, seductively putting the whole half in my mouth and watching me chew. Her finger caught a little mayonnaise on its tip and the next thing I knew she put it between my lips for me to lick it off. She looked at me mischievously with her penetrating blue eyes. She was testing me; these were girls' initiation rites. We laughed and she began talking to me, which, for Jill, was a big deal.

"Why don't you come to my friend Toni's after school?" Jill suggested a week after we had met. When I arrived at the house I came across this scene: Toni with a beret, looking like a street urchin in Montmartre, painting three canvases at the same time. Very dark, rich, blood-like colors, and a lot of black streaks was what I caught at first glance (not wanting to stare at her masterpiece in case she asked me what I thought). And Jill sitting smoking a cigarette and (very slowly) flipping through her books pretending this afternoon might be about studying. These were two cosmopolitan bohemian chicks—a mad artist and a mystery woman—hanging out and communicating in a way I wasn't privy to. Just walking in the door, I felt like an idiot. I sat down uncomfortably with my books under my arm. Within moments I sensed they were going to ignore me and that I was being set up.

"Goddamnmuthafuckincocksuckinasslickinbitch!"

"Fuckfacecumbutttitlovincuntlappingdirtyoldman!"

The words jammed together and flew by me so fast that they were no longer English. They were Aztec or some other ancient language. The two of them were sneaking looks to see how or if their crudeness was affecting me. I was blushing and couldn't hide it. They continued and started to run some graphic and sexual details by me. They were watching. How upset would I get? Then—the big aha!—I got it. This was the test, and the soldier inside me wanted to pass it and enter their surreal army. I joined in with my particular brand of cursing and swearing—"Shit, bitch, bastard!"—and they were amused. It didn't have their down dirty, gruff in-your-face style, but it was a stab at profanity and they liked that I tried. They listened and laughed and I moved that day through their girl-club gauntlet fairly unscathed.

My true initiation came two weeks after meeting Jill.

"Peggy, I'm taking you to a party tonight," she said, without a hint of what was to come. When she came to my parents' house to pick me up. I was dressed conservatively in a skirt with flats. And I was worried. But Mom had great taste and discernment and adored Jill right away—really good points for my mom. And Dad, of course, loved whatever Mom did because he was so in love with her. Jill was always welcome at my house. My mother would laugh the entire time Jill was there. Her movements were so slow and deliberate, they tickled my mother and reminded her of a Chinese dance. She knew how to please and entertain my parents just by being her own kooky self.

Jill drove a little Nash Rambler. She never carried a purse. The only thing in her possession was a car key dangling from a tree branch with "Jill" carved on it. Nothing about her seemed extraneous. She was just Jill. The girl with the crush on Marlon Brando. This beautiful, strange, enigmatic girl I wanted to make my friend.

We got in her car and headed toward Bel Air. Jill was doing her lips in the mirror. Getting pretty tarted up, I thought. I didn't ask where we were going; basically, I was afraid to. We drove up to a typical Bel Air '60s noveau riche extravaganza with Rolls-Royces parked in twos in the circular driveway and a cherub stone statue displaying his wares.

The door swung open and a woman stood there—stark naked. I tried to look everywhere else but at her nude body. Her teeth, her blond hair, anywhere else. But by now her vagina was the only thing I could focus on. And there wasn't a hair to be seen on it.

I wonder what expression I had on my face—probably just the one Jill wanted to see. She'd brought me here to find out how I would react.

"Why, hello there!" said our hostess, as blasé as if she were wearing a shirtwaist dress with three crinolines underneath. We kind of shuffled into the house, and inside everybody else was, lo and behold, naked, too. Sitting around drinking and talking and passing hors d'oeuvres—all in the nude. Otherwise, it was just like a regular, boring, middle-aged cocktail party.

This was over my head. What was the point of this party with Jill and me sitting there completely clothed? I tried to act as nonchalantly as I could under the circumstances, trying not to seem alarmed at the penises and breasts in the room. I prayed that nothing was going to happen, that we'd get out in time—before this party turned into an orgy. You can imagine how everyone was eyeing us, waiting for the moment when we felt embarrassed enough to take off our clothes, too. But Jill was my protection. I knew that whatever wild scene she threw me into, Jill was in some way taking care of me. And if she wasn't going to take off her clothes, I certainly wasn't. Jill liked to test the limits. She was controlling the room by keeping them guessing if she and I would finally give in and disrobe. I hoped this was just another test from her and if it was, I could just remain cool and pass it. When we got home unscathed, she turned to me with delight and said, "My my, wasn't that interesting?"

12.

Enter Earl

Jill didn't have a regular job. She sometimes acted in movies or soft porn films. She lived with her mother but spent most of her time at Earl's, a man in his fifties, which of course seemed ancient to us. Jill was his princess.

Earl was fun. He took things lightly. He'd been a war correspondent and seen his share of suffering. Now he wanted to live in the moment like a teenager would. His bohemian life revolved around a two-room rustic shack in the Hollywood Hills. Scores of black-and-white photographs he'd taken during his career covered the walls. Dozens of cats dripped from the ceiling beams or scrambled up the ivy that had grown into the house from the outside. He was an original. He took life as it came and he had a generous soul. And now in 1963, he was living for us. Before he had lived for Jill, but once I was there, it was double trouble.

Earl liked to have the two of us come to his pad to arouse him by describing our teenage sexual fantasies. Being a good Jewish girl, I was still a virgin at seventeen, but I could always spin a good tale. Earl was a bit of a voyeur; he liked seeing us hang out together because we were like photographic negatives of each other. Me, blond and tan. Jill, dramatically pale with black hair. He could let his imagination run wild, but his dreams about being with us sexually were never going to come true. I didn't know Jill's personal relationship with Earl, and didn't want to. What was between them was their own business. I just liked being at his crazy pad in the hills, and I started going there every day after school.

Jill and Earl were like characters in a movie. It was as if they had invented themselves. Jill seemed to come from nowhere. She had no father. No sisters. No brothers. She lived with her mother, but in all the years we were friends, I never met her mother or even talked to her. They came from Iowa farm country and her real name was Mary Kay—that was all I knew. That's all I ever knew. The fact that we were so different from each other in our looks, our backgrounds, and our personalities had a profound magnetic pull on our relationship.

We became best friends. Every day after school, the two of us took our positions on Earl's ratty couch. Her head on one end and my head on the other, our legs intertwined, drinking Coke and smoking cigarettes, petting the cats, and just fantasizing about our lives.

We'd make our plans. Who we wanted to kiss and tease, who we could call and invite over. Jill wasn't a virgin. When I was growing up, you didn't sleep with anyone before you married them. Girls in those days were sternly warned not to "spoil" themselves or would-be husbands might reject them as "damaged goods." If you did, you were considered a slut. People got married right out of high school. That was the last thing I wanted—to be married to someone from high school and get stuck in the Five Towns forever. For countless, shadowy reasons, it was hammered into us that premarital sex would ruin our lives. No one, of course, ever told us about the pleasure. But what scared me most were not the threats but the suspicion—warranted, as it turned out—that sex would awaken in me ferocious passions.

13.

Chez Rock Hudson

My introduction to the legendary Hollywood and the stars in their gated mansions came when I went to my first dinner party at Rock Hudson's house. I went with Clive, a friend I'd gone to Professional Children's School with back in New York. He was a Broadway singer and dancer who had moved to L.A. for work. He had beautiful manners, and was the ideal escort to the strange and elegant world I was about to enter.

At least once a week I accompanied him to Rock's hilltop home in Bel Air. Arriving at Rock's house was like entering the palace of a very chic King. The house was neither large nor ostentatious; quite the contrary. From its brown, velvet Regency-style armchairs and polished dark wood floors to the art on the walls and the crystal and china place settings, everything was in unpretentious good taste. His house was done in the California contemporary style of the time—built on one level around a pool. Everything opened out onto it. Not a grand house by any means, just comfortable and beautiful. Rock—or Roy, as his friends called him—was never pretentious; he just seemed to be a regular guy who loved to entertain.

I silently watched and took everything in. The guests at these congenial gatherings were sophisticated and relaxed. They could sense I felt out of my element and always took pains to make me feel welcome. As it all became more familiar, I began to relax. The food was delicious and I was slowly becoming more adventurous about trying new dishes. One night as the butler served dinner, I noticed a strange green substance carved in crescent shapes and meticulously folded into the salad. I cringed at the thought of eating whatever this strange thing next to the red onions was. I had grown up eating meat and potatoes and this exotic delicacy on my plate didn't look too appetizing. Clive could see I was hesitating and leaned over and whispered, "It's an avocado. Try it." Never had I tasted anything this good. It would become a staple of my diet for years to come.

In the corner of the sunken living room was a shiny black ebony grand piano, and after dinner the guests would gather in a circle around it. Someone would play show tunes by Rodgers and Hammerstein or Cole Porter. Everyone would laugh and sing along, and in this way each dinner at Rock's ended with a little celebration.

Rock was affable, charming, and shockingly good-looking. Tall, lean, and tan, he would greet you at the door with his dazzling smile and the warmest hello, wearing a button-down pressed cotton shirt and chinos. He was so casual, and easy, there was no way you could help but be enamored of him.

A frequent guest at these soirees was an actor named Tom Tryon. He too was extremely handsome, and a talented painter and writer. As fun and interesting as it was seeing all these gorgeous men together in one place, I began to wonder: Where were their dates? Where were the bevies of Hollywood starlets that you'd expect to find hovering around them like bees? It was a mystery. I felt a different energy among this group, but didn't know exactly what was going on—not that there was ever any sense that something was being hidden. It took awhile before I realized most of the men at Rock's dinner parties were gay. If you were gay in Hollywood in the early 1960s, you were definitely in the closet. Nobody was out.

Gay actors had to be constantly vigilant. Their contracts with the studios would have been terminated in a flash if these men hadn't escorted women to their movie openings. Studio publicists linked their names with stars of the opposite sex for the benefit of gossip columnists like Hedda Hopper and Luella Parsons, and spent much of their time keeping revelations about their clients' sexual preferences out of the tabloids. One slip, one confirmed rumor and their careers would have been ruined. Two decades later, being openly gay in Hollywood would be somewhat more acceptable, but by then AIDS had taken the lives of many.

One night Rock and his friends threw a party for about a hundred people. A live band played and everybody got up and danced. And whom did I find myself dancing next to but Jane Fonda and her agent.

"That's Dick Clayton," Clive whispered in my ear. "He brought James Dean to Hollywood and he's the best agent in town."

When I was introduced, Dick turned to me and said, "When you're out of high school, I'm going to be your agent." Wasn't this the kind of thing that only happened in the movies? As unlikely as it seemed at the time, I felt like I *was* living in a Hollywood movie when Rock, Tom, Clive, and Dick Clayton all showed up at my high school graduation party.

Dick kept his promise and before I knew it he put me under contract to Universal Studios—a huge break for someone who had never done a film or TV work before. This was 1966, the tail end of the longstanding Hollywood era of contract players; I was signed to an exclusive deal at Universal for $175 a week.

At Universal, I encountered a tough mentor in Monique James, head of casting. The more afraid I was, the more she threw me into the fire. My stutter didn't stop her from promoting me for every available ingénue part at the studio. When I'd balk, she'd just get me more parts and if I stammered, she sent me off to the speech coach. Her department was boot camp for actors, an intense and disciplined training ground.

When I went in for my first TV job I was petrified. I got a tiny part on *Bewitched* as Darren's secretary. Basically I got the job because it consisted of just two words: "You're late," I said to Darren as he was going into his office.

Whenever I got cast in anything, I always felt people might realize at the last minute that they'd made a mistake and cancel me. Monique and Dick Clayton were the glue that held me together during that first year of working in Hollywood.

14.

Smile

I n 1966 I was a Clairol Deb Star of the year. There was to be a televised Hollywood debutante coming-out party for young, up-and-coming stars. And what did Clairol think Deb Stars should wear? Ball gowns. They stuffed me into a frou-frou gown, put my surfer-girl hair up in a Mme de Pompadour high rise and said, "Smile." I wanted to wear my hair long and straight and pad my bra. I wanted to wear a curvy body-hugging Grecian gown. But they wouldn't go for it. One of the very few things I was sure of was my look—what suited me and flattered me most. Turning me, at that age, into something I wasn't irritated me and made me sulk. Why were they so intent on changing me?

Actresses today have so much more say about how they look, but back then being under contract to the studios allowed no leeway, even for the biggest stars. Images were shaped and molded by the heads of studios. I didn't want to put up with it, but it seemed I had to. In between small parts on shows like *The Alfred Hitchcock Hour, Chrysler Theater,* and *The John Forsythe Show,* the powers that be had me report for a fitting. I was to model in a short film that would be shown to visitors taking the new Universal Studios tour. They put me in a Jean Louis evening gown, a pink taffeta concoction. Jean Louis was a world famous costume designer whose exquisite dresses for many famous films always won awards. All I knew was that my gown itched and I couldn't breathe. I was a hippie, for chrissakes, a T-shirt and jeans girl. I was too young to do glamour. As an actress for hire I couldn't exactly be confrontational, but the rebel in me wanted to jump out of my skin and shake the bony shoulders of any and all authority figures.

15.

Back at
the Ranch

By this time I'd made up my mind not to be a virgin anymore. It was a clear decision. I decided to put a plan into action. I was ready. My sexual drive was strong and I needed to have the act consummated if I was to explore these unknown realms of love and loving. I had been attracted to so many boys since I had reached puberty, and wondered what it would feel like to go all the way. Although I was a little apprehensive, basically I just wanted to get it over with. It was the '60s and free love was everywhere. Being a virgin was outmoded and prudish, and I felt like I was missing out on all the fun.

"When you have an orgasm, it'll take the top of your head off," Earl used to say.

"How do you know if you've had one?" I finally asked. "What does it feel like?"

"Baby," Earl said, "you'll know when it happens, believe me."

I was so curious about sex that Earl finally said, "Alright, I'm going to show you how to do it."

He invited over a stunningly beautiful partner named Andrea, who in retrospect was a hot R. Crumb cartoon version of a big busty babe: huge breasts and hips, big butt, and a big hairdo. Just pulsating with sexual energy. She was way too much woman for our little brains to absorb. She and Earl got into the bathtub and started going at it. Jill and I were supposed to be getting a lesson on how to, you know, be sexy and please a partner. Our eyes were popping out. All of a sudden the two of them started to get hot and heavy, and Jill and I looked at each other. I was hyperventilating.

"Let's split," Jill whispered, and we fled the house and raced down the hill in our cars. We never discussed it. What had started out as a game of show and tell had become too private and intimate for the two of us—we suddenly felt like intruders.

Finally, Earl and Jill made a plan to help me out. A young friend of theirs—who'd taken on every red-blooded male's classic dream of initiating eager young women—was going to come up to Earl's on Tuesday after school to "devirginize" me. It was all moving quickly now, and I was getting a bit nervous. What would it feel like, I wondered, and what would he look like? If he turned out to be cute and attractive that would be an added plus. He was, and he knew his assignment.

We were introduced while Jill and Earl hung around, gloating like proud parents. "Come on," the young man said, "let's go to bed." I let him undress me. I fought the urge to feel embarrassed about it all. He was gentle . . . and so professional. He had mastered the touching, the kissing of the mouth and neck and breasts. He knew when it would be okay to enter me. I tried to close my eyes but they were riveted on Earl's bedroom ceiling above. The raggedy beams and the cats hanging off them was my view at the moment of penetration. It hurt, then it felt good, then it was over.

I slept with my first lover only once after that. I had achieved my goal; I was no longer a virgin. I felt I had shed an old layer of skin. I'd giggle to myself when I thought of it. Now I wanted to experiment with my newfound freedom. I wanted to sleep with as wide a selection of men as I could. It was liberating, and I felt a certain euphoria, similar to when I was finally out of high school, or when I left New York—where I could feel my body release. I had no guilt or shame about having sex. Through it, I was somehow going to discover who I was. Somewhere in the back of my consciousness I knew I could use sex as a way not only of getting what I wanted, but *feeling* the way I wanted. Being acknowledged and cared for and, perhaps most importantly, being the master over of my own body and desires. This is how at eighteen I began my pursuit of sexual power and pleasure. But as time went on, there would be a price to pay.

16.

Married Men

Under contract to Universal Studios, I was compelled to take all jobs I was given, and say lines I couldn't get out because of my stutter. I'd fret and stay awake all night worrying about how to ask the director if I could change or rearrange a sentence just so I wouldn't have to say a certain consonant. A "p" or "g" at the beginning of a word made me break out in a cold sweat. With everyone ready to shoot the scene I was sure the smell of fear was emanating from my pores. Rarely would anyone let me change a line so I would just pray and turn completely inside out with trepidation. I'd stammer, freeze, or fake that I had forgotten the line. I would feel like I was about to pass out, until by a miracle of determination and detachment, I'd catch a wave and ride its smoothness into the moment and dive into the dreaded words. Out they came. I had summoned up the gods. I learned to do this over and over. No one cared or lost patience and it didn't show up on TV, but I was acutely aware of what I had to go through.

I met my "first married man" on the studio lot. He had been a comedian in a hit series and was now directing. Easy and altogether loose in his tall frame, he was also very funny and much older than me. He rented an apartment for us on Doheny Drive in West Hollywood and there we met on many afternoons. I became his very young mistress and he, in turn, my tender and passionate lover. I don't remember how long it lasted, maybe a summer. It was the beginning of feeling strangely uneasy and comfortable at the same time. The fantasies I had indulged in as a teen were mine for real and they were free to run rampant. I reluctantly moved on. He had a wife to get back to, and I had to get on to my next conquest: a tortured but gifted acting teacher. I signed up for his class. My attraction was obvious and I seduced him. Though married to a movie star, he wasn't beyond squiring me, his young student, to Restaraunt La Rue in Hollywood, the last of the great romantic spots above Sunset Boulevard. There, he openly courted me. Kissing and touching me between vodkas. The violinists serenaded us with melodramatic snippets of familiar Russian overtures I felt sophisticated and worldly. He was older, experienced, and as intelligent as they come. He could quote English literature, characters' lines from great American plays, and tell me "What a wonderful actress you will become." I went to bed with him right away. I attended all of his classes and for a short time felt like the chosen one. All his words and gestures were seemingly meant only for me. But as the glow wore off I was keeping busy with more TV work and more affairs. So I ended it with him and moved on to my next conquest.

Now under contract to Columbia Studios, I was assigned as the traveling companion to a popular actress who was starring in one of their newly released films. She was four years older than I was. I had to be on my best behavior. Up early every morning I'd accompany her to all her promotional events and be there for her makeup and interviews. I keenly observed everything that was going on around me including the great fuss that was always being made over her. I secretly wished it would happen to me. We went to New York, Miami, and ended up at the Ambassador Hotel in Chicago. Being dutiful, I made sure the days were devoted to her but at night I took on the persona of a vixen. Her costar in the film was a very sexy married man and I couldn't resist being with him. At night I'd go to his room and we'd push a little canvas menthol-smelling bomb called amyl nitrate up our noses while we made love. It enhanced the basics and at the same time, blasted you out of your brain and body so all that was left was the spinning room and your way-too-fast-beating heart. The actress found out and gave me the older sister talk. Humiliated, I happily carried on seeing him. Desire like this was nothing new to me but fulfilling it was. As I began establishing my sexual power, I used the married man as he used me. It was a rush to see how much I could manipulate and lose myself in love and the intoxication of being desired. Each meeting held such great anticipation that I became addicted to it. But each affair was undermining an already shaky foundation. And there would be more to come.

17

We've Got a Ticket to Ride

Within the first month of knowing each other, Jill and I were whipping up schemes to meet the Beatles. Like generals planning the Normandy invasion, we plotted the thing every day for a year. Like most of the world, I wanted Paul. Jill wanted Ringo, which was just...so Jill. She had this screwy idea that Ringo was the *real* Beatle, the soul of the Beatles—and the fact that he looked so goofy proved it. All the other shallow fans fell for the dreamboats, the lead singers, the cute guitar players—but Jill was not deceived.

We were cunning teenagers wanting to cross over the threshold into womanhood. What would get us there? Love. Giving it. Getting it. We weren't doing drugs or drinking. We didn't go out at night. We kept our plans to meet the Beatles to ourselves. Every day after school we worked on it. This was no prank, no whim, no flaky teen daydream. It was cool, calculating strategy—a business project—and our mission in life.

We had to get Earl involved, that much we knew. He was the linchpin of our plan. He had the connections. He was an established photojournalist with press passes. And he was old. No one would ever suspect him of trying to crash a Beatles bash.

Our scheme began with our going to the Beatles concert in Las Vegas. Earl would get us backstage passes and we'd meet the Beatles. That, we decided, was how it was going to happen, and believe me, it *was* going to happen. Of course, there would be ten thousand kids at the concert—all wanting exactly what we wanted—but Earl was our trump card. He was going to get us into some informal party to be held before the show. That's what the two of us decided, anyway. We played on Earl's nerves to the point where he would go, "Please, my little darlings, I can't do it. Don't ask me to do it!" and break down in tears.

"Listen, Earl!" we'd say. "You're doing it. You want a flash, we'll give you a flash." We'd open our blouses to expose our bras and quickly close them. That was all we'd show and as far as we'd take it. We drove the poor man crazy but, of course, he eventually did it.

We were relentless. The fact that he actually drove us to Las Vegas is evidence of the kind of brainwashing we inflicted on the poor guy. The two of us sat in the back and plotted and planned all the way there. Earl had been listening to us fantasize about the Beatles for the last year. He drove the entire eight hours in the heat listening to our frothy tales.

The hot desert air blew in our faces as Jill shouted out to passing cars, "Ringo is god!" and I screamed "Paul! Paul! Paul! Paul!" We had overdone it on the clothes and makeup, the way teens tend to do when overcome with the need to impress. We thought we looked *great*. Jill made a gorgeous floozy; I affected the nymphomaniac schoolgirl look. Pickup trucks swerved off the road as rednecks caught a glimpse of two scantily dressed, Beatle-obsessed young tarts in the skimpiest of outfits. As we entered Las Vegas with Earl, the classic dirty old man beaming at the wheel, we resembled two sex-crazed, doped-up, out-of-control groupie call girls with their rumpled pimp on a rampage through Sin City.

Poor Earl. We didn't even let the guy take a nap when we got to Vegas. As he moaned, we barked orders at him: "Earl, we told you what you had to do. Now stop dawdling around and get on with it!"

"Oh my god, I can't believe you girls really expect me to—"

"Earl! You're pathetic!"

"Okay, okay. You win."

The idea was for him to get us into this preshow party, and come hell or high water we were going to be there. Well, Earl came through—I haven't the foggiest idea how, and I didn't ask. Somehow we expected everything to just come to us, and it usually did. That night we ended up at a preconcert cocktail party in a sleazy hotel room with too many middle-aged A & R men. The kind of balding, paunchy music-biz types in sharkskin suits you see in industry trade papers. Freeloaders, lushes, and loud boring guys in golf shoes telling stupid jokes. No Beatles.

A lot of letching took place but we had to do what we had to do. Which was to just go in there and charm them. Jill was shameless. I remember her sitting on one guy's lap. Grimacing and brushing away hands that were groping me, I caught her action from the corner of my eye. I hadn't really seen how outrageous and blatantly sexual and flirtatious she could be. I knew it lurked there somewhere but it was still a bit shocking. She took over in the places I just couldn't go. Like hiking up her skirt so it slid across her thighs and stroking their eager faces with her long white fingers. We were going to do whatever it took short of sleeping with these men to get what we wanted. We would tease and pretend. We were used to that.

That night we went to the concert. It was mass hysteria: girls screaming, wailing, tears streaming down their cheeks, pulling their hair like some bad production of a Greek tragedy. It was full teen-cult frenzy, and we were screaming and yelling along with everyone else. We screamed from the first instant the Beatles appeared until long after they'd left the stage. We lost our voices. Every one of these girls wanted in the most fanatical way to get as close to John, Paul, George, and Ringo as humanly possible—to physically merge with them.

"No one here is going to get anywhere near them," we were thinking. "THEY'RE OURS!" We were a hundred percent sure. Confidence fueled us forward; we couldn't let our elaborate plan fail.

The next day Earl drove us all the way back to L.A. in the heat—Jill and I sitting in the back sweating, Earl talking to himself the whole time: "I must be crazy! I *am* crazy! I was a reasonable, sensible, highly respected member of the journalistic community and you two lunatic girls have turned me into a sniveling, pandering Beatle pimp! You've driven me crazy."

"C'mon, Earl," we told him. "You love it. Without us you'd just be a dirty old man dreaming about driving two gorgeous chicks to Las Vegas. Woooweee!" Jill and I sat in the back fantasizing about how we'd kiss and hug our Beatles. Make them crave our cute little bodies and more! Taking our vision to the limit, and, of course, never letting Earl off the hook. We were two obsessed girls in the grip of Beatlemania, and Earl was our ticket to ride.

When the concert had come and gone, we knew what the next step had to be: close encounters of the third kind. We knew because we had plotted it for a year. We knew that after playing Vegas, our future boyfriends would be coming to California. Fuck the concert! We were totally *over* the concert; it wasn't about the concert anymore. Just sitting and screaming and seeing them from so far away was never going to do it for us. Now it was about how we were going to get to them *physically*. Project Meet the Beatles (part two) was under way.

We wore Earl down with our angelic pleas until he finally got to the president of Capitol Records. Earl asked to be invited with his "nieces" to the party that was being given for the Beatles in his backyard. The only people who were invited were celebrities and their children. That was it. We weren't celebrities—just working actresses—and I certainly wasn't a child. This was a quintessential Beverly Hills party. A tea party, no less, with movie and TV stars and their families. There were no Peggy Liptons or Jills required. We needed a solid invitation. A year in the making; the rest would be up to us.

But soon our plans went haywire. When Earl finally came through, as we knew he'd have to, Jill was working on a movie and couldn't go. Oh my god, I was going to have to handle everything myself. How could she— my partner in crime—do this to me? Okay, I told myself, calm down. Go with plan B. What plan B? I didn't have one.

18.

Meeting Paul

arrived at the party wearing a pink silk skirt and my mother's Emilio Pucci checkered jersey top and little heels. I just walked in and pretended to be very blasé, like I wasn't about to expire with every step. Well, I *am* an actress, so I said, "Peggy, imagine you're a very composed, cool character who is not in the least inhibited by all these famous people and what's about to unfold." It worked. I began snaking my way through the crowds that had gathered on the lawn in anticipation of greeting the world's most alluring popstars. I found myself talking to people. It was better than chewing on the inside of my mouth, which by now I couldn't stop doing. I talked to everyone . . . anyone I met. The lovely Eva Marie Saint said hello and told me that she thought I resembled her! I felt extremely flattered. Enough to momentarily drop my *raison d'être*—then it all hit me again. I'm going to see *him*. My heart was ready to burst open with my secret. I'd just have to stay cool for a little while longer.

I started aimlessly floating around. I could no longer concentrate on talking to people. I don't know where *they* were or where *he* was, but I was feeling it, believe me. Without warning, the four of them appeared, sitting on high wooden stools under a big tree. Someone politely announced that children should come forward now and say hello. To my dismay I saw a line forming—a line of little kids! They were all so small—their moms sending them off with tears in their eyes. I was obviously not a kid but a woman towering ridiculously over them in my slick Pucci getup. The only thing I had in common with those kids was that we'd all been outfitted by our mothers. Sweating rivers through my clothes, I was feeling somewhat humiliated but unerring in my determination. The whole year of longing culminated in this moment. Adolescence was over forever. I was in line to meet the Beatles.

The Fab Four under a tree. They looked cute. Just like the photos I had strewn across the walls of my bedroom. But I knew they weren't the cuddly mop tops they were pretending to be. You knew that when you got up close. John's twisted smile, for one thing, suggested a lot of strange thoughts could be going on in his head. Ringo, sporting a huge grin, seemed utterly bemused and nonchalant about it all. George was wiry and agile, adjusting his body to shake as many of the little hands as he could. I watched Paul. It felt like he was doing a sort of music-hall soft shoe routine for the crowd.

He was being a showman, a carny. The nice one who could engage the multitudes. I didn't know if I'd be able to talk when my turn came. What was there to say? My mind went completely blank.

Okay, so John greeted me first, then George took my hand. I hardly remember them. Paul was the one I was watching and my heart was pounding too loud, sounding like thunder in my ears. "Look, Peggy," I said, trying to get a grip on myself. "He's being really sweet with these kids." I was admiring that while he was looking down and patting them on the head. All of a sudden I felt him looking at me and it was a totally different look. It was filled with promise and sexuality and I was stunned.

"Come on, Peggy, you can do it. Shake hands!" Earl was shouting as he was photographing me. I was embarrassed. "Please stop, Earl," I thought. But this was a great moment for him, too. He actually saw his diligent work paying off. I wanted Paul at that moment as much as I had ever wanted anything in my life. I came face to face with him.

"Hello," I said, and he shook my hand and looked at me.

"My god, you're beautiful," he said.

"You're not so bad yourself," I replied, like an idiot. A year in the planning and that was all I could come up with?

My knees under the pink silk skirt buckled. I was madly in love with Paul McCartney, or should I say even *more* madly in love—knowing full well that disaster lay ahead. How could it be otherwise? *Every* woman wanted Paul.

"Well, move on. Next person," said a disembodied voice from hell. I went to the next person who was George Harrison or whomever. I couldn't have cared less. I had made the connection. Paul had looked at me with his puppy dog, long-lashed, beautiful eyes and that was it. Paul moved on with his conversation and charmed the next fan in line.

I grabbed Earl, who was positively gleeful. "What am I going to do now? You have to give him my number." Poor Earl. And then I realized I also had to work it out so that Jill would be able to come with me.

Earl slipped a note to somebody. "Peggy really likes Paul," it said, "and here's her number." Later on, the band's press agent called Earl to hook up and I was asked to come to a bash that evening. Bliss now and a mind going wild with anticipation. But I was worrying about Jill. I *had* to get Jill in.

Thinking Jill would be furious with me for scoring without her, I miscalculated. Somehow I let it be known that Jill wanted to be with Ringo—just blurted it out to the press agent who invited me. How crass! How childish. How could I?

Well, she didn't talk to me for a long time after that. After all our planning, I'd messed the whole thing up. I had no class, no common sense, no feminine wiles, no criminal mind. Jill wanted to do it on her own. As close as we were, she expected me to know that. Jill didn't need me to set the thing up, she didn't *want* it if it had to be that way. She figured if she met Ringo under those auspices, when she got there, he'd just say, "Oh, *you're* the girl. Let's go fuck."

I'd ruined everything. Even worse, I'd gone against her carefully crafted script! After all, Jill had been writing the play in her mind for more than a year. We each had our own sacred fantasy. Jill never would have been so crude as to ruin it for me. If only I'd considered things for one minute! I thought I had to take care of her, but actually it was Jill who had to be in control—and suddenly with Ringo, the most important thing in her life, she wasn't in control of anything.

Before I left for the party, I told my parents where I was going. They were genuinely excited for me. Little did they know. I got dressed up in a perfectly sweet little shift with heels and gold hoop earrings. I looked pretty and demure and different. I went by myself with all the confidence I could pack in the little clutch bag gripped tightly under my arm. The Beatles were staying at someone's very large home in Bel Air. I arrived almost sick to my stomach with butterflies. I had lost my virginity only six months earlier and I'd been thinking about Paul day in and day out for a year. He greeted me sweetly and checked me out with a quick once over. He liked what he saw. We sat downstairs. He played the piano. The next thing I knew we were on our way upstairs. Upstairs, we both knew what would take place. I tried to stretch it out. The fantasy was all playing out a little too fast. He took me in his arms and kissed me. May I say that this was the kiss of my dreams? As good, passionate, tender and exciting as I ever could have imagined. Kissing his mouth was delicious. I took a shower to slow things down and when I came out wrapped in a towel, he caressed me in front of the window and let the towel fall to the floor. This to me was an utterly romantic gesture. Paul was a romantic. A confirmation of how I had pictured him for the last year.

During our lovemaking, I caught myself . . . thinking. How was this making me feel? Special? Connected in any way? I didn't have to pretend how attracted to Paul I was. My body felt like it was being covered in molten lava. Every touch, every movement of his was erotically plugged into my psyche. It went on like that for much of the night. But I was also starting to navigate outside my sensations and becoming the observer. I couldn't seem to help it. I couldn't just *be*. I had too much riding on this one encounter. We carried on for a long time. I liked absolutely everything about him, yet when we walked downstairs together I wasn't feeling too good. I saw myself as just a young girl he had taken to bed and that was it. I wasn't imagining this. It had less to do with the sex then just feeling starved to be comforted after pursuing him in the unabashed way I had. Wanting the feelings to be mutual. Uhn uh. Not realistic. It was all predicated on too much fantasy. He could never feel the way I did. The whole world was open to him and he intended to experience it.

He sat at the piano and played me a song. I got the feeling it all applied to me. "If when he calls she runs away and he calls her back, she comes. If there's a next time he's okay 'cause she's under both his thumbs." We had slept together; I had succeeded in my mission and the evening was over. Finished. I left. Oh, it was a bad night. Constantly searching in my head for anything I had done, or word that I had uttered, that might have been wrong, naive, stupid, or needy.

Paul called the next night and I went back. Well, of course I did. Once couldn't be enough. The second time we were together, I was even *more* nervous and upset. I wanted to make love to try to cement a bond. Once again it was sexy and I felt even more reeled in. But by the time our tryst was over I felt chilled and just wanted to go home to my own bed in the comfort and safety of my parents' house. I was no longer willing to be transparent with my feelings. When you have a hyper critic living inside your head, it doesn't matter if words are spoken or not. You hear yourself and you're sure the whole world is in on it. At this point, it's time to gather your wits and get out. Which is what I did. I slipped away to my car and headed home. I didn't see Paul again that summer. He left town as the tour moved on.

I was devastated. Jill wasn't speaking to me although I kept calling her in tears. Eventually, she listened to my misgivings. I poured my heart out.

For months I moped. I was still living at home and didn't want my parents to see me this depressed. I'd hide in my room at night listening to music or reading, but they knew. Being under contract to Universal Studios, I was working constantly. This helped because no matter how sad I was, I just had to get up and go to work—I had no choice.

19.

Same Time, Next Year

A year later, the Beatles came back to Los Angeles on tour. I had pulled myself together. I was working on a consistent basis. I was dating and going out. But somehow I knew I would see Paul again. He had a serious girlfriend in England, Jane Asher, but when he called me I went to see him with hardly a hesitation. The Beatles were renting a house in Benedict Canyon, and it was there that I first smoked grass.

I came for dinner, and I was the only girl there. John definitely didn't like that. He didn't like me being there at all. He was mean and sarcastic. As far as he was concerned, I had no business being invited to dinner with the four of them. For him this was an exclusive boys' club. He was purposely making me feel uneasy. Around Earl and Jill, I could be outgoing, but at the slightest hint of confrontation I would wither. Well, I was withering. With all my so-called sexual bravado, I was completely insecure at my core.

At one point, the boys were handing around a scrapbook—looking at pictures of that first tour. John made some snide comment like, "What is *she* doing here?" I got the idea that he thought Paul was an idiot to take a girl so seriously he'd actually invite her to dinner, when all he really needed to do was fuck her *after* dinner. Get me away from this, I thought to myself. When Paul suggested we smoke a joint, it sounded like a great idea.

We ended up smoking in the bathroom before other people arrived. Ringo, George, Paul, and . . . Peggy. We hung our heads like balloons tied together over the toilet silently blowing out the smoke. This was illicit business and we were having fun. I had been temporarily cowed by John's gratuitous attack, but it wasn't until I got high that I got *really* paranoid. At first I felt great and giddy. Paul and I emerged from the bathroom and floated into the living room where there was a film being screened. We had a few laughs in the dark; he held my hand. But I was way too high. A sinking feeling began to take over; Paul was tuning out.

Every thought of mine now magnified. Did he care the way I did? Would I be able to captivate him enough sexually? Would he ever want to be with me again?

Usually talkative and animated, Paul became silent in bed. We made love, and for a while my anxieties receded, but as he drifted in and out of sleep, I knew I was losing him. I lay there for a while crying—without him knowing—and then I got up, gathered my clothes and silently slipped out the door.

This was really terrible. Horrible. I should never have gotten high with him, I thought on the way home. I knew that Paul didn't want me anymore, that it was all over—my life was over.

I didn't see Paul again on that particular trip. For one thing, I wasn't about to compete with the new breed of overzealous groupies. By now, they practically had their own union. They had honed it so finely, its rules were byzantine and strict, and no one got in their way. Some famous groupie came in and took my place. Someone beautiful, sexy, and everything I wasn't. I was this skinny nobody fresh from high school who had taken the whole thing too seriously.

By the time the Beatles left town that week, I had to face the truth. I wasn't going to have a future with Paul. So obvious, yet I was utterly consumed with grief and loss. Even so, I couldn't blame him. He had skyrocketed from being a working-class guy playing in a Liverpool bar band to being one of the most celebrated and desirable men in the world. I was just sane enough to recognize the sexual attachment and impossible expectations I had invested in our relationship—was it even a relationship? I had set myself up for a hard fall. It wasn't the first time I'd succumbed to an obsessively passionate love affair, and it certainly wouldn't be the last.

20.

Don't Open
the Door

One night about three months
later, I went to the Daisy, a popular nightclub, after shooting a
guest role for *Chrysler Theatre*. We had been
on location all day. I needed to move to my
own rhythm, so I danced alone. A tall
blond surfer type was eyeing me from the
bar. His name was Rick. He was very
good-looking and dressed to the nines in a
blue and white sport shirt with the collar
turned up. Not necessarily my type but his
sex appeal was undeniable. He came over
to me on the dance floor and asked me to
sit and have a drink with him. I did.
Within minutes he was telling me a sad
tale of woe about an affair he was having
with a very big star's wife.

My self-esteem had hit an all-time low.
I didn't know that he was a raging alcoholic.
He wanted to take me home and when we

got outside he accused me of flirting with someone else and slapped me across the face. Incredibly, I still went home with him. What was I thinking? The day after it happened I went into my mother's studio while she was painting. I guess what I was truly yearning for was her comfort and for her to tell me she understood. I told her what had happened and she didn't handle it very well. In fact, she kind of freaked out. It must have had something to do with her own fears. All support or hope of her intervention went out the window and I moved into his house within a week, diving headfirst into a destructive and violent relationship. I spent almost every night of the following year with him, and most of those nights he was drunk. The sex, the making up after he hit me, became an addiction for me. Like most enablers of alcoholics, I fully believed that he could change, miraculously get sober, and become a nice guy who loved me. I didn't have the confidence or tools to deal with the undeniable truth: that he was an abusive drunk who became violent and took his rage out on whatever was in his path. I couldn't tear myself away.

It was the same thing over and over again. Ricky would get very drunk. I'd be frightened out of my mind, not knowing what he would do, and then we'd end up making love. He didn't have these rages all the time. Or should I say, I learned how to sometimes diffuse the tension before he became violent. He also had other girlfriends. He went to see them or he'd just sink into a fit of drunken tears and pass out. But the violence was escalating, and I was starting to show body and facial bruises. We would break up and I would go back. The sex after these tirades became addictive in its own way. He needed me more. He was arduous and apologetic. Ricky would swear it wouldn't happen again and pledge his undying love. These acts of passion felt good only at the time they were happening. Then, like any addict, the need and desire to recreate them would take over all my senses and my basic common sense. And I'd stay and stay, waiting for those passionate moments to happen again. I couldn't go out with my friends. They would see how obsessive I was and the state of my injuries. Shame took over. I hid it from my parents as best I could but they were beginning to figure it out. Maybe they weren't aware to what extent it had escalated, but I would stay away for weeks and then when I'd finally come home, I'd avoid eye contact and hide in my bedroom.

One night after finding out—through my own admission—that a year before I'd had an affair with Arthur, a married Englishman who'd once been a publicist for the Beatles, we ran into him and his wife at a popular restaurant called the Luau. It was some kind of Polynesian watering hole where drunks hung out and mobsters made deals and passed money under the teakwood tables to movie stars and producers. Usually we went out with his friends in tow and they would act as a sort of buffer for me. Most of Ricky's friends were alcoholics so they tended to play well together, mercifully taking the focus off me. On this particular night, however, we were alone, and I started shaking almost uncontrollably when he called the English couple over to have a drink at our table.

The Englishman and I said cordial hellos, acting as though we had met only once before. I watched them both guzzle down the scotches and brandies. I had tremendous trepidation about where this was going. I tried to remain calm. Underneath that exterior was a frantic child screaming and praying, "Please don't let anything happen tonight." Before I knew it, Ricky had invited the couple back to his house for more drinks. He was silent with me in the car, racing his Stingray Corvette up Benedict Canyon. He was all over the road. What would be a worse fate at this point, I wondered: crashing in this car or ending up at his house in what I knew was going to be a disastrous situation. The choices weren't good. I was immobile. Frozen. I just kept praying and calling on an imaginary angel to protect me. When I got to the house, I started thinking of ways to escape—just in case.

It all seemed to be going fairly smoothly as we hung around the bar—until, that is, Ricky took a huge gulp of J&B and turned to Arthur.

"So, I heard you fucked Peggy," he said, point blank. Shit! It was three A.M. The little bar in the corner of the living room was lit by one lamp. Arthur's wife was demurely sitting on her bar stool. The Beach Boys were playing as background music. To someone looking in, we would have seemed a foursome in a very cozy setting, having nightcaps and a friendly chat.

Ricky lunged at Arthur. I ran into the bathroom and locked the door. Someone could get killed here, I thought to myself. I made up my mind that if I got out in one piece I would never be with this maniac again. Through the open window, I heard the footsteps. They were all running down the street. I heard Arthur's wife scream out, "Somebody call the police. He's going to kill him!" Then silence. Within a minute or two, an out-of-control alcoholic in a furious rage tried to kick down the bathroom door. Luckily Ricky wasn't capable of using his full strength, as he was exhausted from the chase. I assumed Arthur and his wife had gotten out safely because Ricky was alone and now moaning and crying after an hour of trying to get in. He begged me to open the door.

"Don't open it, Peggy," I heard an inner voice say. My teeth were chattering. I was petrified. I was experiencing the very real possibility of being beaten to death. Yet it took all the courage I could muster not to let him in when he swore to Almighty God that if I opened the door, he would never hit me again. Ricky said he loved only me and he was sorrier for this than anything else he had done in his life. He became delirious and started sobbing about the way his father had beaten him when he was a child. After two hours of my waiting out his rage, I came out of the bathroom and found him passed out in a heap right outside the door. I grabbed my little suitcase, ran to my car, and left. It was over, or so I thought.

21.

Exit Adonis, Raging

moved back into my parents' house and started seeing Jill again. Jill, my beautiful, dark, protective angel. She was so important to me, yet I had told her almost nothing about my last year. When you are in an abusive relationship, windows to the outside world close. I had shut her out. It was pure joy and a relief when we started seeing each other again. I told her everything. One night we went to the Daisy together. It wasn't what we usually did, but I wanted to show it to her. After all, it was a very hip spot with good music to dance to. We were standing at the bar when Ricky walked in. He tried to talk to me.

"Get away from her!" Jill yelled, after taking one look at him. I couldn't believe what was happening. It seemed like he wanted to apologize. Suddenly Jill was acting like a protective mother hawk swooping down and pushing me out of the club.

"You must never let that guy near you again," she said, when we got back to my parents' house. She was furious; I was still trying to make excuses.

"But it seems like he's better," I said, half believing it. "It's really okay now."

"No," she said. "It's not okay."

I said nothing.

"Forget it," Jill kept saying. "You can never see him again." Someone was finally standing up for me. Someone was finally talking to me with the voice of reason. I was taking it in, but as an enabler, when you really have to disconnect from an alcoholic and abuser, you come face to face with trying to break another addiction, and it's your own.

Suddenly there was a car in the driveway and then a fist banging on the sliding glass door to my bedroom. Ricky had followed us home. I opened the curtains and saw him standing outside, no longer the tall, handsome Adonis I had first perceived him as, but more like the pitiful, self-loathing, defeated drunk he had become. I had the hugest pang of feeling sorry for him.

"Please let me in. I love you. I can't live without you." He was crying.

Jill stood behind me and in a beautifully contained way said, "Don't open the door." She was definitive and said the exact words that I had said to myself weeks ago: "Don't open the door." It had now become a catch-phrase for self-preservation and survival.

"Please, I love you so much. Please, baby let me in," he pleaded.

Something awful clicked inside me, a thought: "Things will be different this time." I opened the door. The moment I did, he grabbed me by my neck, threw me over the desk and started choking me. Jill ran and got my parents out of bed. My dad pushed him up against the wall with one hand and started calling the police with his other. Ricky broke free from my father's grip and ran out the door with his tail between his legs, never to be seen again.

22.

Blue

first saw Terence Stamp at a full-moon
party in Malibu. In his autobiography he
wrote this pipe dream about me:

*Then I saw a fairy. She floated across the
hall from room to opposite room. Something
from* Les Sylphides. *How strange, I
thought, distracted, and made my way into
the room she'd entered. It was dim and appeared empty: I looked around, seeking another exit. There wasn't one. I looked up the
chimney and then sat on the floor. . . . I
leaned my back against the wall and closed
my eyes for a moment. When I opened them
the fairy was standing in the door.*

That was back in 1967 when I could
still vanish and rematerialize at will. And
Terence was just so stoned. Sheepishly he
admitted he'd been smoking quite a bit of
Acapulco Gold, and, in his quaint Cockney

manner of speaking, did a little commercial for the sacred herb: "You know, they say it's so good you can actually hallucinate from it."

In 1967 I was in a movie with Terence Stamp and Joanna Pettet called *Blue*. When the film came out, much fun was made of Terence playing a Mexican bandito who, halfway through the film, delivers his first words, "I'll do that," in a thick Cockney accent. "Where is this cowboy from?" one incredulous commentator asked. Why, from the '60s, of course! *Blue* was a classic '60s western. No good guys, no bad guys, the hero is—what else?—an antihero, a mildly schizophrenic character who doesn't fit in anywhere and has temporarily lost the power of speech. The movie's tagline was: "To escape his past, he had to destroy it." Hilarious stuff in retrospect. Terence played Azul (Spanish for "blue") and Joanna played Joanne Morton, the beautiful woman whose love changes him.

Terence had dyed his hair white-blond for the film. He was gaunt and sexy with deep creviced dimples and turquoise eyes. The most attractive thing about him, though, was the contrast between his street energy and his patrician refinement. Nothing got by Terence's radar. He could out-match you at any time discussing art, history, literature, film, and the occult. He was the most magnetic man I'd ever met. I fell madly in love with him on the spot. But then, every woman—and man—was in love with Terence. I was introduced to Joanna Pettet that night and I knew immediately that he was going to fall in love with her. Compared to her I was a mere peon, a shy teenager. She was a self-possessed sophisticate and he was an intense romantic. So much for my wild fantasies. Once in a while I won the race because I was a good runner, but this one I knew was hopeless.

For *Blue*, I went on location for two months to Moab, Utah, in the heart of Mormon country and was immediately thrown into a wild scene. I was nineteen years old and still living with my parents. My brother, Bob, also under contract to Paramount, had a part in the film as Antonio, one of the banditos, and for two weeks I was comforted by his being there. Then he went home and I was really on my own.

Mike Nader, a friend from my acting class, was also cast in the movie and when we both were on hold for the day's shoot we'd make little side trips to shop for Native American artifacts, go bowling with the locals, or horseback ride across the expansive plains during the early evening hours. Being friends with Mike made the days when we didn't work pass happily. Silvio Narizzano was the director of *Blue*. The first day of shooting his lover died in a car crash on location. How he dealt with his grief and kept shooting the film, I'll never know. How do films ever come together, anyway, with so many disparate elements making the whole undertaking seem like it's always at risk?

I had a very small part in the movie. Being under contract to a major studio, you did what they told you to do. I played a young pioneer girl and had no dialogue. I cried every day because I missed my parents and home and couldn't get over my crush on Terence.

We filmed during the blistering heat of mid-July, when insects the size of birds came at you all day. We all assembled on the soft banks of the Colorado River for weeks on end. The marvelous and musty smell of clay and the perpetual blue skies above the very red canyon peaks were intoxicating enough, but I enhanced the daily experience by rolling my own joints from the stash of Acapulco Gold. We weren't only smoking it; we also brought it with us to the set baked in cookies. The Pillsbury dough kind. We'd clean the grass, roll it in the mushy sweet dough and bake a hundred of them at a time. We smoked and baked that entire summer.

My costume was heavy with crinolines and petticoats under a long full skirt. When we went in the river for the "pioneers crossing" scene, the director, high on a camera crane five hundred yards away, shouted for us all to get on our knees. The waters were too low, so we had to get down on our knees to look as if we were nearly drowning. Then the most joyous thing happened. The current took me swirling in its warm waters down river. I kept trying to stay upright to look as if I were standing, but I tilted and tanked, and came up with Colorado River mud oozing from my mouth and dripping from my hair. The shot was ruined. Who cared? It was a delicious afternoon.

By now, Joanna and Terence, Terence and Peggy, Mike Nader and Peggy, and Joanna and Mike Nader were a close foursome enjoying each other as friends.

Each night when we got home early enough from the set, we ate at the local diner together—cheeseburgers and western omelets were the specialties. We were cowgirls and cowboys enjoying ourselves. One night we heard about a place called Scofield's. A new place to eat! We were so excited that the four of us immediately got into a jeep and lit out over the rough dusty roads and boulders, dodging coyotes and snakes. It felt like real freedom to be away from the set and out into the magical wilderness. Terence drove like a maniac under the stars—billions and billions of them. It was a light show of sparkling diamonds. The magnitude of the open sky and its vastness was something I'd never seen before. I lay back with my head looking up and counted my blessings. God was everywhere.

When we got to Scofield's an hour and a half later, the owners welcomed us with a delicious meal: steak and french fries. A fortune teller appeared from nowhere with cards and a crystal ball. She told Terence that he and I might fight but would always keep a deep connection. She saw he was a seeker and something of a mystic. She told me that I had been sad as a child and not to worry, that my path would be a spiritual one at some point in my life. After having our fortunes read, we drove back in silence. Some door had been opened to another realm for all of us and we didn't want to discuss it. We were peaceful under the billion stars.

23.

Moonflowers

On the set, the hired extras were young teenagers who read their Boy Scout manuals in between shots. They looked innocent enough, but the way they kept eyeing us as suspect Hollywood freaks told me they weren't. They must have gathered we had more than a botanical interest in the local flora and fauna because they started confiding in us.

"Hell, you can go up on the Colorado and get the best drugs you ever had in your life," they said.

At dusk, Joanna and I were assigned to go to a spot they had described and went out to pick the moonflowers, as they were called, and bring them back to our motel to make salad. They had been used for centuries by the Native Americans for rituals and ceremonies to evoke their totem gods and spiritual ancestors. Joanna and I, still dressed in costumes from the day's shoot, proceeded with caution as we gathered bunches of moonflowers. Sundown, when they opened, was apparently the only time they could be harvested. The stems, we were told, were so poisonous that if you touched them you could die from the contact. Adventure!

We put on heavy cowhide gloves and stashed hundreds of white flowers in the folds of our voluminous prairie skirts. In a manic flash of giggles and screaming our mission was accomplished. Back at the motel we picked the petals from the flowers and very carefully washed and cleaned them. Terence, Mike, Joanna, Silvio, and I had a most unusual dinner that night, one that we could never have seen ourselves eating a month before: a lettuce and moonflower salad.

Hours passed. It was taking forever. Nothing happened. We were sitting around waiting for the big moment to arrive and, in unison, they all said, "Well, we're going to go to sleep."

"How can you go to sleep when we're just about to have a mind-altering experience?" I asked. "Just wait, something will happen."

"Oh, Sunflower," said Terence. "You're such a hippie."

I went up to my room and lay down. Nothing was going to happen, I thought, and got into bed to go to sleep. Maybe these Boy Scouts were just having a bit of fun with us Hollywood prima donnas—they were probably having a good laugh at us gallivanting across the river banks.

Quite suddenly every inch of my bed was moving, hundreds of tiny bumps pulsating to individual rhythms. And thousands of iridescent insects were pouring out of the ceiling. While I was looking up at the ugly light fixture—the one with the gold chain that hangs over the round table in every motel room in America—it morphed into a giant ancient insect that began coasting on scintillating molecules of air towards my bed. It was classic psychedelia and I wasn't afraid. I was watching a movie in my head in brilliant Technicolor. Never had a drug trip taken such a clear path away from my worries and allowed me to just ride it like a wave in the surf. Easy and fearless. I didn't want to go to sleep, but my eyes became wonderfully heavy—the movie was over.

The next day I excitedly inquired of everyone who had eaten the flowers the night before, "Didn't all of you have the best trip?"

"What trip?" they said. "Peg, absolutely nothing happened."

No one had had this dream. In a way I was glad that the moonflower experience hadn't happened while I was with them. It was my own little secret that whole summer.

After the movie wrapped, Terence and I went to Haight-Ashbury in San Francisco. Long-haired radicals on the street were yelling peace slogans: "Stop the war now!" "Get our soldiers out!" On every corner, beggars, high and hungry, were shaking paper cups that held only a few coins—panhandlers with improbable hustles: NEED BREAD TO RETURN TO HOME PLANET. Psychedelic shops with acid-green-painted doors were hocking posters, bongs, T-shirts, and tie-dyed everything. Incense and pot and patchouli wafted from the doorways. Jim Morrison and Janis Joplin screamed from stereos, beckoning you to come inside.

Terence and I were dancing down the street, our green, gold, and purple love beads jangling as we went. We were in love with the day, the times, the high. We bought each other two vintage Navy peacoats and wore them that whole year, even in the summer heat. We felt blessed and a part of it all, riding this incredible wave on a chromatic sea of thoughts, sounds, smells, and emotions. We stayed in a hotel in San Francisco and made love all day. But coming down from any high means facing reality. Terence didn't love me the way I wanted to be loved—in that all-consuming way—but deep friends we would become, and as we walked arm in arm down Haight Street, I sensed that Terence, the enigmatic lost boy, would always remain a part of my life.

24.

I Heard the Word

Terence's whole family were geniuses —and very flash. He and his brother Chris were East End boys with a touch of menace. I had a fling with Chris, too. If I couldn't have Terence, I'd have Chris. I spent a lot of white nights with Chris and Terence and Pete Cameron. Pete and Chris were managing the Who. Pete was a rascal, brutally honest and seemingly very much in control of his own wild lifestyle. He was the older man, the friend, the adviser. Filming on *Blue* was over, but Terence, Pete, Chris, Mike Nader, and I had become like a little family, and we were trying to carry on the mood.

It was at one of those draggy, druggy events that Pete said to me, "Y'know what your problem is, darlin'? You're compulsive." It wasn't meant to be insulting. But he knew me well enough. In Cockney argot, he'd "sussed" my problem. He knew I'd slept with Chris Stamp, had un-containable feelings for Terence, and had had a fling with Keith Moon, the Who's totally over-the-top drummer (though I had tried to keep that one a secret). He knew that in my pursuit of love, I was leaving wreckage in my wake. It was just Pete's raw, uncensored observation and he was right. In his own inimitable way he was trying to make me see that part of myself. His remark set off an alarm in my mind that rattled it like pots and pans. I had never heard the word before, much less applied to me. But for a kid who wanted to be accepted and perfect, it was shattering. Then again, having to be perfect *is* compulsive.

Five minutes after this happened, I saw a girl come out of the bed-room. A lithe, nonchalant beauty, the epitome of '60s easy cool. For a second I thought, "Oh, I wish *I* could be like that!" She was the very model of glamorous detachment that I was looking to emulate. But when she turned around in her mini halter top, her back and arms were scarred with pockmarks and pimples—a minefield of red holes and pus. She was shooting speed. Methedrine.

There was a part of me that wanted to escape into that world. I'd never gone near methedrine or heroin, but I easily could have. I wanted to be high all the time—on anything. Maybe it was to court oblivion, keep memories buried or communicate with God.

Still, seeing what I could become—a full-fledged addict chipping away day after day, saying "Fuck you!" to the outside world and diving into oblivion—made me very sad. And as I stared at that drug-ravaged girl, I told myself I was never going to let that happen to me.

25.

The Train Was Coming Right at Us

There had been other drug escapades that frightened me. One of them was shortly after I'd met James Fox, a blond, tall, good-looking young Englishman. Although he had the looks of a surfer, he was anything but. He was well-educated and a brilliant actor. He was also quite ethereal; I don't think either one of us at that moment had very strong ties to earth. He took me to a party at the David Selznick and Jennifer Jones estate, a glorious mansion filled with antiques juxtaposed with 1940s California chic. Massive blue and white Chinese vases, the chairs and couches pattern-on-pattern in chintz. It was dazzling eye candy, the living room bathed in the gold light of candelabras. All heads turned as we entered in our striking

Sgt. Pepper jackets and with kohl-rimmed eyes and dashed out to the fresh air of the terrace.

I saw my agent, Dick Clayton, there, and a number of famous old movie stars. It was going to be a typical Hollywood party, and we just couldn't hack it. When we spied James Coburn unruffled and smooth as ice, quietly smoking a joint on the balcony, we casually introduced ourselves. This was a very cool actor and James Fox was in awe.

He asked us to sit with him on a patio couch. Then, right in the middle of the conversation with James Coburn (the usual Hollywood talk about agents and restaurants), I took a hit off a joint that must have been laced with DMT or PCP. Before I knew it, I looked across the lawn and thought I saw an out-of-control passenger train heading toward us, careening from side to side. I could hear its powerful engine roaring through my head, in one ear and out the other. All other sounds became muffled as this train ripped through my eardrums.

Everyone else seemed fine, so I tried to appear cool, like none of this was going on. But I was anything but cool. I locked myself in a bathroom nearby and couldn't move. I wouldn't open the door when guests needed to use it. The viselike pressure felt like the whole universe was sitting on top of my head. Every time I thought I could stand up and get out of the door, I collapsed into the fetal position. Dick Clayton had been looking for me for more than an hour. Finally, he found me in the bathroom and told me it was okay to come out. He pulled me out of my nightmare with a very strong cup of black coffee. I caressed his face with my shaking hands and repeated thankyouthankyouthankyou. A few minutes later, James Fox and I took off in a little red sports car, driving at seventy miles an hour down Sunset Boulevard. We were young and immortal.

We ended up at someone's beach house in Malibu, and the following day James and I made it back to our own homes. Within a week he was on his way back to England and we never saw each other again.

26.

The Peyote and the Plumber

moved out of my parents' home and found an old, dilapidated house in Topanga Canyon, one block from the beach. In 1968, drugs were still a part of my life when Terence arrived at my house with two tabs of peyote.

"We've got to take this, luv. It's supposed to be the best, most natural high of all."

I had never done peyote before but I agreed. Terence popped his tab and I brought mine into the kitchen to take with a glass of water. I looked at the peyote pill and thought, I'm not taking this whole pill. Where had Terence gotten this drug and more importantly where was it taking me? I cut it in half but told him I'd taken the whole thing. Terence had a will of iron. I didn't want to go up against it.

It took effect within the hour and I

started gagging. When pure peyote hits your system, you want to throw up. The gagging went on for six hours. Fortunately our stomachs were empty. But the retching was so intense that for two weeks afterward my stomach muscles were sore. We couldn't do anything once the peyote kicked in but just lie there on the living room floor. The room was spinning and we had to concentrate on not throwing up.

Terence started talking. He'd only recently broken up with his girlfriend, Jean Shrimpton, the top fashion model in the world during the '60s, but he was still very much in love with her. He talked about her as if he were under hypnosis. Everything he was feeling, everything he had gone through, every way he had tried to get her back. Hours and hours of it. We were lying on the floor as he talked on and on about Jean. I wasn't that thrilled listening to Terence's lament for Jean Shrimpton, especially while I was high. He started to weep and writhe on the floor. I felt helpless to comfort him.

Finally he stopped talking and crying, got up, and walked outside. I followed him out onto the deck. He circled his arms wide and his hands met in front of his chest in the Indian greeting of Namaste. He stayed there for a few seconds in reverence of the moment and then whipped his head around to face me.

He looked at me accusingly with those piercing eyes of his, and said, "You!"

"What?"

"You're on a different beam, baby. I knew it."

"I am?"

"You didn't take the whole thing, did you? You didn't take the whole tab of peyote!"

He knew. His hair was standing on end and he was beginning to flush with anger. We had been through enough this evening. I didn't want to argue, and breaking that pill in half was the wisest choice I could have made. A self-protecting, smartly paranoid choice.

"If I had taken that whole damn pill, I wouldn't have been able to take care of *you* for the last eight hours," I responded calmly. He got it.

We tried to make love, but all the passion had been spent. That was funny to us and really sort of friendly. We stayed in bed for a while but couldn't sleep. We went to shower and use the bathroom. The toilet was broken (or at least we thought it was). It was 3 A.M., but we called a plumber from the yellow pages and quite unexpectedly he said, "I'll be right there." It was ridiculous.

Perhaps we had just gone out of our minds, but the plumber coming up the winding stairs to the door looked like an alien. My house was located in the middle of nowhere, and we became paranoid and wary about the plumber—even though it was we who had called him. Why was he here in the middle of the night trying to fix an old toilet? In any case, attempting to engage with anyone when you're that high is a lost cause. The man chatted away and fixed the toilet as we stood around watching and pretending all was perfectly normal while trying to get our mouths to move.

At about five in the morning we got into the military peacoats we had bought in the Haight.

"Let's go out," I said brightly. "Let us go forth and greet the day."

My house was in a ravine behind a creek across the Pacific Coast Highway from the beach. We traipsed through the long grass, laughing. Two beautiful freaks. By now my hair was matted and tangled and my eyes huge and glued open. We started across the highway—it looked as wide as the Ganges—when suddenly we saw a police car coming. At least we thought we saw a police car. We panicked and ran back to the house and waited for Señor Peyote to wear off.

For all his Cockney mockery, Terence was a seeker after profound truths. Once, on a flight from London to Rome, he scrawled me a note:

My dear Peg,

It seems in my new dimension, that you are here talking with me and I like that feeling. I generally do most of the talking. I guess it's okay with you, right? Why are my nails breaking? Is it the life I lead? This flight over the ocean is satin smooth, like a butterscotch sweet. Clouds and mountains beneath me and my thoughts are to you my dear Sunflower. If this letter arrives it means I have.

Yours,

T

I saw Terence once again in 1986 when he had grown up. He was still handsome but he had lost his boyishness. The rigors of his life and many spiritual quests had taken their toll. Still, his twinkling blue eyes made me laugh. He'd been a tremendous influence in my life, but it wasn't until I read his autobiography, *Double Exposure*, that I realized I'd also had an influence on him. I was his "unwitting medium" at the beginning of his spiritual journey. In the book, he makes great fun of me as the "fairy from Malibu" saving bees from the swimming pool at the motel, and talking about the hole at the North Pole—where all the vibrations resulting from the shift in the earth's polar axis were pouring in from space. Well, aren't they?

I Was a Hippie Cop

27.

I Met Him at the Slave Girl Market

Aaron Spelling was always at the Daisy, the private little nightclub in Beverly Hills. He was as much a fixture there as the grand pool table and the room-size bar overflowing with actors, boozers, and letches. I'd show up a few times a week to dance. I was too young to drink, so I'd go off to the tiny dance floor and watusi, frug, and monkey the night away, whether I had a partner or not.

Everyone knew Aaron. He was peculiar-looking: an elfin man puffing on his pipe, very much the stereotypical image of a producer. Aaron sat nightly at a back banquette watching the beautiful young actresses as they strutted their stuff in front of him along with other industry types who might be important. Plenty to drink and plenty of stars made the Daisy jammed every night. When I was eighteen, we were introduced. I knew Aaron was a producer, and he must have guessed I was an actress. When the time came for auditions for *The Mod Squad,* he remembered me from the club.

Aaron was known as a perfectionist, taking meticulous care of his shows plots, sets and especially their characters. The first show he had on network TV was called *Burke's Law* with Gene Barry. Then came *The Mod Squad* and after that *Charlie's Angels.* He was a teenager at heart. He loved young people and wanted to write about them. He'd started out as a writer and along the way had evolved into a big-time producer.

Sometime in 1968, I got a call from my agent.

"There's a really good Aaron Spelling show that's going to be auditioning in about two weeks," he said. "I've got the script here. It's for an ABC pilot about three young cops, hippie cops."

"Well, that's different," I said. "Don't go anywhere. I'll be right over."

I guess the whole point of dancing in front of Aaron Spelling and the rest of the ogling producers and directors had been to get them to put you in a series or a film, but when my agent actually called, my nerves got the better of me. Every audition put me in this state initially and still does. Until I can settle down and focus on the part, I imagine every horrible outcome and embarrassing moment. Can I avoid stammering? Can I remember my lines and the beats of the scene—and connect with the casting person I have to read the scene with? Can I be the crowd pleaser in the room with the producer, director, and writer—and still remain true to the character? It's tough. In any role you go up for, someone's going to get the part and it's probably not going to be you. Those are just the odds. After the usual auditioning experience, you've probably burned up a thousand calories and sprouted some grey hairs. If you survive all this and still believe you did pretty damn well, you'll at least go on to the next audition.

I was at my parents' house when I read the script. As I read, lights exploded in my head and for once it wasn't as a result of drugs.

"I want this part," I said to myself. "I want it badly." I could taste the excitement in my mouth as I danced around my bedroom. It was a terrific script about three young people who worked undercover for the Los Angeles Police Department. It was cool, hip, and different from anything

I'd done. My repertoire until then had consisted of playing a teen at a boarding school (sporting a uniform and a beanie), a seventeen-year-old southern Civil War bride, the young daughter of a homesteader in the wild west of 1860, secretaries, nurses, a teacher's pet in a public school, and a ditsy college coed.

These were the kind of generic parts a young actress got cast in, but this character Julie Barnes *was* me. She was me in my other life, my counter life. She didn't really have a family and had lived on the streets; she was tough and withdrawn and prime for opening her heart to two other misfits like herself. I couldn't stop thinking about her.

28.

How Not to Audition

The day of the audition came. I woke up, yawned, showered, and pretended it was a normal day in my hippie house in Topanga Canyon. What would I wear? The morning had started in a sea of calm; then I decided to smoke a joint, thinking, "This'll get me through the day." Not a good idea.

It took me five hours to get it together. I went into a frenzy trying on and rejecting outfits. It became a kind of existential quest for the perfect look. What would Julie wear? Jeans and T-shirt—and beads. But love beads and granny glasses or just the beads? I dealt with my nervousness by getting more and more stoned and trying on more and more outfits. Perhaps a dress would be better. A tie-dyed miniskirt, maybe, or an Indian wood-block print sarong. I didn't know. Did I even own a skirt? Okay, jeans with boots. Or jeans with sandals? Wait, how about leather? The word insinuated itself into my mind as if spoken by the fashion devil himself. Leather, that's very cop, right? But leather pants or leather jacket? I know, I'll mix and match, sort of cover the whole hippie spectrum. Leather jacket, T-shirt, and sarong, with ankle beads. Peggy, stop! You can't wear something that convoluted. You'll scare the ABC executives. You're not applying for membership in a Marin County commune; you're auditioning for a part. Remember who you are: a runaway, a felon, a street kid. Sneakers! That's it. I'll put on sneakers and it will all come together. I ended up in what I started out in: T-shirt, jeans, beads and dark-tinted granny glasses. The final touch was the sneakers. Five hours later.

I was feeling no pain as I stepped into the sunshine on my way to conquer the world. It was a classic California day and I was a typical California girl. I was out of the house and driving from Topanga to Hollywood. Me, my *Mod Squad* script, and my little red Porsche flying like the wind down the freeway.

I was somewhere in the ethers when I entered the office. I faced a row of network executives in suits. They were a blur. Aaron sat on his couch with a welcoming smile. He was simpatico with me. Despite my nervousness, I picked up on that right away. The first thing the ABC people said was, "Take off your glasses." Darn, I knew it. That's okay, I thought. My ability to stay in the moment as the vulnerable yet cautious Julie Barnes seemed hardwired. Absolutely nothing could steer me from my course. I forgot I wanted the part and succumbed to the dynamics of the scene. In my next conscious moment I heard them ask me to read again and then they all stood up and changed seats. Something was up. The energy was electric. I read the scene again.

"Thank you, Miss Lipton, that was wonderful," they seemed to all say in unison while telling me to wait outside. It's always a good sign when they don't send you home! I was quickly whisked off to a sound stage to stand between Michael Cole and Clarence Williams, both of whom had already been cast—as the characters Pete and Linc. They were warm and adorable. People moved us around, fixed our hair and body positions, and just stood and stared. Even though I was still mildly stoned, I suddenly had a strong inkling that I'd gotten the part. When I looked out at Aaron and the execs now buzzing like bees around a hive, I saw in their faces that something they hadn't anticipated had occurred.

I heard later that they'd seen 150 young women for the part and had already decided on another actress. My audition had been an afterthought, a last-ditch effort to find the character they'd envisioned. They had put a lot into this search and I was feeling the pressure as I waited for what seemed like an eternity outside Danny Thomas's office. He was the show's executive producer. Once more they called me into the room where Aaron was sitting with his pipe and a very nice smile on his face. And so, an hour after I came to the Paramount lot, faced the executives, read my scene, and met two very excited actors, I was Julie Barnes.

Danny Thomas walked in, shook my hand, winked, and said, "Congratulations, kid. You got the job." A wonderful "old Hollywood" moment. At that instant I felt, like a character in a folktale, that I'd been transformed. At the wave of Danny Thomas's wand, dross turned into gold and the milkmaid became a princess. It was too far to travel back and forth to the studio, so I packed up my little house in Topanga, put everything in storage, and moved back to my parents' nest.

29.

The Zeitgeist Kids

We made a two-hour pilot to set up the show's premise: how three outsiders come together and get hired by the police department. One of the scenes was shot on a cold night at the Greystone Doheny Mansion and was consciously modeled on the one filmed in the old mansion near the Griffith Park Planetarium in *Rebel Without a Cause* (starring James Dean, Natalie Wood, and Sal Mineo). Like the characters in *Rebel*, three disenfranchised youths spend their last moments together before being spun dramatically into the violent unknown. They share their fears and lifelong dreams.

We were huddling together against an old stone wall, waiting out the villain's next move, and we began to talk about our backgrounds. Our different personalities started to come out when Pete Cochran (played by Michael) talks about his past—how, although coming from a privileged Beverly Hills home he'd always been rebellious. He'd been disowned by his family after stealing a car just for the hell of it. Being on this team is his way of breaking away from a world of boredom and limitations. Streetwise Linc Hayes (played by Clarence) comes from the ghetto where nine people sleep in one room. His famous line (written by Aaron) was, "Our house had one bathroom and wall-to-wall people." *The Mod Squad* was his way of getting out of that world after he'd been arrested during the 1965 Watts riots. Julie Barnes is a hippie chick from San Francisco. She tells the others she fled her home and joined the squad to work off a vagrancy charge. But she doesn't initially reveal the most surprising thing about herself: Julie's mother is a prostitute.

The *Mod Squad* pilot established our characters: who we were and why we came together and what we were going to be doing as cops. In one scene, we are told that the chief of police has never used kids from the street before and that the department is breaking new ground by having us join the force. They tell us we'll work undercover and carry guns. At which point, we say, "No guns, man." We actors tried to make our language as contemporary as possible, using the street jargon of the time: "Solid" (a Linc specialty), "Groovy, baby," "I'm hip," "Cool, man," "Dig it," "Power to the people," and "Peace, baby, peace." It was very 1969.

Some of the scenes in the pilot were embarrassing for me because of the clothes I had to wear. I felt awkward in the costumes the wardrobe department put me in. Working undercover in a nightclub scene, I was dressed like a Playboy bunny knockoff in a leopard-skin bustier and hat with rabbit ears. Worse was the scene in which I had to appear in a bikini. I was terribly shy and self-conscious about my body. I was tall and so skinny that I couldn't buy women's pants; I had to shop in the kid's department.

With the help of Joanna Pettet, my actress friend from *Blue*, I hit every clothing store in the city in search of the elusive bikini. Joanna was half French, half English, and stunning. In those days I could easily get into idolizing girlfriends, projecting onto them everything I thought I wasn't. The less like me they were, the more I idolized them. Joanna and I went shopping at Saks Fifth Avenue, where we finally found a bikini I could live with. It wasn't easy; I wore a boys' size ten. You could have exhaled and blown me over in that bikini.

30.

Canary with a Broken Wing

After all the struggles with acting and the stuttering and being shuffled around the studios, I finally felt at home on a set. I was one of the stars, which helped to alleviate my insecurities.

Getting the part of Julie Barnes in *Mod Squad* gave me a feeling of euphoria. I felt taken care of. It was very liberating and a change from my usual apprehensions: worrying about who was looking over my shoulder, who might be judging me, and wondering if I had any real talent.

I loved my costars and our crew. I loved the still-friendly Aaron Spelling. Here we were at the genesis of a new, groundbreaking series, and we were being asked to help create our characters, the dialogue, what we would wear. It was as if you could project your idealized self on the screen and have millions of people identify with it.

In interviews Aaron gave about the show, he always described Julie as "a canary with a broken wing." That's the way he saw Julie and it was certainly the way I saw myself. Wounded, but tough enough to hang with two guys. There *is* a tough side to me—the person who will do whatever it takes. I tend to manipulate through my mind before I take action, and I can muster almost superhuman strength when it comes to getting what I want. As Michael says, it's more like I'm an eagle than a canary with a broken wing. He liked to quote Oscar Levant's sardonic remark: "She's as winsome as an iron foundry."

"That's you, Peg," he'd tell me.

Julie had come from a very tough background and she carried that within her, but it was hidden. There were a lot of things about Julie that were just like me, so I didn't really have to adjust my own behavior too much to merge myself with her.

Julie had a deep-seated sadness about her. She was a loner with a damaged past. That was something I had no problem identifying with. Of course, there were pieces of her past that clearly weren't my reality. Julie had been a street person; her mother was a prostitute. But the details didn't matter—the details were really just cultural metaphors. Julie was my alter ego.

Like me, Julie Barnes was always finding herself in sticky situations—although my own near-disasters were different than hers, and certainly not as physically threatening. Then again, hers were scripted! It was the idea that I was putting myself in jeopardy that the audience identified with, as did I. I reveled in the peril and danger that the part called for—whether it was being pursued by a homicidal psychopath or being kidnapped to keep an eccentric old man company. I became involved in these menacing scenarios in much the same way someone watching them might. When my costars would come to my rescue at the end of each episode, I was genuinely relieved.

I wasn't very good with a lot of dialogue or exposition of the plot, but

I knew how to get inside the words. The paradox of my becoming an actor was that I was pathologically shy. I was in my own world, and I knew how to escape into my deliciously detailed fantasy life.

Sometimes I would imagine what Julie Barnes would do if she were me—how much better she would deal with my problems than I ever had. As Julie, I'd fantasize myself delivering withering put-downs to the various overpowering people in my life, and all those stupid guys who were giving me trouble would sit there open-mouthed as Peggy/Julie turned on her heels and walked off into the sunset. Another useful aspect of my role was that I could see Julie as beautiful—something I could never see in Peggy.

By now I was beginning to realize that much of the way people reacted to me had to do with my looks, so when I began to feel insecure I'd retreat into my customary fantasy world. I'd lie in bed late at night and draw an imaginary circle around myself. My body would start to vibrate.

The seduction scene would be set when I'd choose the last man I had obsessed over and pull him toward me by offering a light touch on his hand or a sultry kiss behind his ear. All the words I longed to say would be spoken and he would find that irresistible. Then by the alchemy of my own imagination, a mixture of what could be and what I would eventually be able to make happen, I would become ... him ... loving me. In this very specific and erotic way, I had control over my destiny. And for that hour of indulgence I was no longer the little girl who had been manipulated and molested. At those moments something else in me took over. I was a cat on the prowl, a master criminal plotting her next crime. I invented these little plots to prove I existed, to regain some control. Sex and seduction proved to be an astonishingly effective technique. At least in the beginning.

31.

Love Stinks

I didn't go out on actual dates during *Mod Squad*, if a date is where one goes to dinner, talks, and gets to know someone. Sleeping with someone right away was the only way I could determine if there was anything there. But there was more to it than another body being there. It was the words spoken, the touches given, the feeling of merging into another human being. It was being inside the lover when the passion takes over and nothing else exists. If I was attracted to someone, I wanted to see them that night. I couldn't wait. If I had to wait, I would fantasize the encounter until all the details were in place. My love affairs were often more about the fantasy than the actual person I was involved with.

One of these affairs was with a very attractive talk-show host. I had come to New York during my first year of *Mod Squad* to be a guest on his show. I wasn't particularly good in these situations. I just wanted to sit and observe, not talk about myself. I flirted with him on the show. He was well known and very married. That didn't stop me. He was flirting, too, and I felt the doors of possibility open like I had so many times before.

I plunged ahead, regardless of his martial status, and during the commercial break, delivered my standard line: "What are you going to do later?"

"Be with you," he responded.

I was staying at the Waldorf-Astoria. The network had booked me a huge, beautiful suite. I felt on top of the world that night. I paced like a cat ready and waiting. I wanted him there and when he showed up—at one in the morning—it was in disguise. He was wearing a baseball cap low, nearly over his eyes, and carrying a brown paper bag. They called me from downstairs.

"Miss Lipton, there's a strange man in the lobby who says he needs to make a delivery right now!"

He sure does, I thought. He came up and we made love. He was a very intelligent man, though there wasn't much to talk about at that hour. Only time to pursue the sexual romp. He recited poetry to me, and I slept with him a few more times. I got hurt, of course. Who couldn't see it coming? In order to stop seducing these married men I would have to face the ways in which I needed to feel in control and continually hide the burden of shame within me. Even my success on *Mod Squad*, when it came, did nothing to improve my chaotic sex life. I just kept running.

32.

Imaginary Siblings

From the start, Michael, Clarence, Tige Andrews (who played the police captain) and I were a family. A healing reconstruction of my own family, as it turned out. With Michael and Clarence, I had an intuitive, wordless communication.

The connection was so strong between the three of us that we could, without ever saying anything, sense a wrong note, a bad vibe. If someone on the set gave off divisive or disruptive vibrations, he or she didn't last, and had to leave or incur our wrath. That went for actors, crew members, directors, or writers. Considering how obnoxious we could have been given our youth and instant fame, only occasionally do I recall our actually being hard on someone who came on the show. We knew intuitively who we should warm up to and who we should be wary of. We protected each other. Sometimes an actor or director would come on the set and mess with us—and end up getting his ass kicked, never to return. Once when a director brought me to tears, Michael and Clarence made his life such hell that he threatened to walk off the set. He'd badgered me when I insisted on changing some lines that I was having difficulty saying because of my stutter. Michael and Clarence demanded an apology for me and got it.

Some of the producers and writers found us annoying and elitist. It's true we could be snobs and perfectionists about our show but, hey, it was our baby and it was our responsibility to make it work.

Clarence was serious about acting, but he'd rarely show how much it meant to him. His work was very much internalized. His roots were in the theater. He had come to Aaron's attention for his intense performance in the play *Slow Dance on the Killing Ground*. Clarence was in many ways a genius. He had a sixth sense about people. He was very well read and you would often feel absolutely ignorant around him and the rapid-fire way his brain worked. But he was ever cautious when it came to who he would open up to, if he chose to open up at all.

Clarence was all about discipline, forbearance, and biding his time. He knew when to have fun and when to get serious. He taught me not to be intimidated by other people's hostility or rejection—their behavior is none of your business.

Behind his shades and intimidating gaze, it wasn't all that easy to figure out what Clarence was thinking or feeling. Though Clarence could be daunting, I always felt I could go to his soft side. His soul was beautiful, delicate, and noble. I saw him as a lionhearted king. Journalists would come with their naive and corny questions—like how did he feel playing a black militant with two white hippie cops—and come up against his brick wall.

"I don't want to talk about that crap, man," he'd say. He was often quite feisty and there was nothing he loved more than a good verbal duel.

Michael, on the other hand, was all heart. At first, he didn't want to do the show. He hated the idea of a "hippie cop" show. He didn't want to be a "good guy" who went undercover to set up hippies or rat out his friends.

"If I did that, I'd be the bad guy," he told Aaron Spelling. A lot of producers would have thrown him out, but Aaron in his wisdom said, "That's not what this show is about. It's about three lost people caring for each other. Besides, that's exactly the kind of attitude we want. The kids in this show are rebels; I wouldn't want an actor who wasn't." Very clever. Michael was hooked.

Michael could fall apart over a lost child or animal. He could break down in tears just drinking his coffee in the morning: he'd get upset thinking about the plight of the poor Colombian peasant who, out of breath from the thin mountain air, had cut his finger picking the coffee beans and bruised his hands grinding them in his thatched hut to support his family. I always called Michael an Irish mush.

At other times he was a powder keg, losing his temper over some imagined wrong. But more frequently he'd turn the rage on himself. Anger and feelings of injustice would overwhelm him. If he ever got mad with someone over some unfairness, his first instinct was to fight it out. Then he'd end up turning it inwards and bursting into tears. Clarence would just laugh when Michael got like this.

"Mick, lighten up, man," he'd say, and Michael would get it and relax.

Michael had a leprechaun's lilting personality and Richard Burton–like Celtic good looks. He was so handsome with his curly brown hair and green eyes that girls and grown women would throw themselves at him. One night we were sitting in our car, the Woodie, waiting for the camera to set up a shot. Out of the blue I leaned over and said, "Michael, you're so cute. I want to kiss you." I did, and he was such a good kisser. We didn't sleep together, though. Despite all of my erotic rampages, I knew that would be a big mistake. For once I pulled the plug on something that would have been a disaster. We could always tease each other, though. There was always that nice sexual tension between us. That's what kept it interesting.

Our on-screen relationship precipitated an ongoing item in the fan magazines and tabloids: Pete and Julie, are they a couple? Are they dating? Are they in love? Michael got so tired of answering that question he started saying, "No, you've got it all wrong. It's me and Clarence." Or sometimes, "It's me and Captain Greer."

Tige, who played Captain Adam Greer, was the best friend you could have in any situation on the set. He was very much a part of our group and took all our teasing because he knew we loved him dearly. He was an old hand at TV and bigheartedly shared with us his hard-won observations on the pitfalls and machinations involved in doing a weekly show— invaluable advice for novices like ourselves.

Tige was quite a bit older than us and had been working since he was a young man, so there was a certain groundedness to him. He looked almost comically straight, like a parody of the humorless bureaucrat, but in his heart he was a kid like us. Many times it was hard to get through a scene together because we were prone to the giggles and wouldn't be able to stop. This drove writers and directors crazy. I empathized with their frustration—it was just that we would get loopy from the long hours we were working and had to fight to regain our sanity through laughter. We'd become giddy just watching Tige rehearse in a deadly serious manner the very boring dialogue he always had to say: the inevitable explication at the end of each and every show.

"His boat exploded, caught fire, and sank. The coast guard saw the whole thing," he'd say with as straight a face as he could muster. We'd laugh just watching. But if someone asked us, "What's so funny?" we had to say, "We don't have the foggiest idea."

The inevitable minicrisis always brought us together. One episode was shot in a cave in the California night desert. We were out there for a week—it was 120 degrees in the shade. On the last day I got bitten by a spider—the sort of quirky plot twist they should've incorporated into the script. I broke out with a hot allergic rash all around the bite. I felt sick. It was one of those situations in which I needed some TLC. They were both concerned and Clarence called for the medic on set. In the meantime

Michael found his own stash of soothing tiger balm, rubbed it on the bite, and calmed me down.

On the way back I was so beat I lay my head down on Michael's lap and fell asleep in the car. That was *Mod Squad* in a nutshell, the three of us in the back of the car together, taking care of each other.

And then along came Lou.

33.

I Enter the Lair

With his hat pushed down on his forehead, and dark glasses even at night, Lou Adler cut a strange figure in the eternal sunshine of Southern California. Lou was as famous as you get in L.A. without being a movie star. He'd virtually created a new wave of the California music scene. With his Lenny Bruce beard and his hipster posturing, he was the kind of mover and shaker any aspiring singer would die to have as record producer.

I had been writing songs since I was sixteen—when my parents gave me a tiny piano with a half-size keyboard for my birthday. My influences came from my old rock 'n' roll and rhythm and blues records, and the Alan Freed shows I went to at the Brooklyn Paramount—and later on, from Laura Nyro and Carole King. I bought stacks of sheet music and taught myself to play piano chords.

My friend Allen Warnick was there to encourage me to have fun and be creative. Over the years when I was composing songs he'd sit with me and gently guide some of the lyrics and melodies into a more pop feel. His plan was to find me a record producer, and in 1969 he took me to see two of them: Terry Melcher (Doris Day's son), and when that didn't work out, the formidable Lou Adler.

Lou had discovered the Mamas and the Papas and produced their hit records. Surprisingly, he agreed to the meeting Allen had proposed. Lou was as intrigued by me as I was by him. Attraction, attraction, attraction. Have I said it enough? That's all it was. At first I just wanted him to hear what I'd written and let me know if he thought it was any good.

I walked into his Bel Air home on a shimmering hot summer day. It took a full minute for my eyes to adjust to the dark, curtained interior. Everything was low to the ground and heavy—the furniture, the lamps, and the giant wheel that served as a coffee table. I was in a subterranean grotto. What moods this man must have, I thought. Lou appeared with a coffee cup in his hand, shirtless. His shoulders and arms were sinewy and smooth. I immediately wanted to touch his skin. He wasn't exactly handsome, but he was definitely striking, and he had a California low-maintenance, it's-all-cool ease about him.

I went to the back room and sang my songs on the piano. They weren't great but the feeling was there: a tormented hippie pop torch singer. That Lou liked my music was flattering beyond belief. My heart and soul were in my music, along with my post-teenage angst. He liked what he heard, and who was I to argue?

Suddenly, Lou was considering producing an album for me—and, needless to say, I was in way over my head. I could write music and lyrics and play the piano a little, but to record with a fifty-piece orchestra as a next step was something I should never have done.

In the back of my mind I couldn't help wondering if Lou wanted more than the producer-artist relationship. I wasn't sure. At the time I didn't even think I wanted it. But I let him court me. He'd bring flowers when he picked me up in his new blue Maserati. He'd tell me it was over with his part-time girlfriend, Tina Sinatra. Lou had all the right moves and just enough flash. His appeal started to grow on me as we prepared to make a record together. He was my mentor now. He owned his own label, Ode Records. He was organized, yet very musical at the same time. I'd see him on his perch in the engineer's booth from my stool in front of the microphone; and the more in control of the game he was, the more attractive he became.

The material for the album was everything I could have asked for—three of my favorite composers: Laura Nyro, Carole King, and Peggy Lipton. I'd written five songs for the album, and we recorded them all. He was one of the first producers to use a synthesizer, a huge machine called the Moog. The size of a room, it had to be rolled into the studio on casters. Everything else on the album was real: the strings, the horns. I had a full orchestra behind me, with the genius Marty Paich conducting the strings. They spent $150,000—a veritable fortune for a new artist in those days.

Clive Davis, who was then the president of Columbia Records, wrote in his autobiography about what a recording disaster the album was and how I couldn't sing to save my life. But Lou had stars in his eyes—that's why he had signed me and that's why he insisted on producing the album himself. Lou wouldn't listen to anybody. Ode was his record company and he was determined to do this record with me come what may. I was surrounded by the finest musicians in the business. I loved every song. Unfortunately, I sang the entire album off key and Lou couldn't fix it. In those days you couldn't electronically fix the pitch of the vocals. *Peggy Lipton: The Album* is now a collector's item—for good reason.

34.

Hide Me!

had very few days off on *Mod Squad*. We'd work weeknights until nine-thirty or ten. On a Friday night, I never got home much before midnight. I would come home, eat some cottage cheese, go to sleep, and get up for the next day. I could easily go the whole weekend without saying a word, absorbing myself in reading, writing, and long walks.

All that time spent alone naturally made me feel isolated. And yet when I went on the set, I was a little girl in my playhouse. Secure and in my element. I couldn't hold on to my weekend blues once I got there because Michael and Clarence wouldn't let me. If I came in behaving strangely, they would say, "Oh come on, Peg, don't be weird," and proceed to cheer me up.

It took us about a year to establish an audience, then the show took off. The first year was sweet. When filming was finished for the day, the three of us would melt with exhaustion onto Aaron Spelling's couch. We'd discuss the day's shooting and where our characters were going in terms of each week's story line. In those days the meetings were still in Aaron's office. We'd go over storyboards and give our input saying, "You know, I think it might work better if we . . ." We got along beautifully. Aaron would sit and write with us. I felt that everything he did creatively for our show came from the heart. Otherwise, it could never have succeeded. He *was* the Charlie in *Charlie's Angels*.

My call was usually at 7 A.M. on Mondays. By one on Friday afternoons I would be so beat I would have to lie down on the floor of the set. I finally got them to give me a dressing room with a bed. I'd leave the set, go to my room, set my alarm, and sleep through the one-hour lunch break. At night I would go home and collapse. Clarence and Michael would often ask me to go out for a drink after work. I loved hanging with them because I felt I could be bawdy, tell dirty jokes, and not have to be the angelic Julie. But most nights I didn't go; I went straight home to sleep. Then it would be back to work the next day at seven.

ABC mapped out extensive publicity tours for us. When we weren't on the set, we were in some city or on an airplane getting there. During the first part of that year we traveled to ten cities with a publicist.

"See the way it is now?" she asked us. "Well, enjoy it because the three of you will never know this anonymity again."

Whoa. Wasn't that a little dramatic? Even though the show was starting to take off in a big way, we really didn't get what she was talking about. And then overnight it seemed we had millions of fans. We were on our way.

Unfortunately, I was hardly able to enjoy it. I was so unsure of myself. Off the set, I didn't know how to talk to people. I didn't know how to smile for the paparazzi. I wasn't good at small talk with the people who'd inevitably come up to me in public. They must have thought I was aloof. But small talk scared me. It made me feel like I was free-floating. I tried to get some perspective on the fact that I was now famous whether I liked it or not, but there was a part of me that couldn't stand being recognized or looked at. It was an ego problem: the way I was perceived by the world versus who I really was. I wanted the attention but I wanted it on my terms—when I felt comfortable with it. Notice me if you like my work. Notice me if you want to be my lover.

35.

Skip to My Lou

The album finished, I moved in with Lou Adler. Almost immediately our relationship began to get twisted. In appearance, he was the king of subtlety—but to me this translated as pure mental torture. Here was another totally unavailable man—unmarried, but still unavailable. Sometimes I became so distraught I wouldn't be able to leave my dressing room on the set of *Mod Squad*. I would have an upsetting phone call from Lou and after I got off, I would be so affected by something he did or didn't say, I wouldn't be able to function. Fifteen minutes late for my call time, stupefied in my dressing room, sometimes rolled up in a ball on the floor, I'd desperately try to get ahold of myself. This tested the patience of everyone on the set. Eventually, someone would have to come and get me.

This happened to me a lot: situations

in which I was incapable of saying, "You know what? They're waiting for me and that's my priority right now. I have to go." I had no boundaries, no way of saying let's drop it or let's leave each other alone—permanently! I constantly tried to elicit feelings from Lou. I'd take it in any form I could get it. He was probably thinking, "Let me just get off the phone," while I was drowning in feelings of abandonment, fearing each conversation could be our last.

Lou came on the set only twice. He assumed a self-important Mussolini-like pose—standing in the corner with his arms crossed, observing. A Balanchine moment with a ballet student, say, or the way I remember once seeing Elia Kazan watching his wife and silently scrutinizing her every move while she was shooting a scene for a film. I had let Lou Adler cast a Svengali-like spell over me; I was in his thrall. I didn't know how to get free and the perverse thing about it was that I wasn't sure I wanted to.

Clarence constantly teased me about Lou. He'd say, "I don't know what you see in him." He would go over to Lou and say, "Hello, Mr. Adler. How are you?" being the polite and cordial man he was, and then turn around and go, *"Shit!"*

"Peggy," he'd ask, shaking his head, "what's wrong with this guy?" I didn't know. I only knew I felt an obsessive pull toward him and the more I wanted him, the less he was available.

Lou had problems of his own. For one thing, he wasn't working. I would come home from shooting and wouldn't be able to tell if he'd even been out of the house the whole day. The lights were dimmed as low as they could go and he'd be sitting there like some doomed cartoon character in a cloud of gloom.

"Hi babe," I'd say, trying to sound cheerful, trying to get through my anxiety about how moody he was going to be and wondering was he going to love me and take me to bed. I definitely wanted the sex. I wanted to consummate our connection. But when Lou felt this down, there wasn't going to be any of that.

We'd order takeout nearly every night from the kitchen at the Bel Air Hotel and sit gloomily in silence around the coffee table. We'd listen to music until I fell asleep. Those were such blue days with Lou Adler, a dismal contrast to my otherwise heady times on *Mod Squad*. My parents came to Lou's house for dinner when I first moved in and they were horrified.

"Why does our daughter choose these kinds of men?" they must have lamented. It was so dark. There was no proper meal. Even when guests came, we wouldn't sit down at the dinner table. Dinner was always served on the coffee table and once again it was takeout. I was certainly no cook—my idea of dinner was a handful of cashew nuts and a couple of raisins.

My parents were extremely outgoing and so game that they could fit in anywhere, but in this disheartening atmosphere they had became two shrunken people. They caught on right away to the dynamic between Lou and me. How withdrawn he was and how on edge and emotionally unstable I was. I'm sure as they sat there, they couldn't help comparing this situation to some of my other bad choices. They might have hoped this one was somewhat better, but I could feel their distress. My parents were overjoyed at my success, but they had yet to experience my being relaxed and happy around a man. Nor, for that matter, had I.

36.

Once More, with Feeling

wish I could say Paul McCartney never crossed my mind. But two years after the last (and I thought final) fling with him, he returned to Los Angeles for a short holiday. My god, I thought. Not again. I'd been through so much crazy pain, and was finally over it—or so I thought. Still, an alcoholic goes back for just one more drink thinking, "Come on, I can handle it."

He called me at work.

"Hi," he said. "It's Paul. I'm in New York."

"Oh, hi."

"I've been looking for you."

"Oh, really?" was all I could say. What I thought was: Looking for me, like, how? Every two years for a few minutes?

"I'm coming out to California and want to know if I can see you."

I was able to spit out a few words, and

for once they were the right ones, even though I was being hypocritical by still being with Lou. I just couldn't help myself.

"I can't see you if you're seeing other girls. I just can't do it."

"There's no one else, luv," he said. "No one. The only thing is, well, the only person who's around is a photographer who's traveling with us. I think she likes me, but other than that, there's no one, honest." Maybe I should have wondered about that long explanation.

"Okay," I said, "but don't bother calling me unless you're really free." With that said, I felt that I had at least put some limits on my obsession with him. I was wrong.

Two days later, he called again. In the middle of the night—a warning sign, right? I quickly picked up the phone.

"Peggy, can you come over to the Beverly Hills Hotel?" he asked. "I really need to see you." He then proceeded to fall asleep while talking to me on the phone. Then he woke up, talked a bit more . . . and fell asleep again. Did this stop me from wanting to see him again? Wanting to feel his kisses and burn in the very hot unpredictable cauldron of love? Absolutely not.

"Please, please come over," Paul said, in one of his waking moments. Well, what else could I do? I went. I actually snuck out of Lou's house and jumped into my little red Porsche convertible, hair flying in the night air, and whizzed over to the Beverly Hills Hotel. I'd been living with this man for a year. It didn't matter now. I had to see Paul.

It was four in the morning when I got there.

"He's sleeping, young lady," one of the band's road managers told me, as if to say, "Really, we can't wake the young prince, now, can we?"

I thought to myself, wait a minute, why did Paul call me to come over? I was trying to be cool about it, but I didn't know *how* to be cool. *Leaving* would probably be as close to cool as I could get at this point, but I wasn't going to give up. I was *there*.

Stuck between the I-should-be-cool Peggy and I-want-something-to-happen Peggy, I just sat there into the night as the road manager chatted me up. He'd seen *The Mod Squad* and wanted to know all about it.

"Well, luv," he eventually said, "we have a boat excursion planned for tomorrow morning and I'm sure Paul will be coming along."

Okay. My mind was speeding. I decided to just sit there and charm the roadie and wait until Paul woke up. And that was exactly what I did. I sat there until around eight o'clock in the morning, nervous as could be. Even worse, I found I still had feelings. Big bad feelings I knew I shouldn't have had.

It was daylight when Paul emerged from the bungalow—and like a scene from a Beatles movie, he was strumming a guitar and singing to me. At least I thought he was singing to me. Was I dreaming? He was by himself, and he had a guitar hanging around his neck, playing a little song for me. We looked at each other and the heat between us was ignited again.

Someone interrupted my moment and announced, "You're all going to the boat." Roadies, techies, P.R. people, flacks, and flunkies were leaving, but the only person I saw was Paul.

As I gathered my things, preparing to join him, I spotted a woman coming out of the bedroom in Paul's bungalow. Apparently, she had shown up before I arrived, and Paul, in his altered state, had conveniently forgotten I was on my way.

Paul and this girl were making a dash for the limousine, hiding their heads as if caught in a sudden hailstorm. It was like something out of *A Hard Day's Night*. I couldn't believe what I saw—they were actually running away from me. Down the path of the Beverly Hills Hotel they went leaping into the limo and crouching down. And I ran, too—I guess because I was so mad. "Wait!" I said, as the car pulled out of the driveway. Paul and the woman crouched down low to avoid seeing me as they drove away.

I had left my boyfriend asleep in our house. I'd come over here—and then found Paul with someone else. I was beyond pissed. I stormed into the bedroom and wrote: "You made your choice" across the mirror in the girl's lipstick, and then I just cried and cried and cried.

I didn't even go back to Lou's, which was probably a good thing. Distraught, I moved back into my parents' house.

I got a call from my agent that week. "There's a card for you in my office I think you might want to see," he said. "It's from Paul." He sent it over. It was a postcard of the fucking Beverly Hills Hotel. Why would I want a picture of the fucking Beverly Hills Hotel? Not exactly fond memories. But at least I was finally finished with this business of loving Paul McCartney.

I never wrote back, of course. That same year, Paul married the girl from the bungalow. Her name was Linda Eastman.

37.

The Dog Days
of Summer

Within a month, and against my better judgment, I went back to living with Lou. Doomed as it was, we agreed to give it another chance.

We rented a cheesy but very expensive beach hut on Carbon Beach in Malibu. I wanted it to be a romantic haven. I imagined us sitting on the beach in the moonlight, watching the waves lap the shore.

But everything seemed to go wrong right from the start. Our landlord, who lived next door, tried to evict us. When I was alone, I'd turn up the volume so loud on Ike and Tina Turner's "River Deep Mountain High" that the enormous studio speakers jumped off the carpet and the base woofers kept the neighbors up all night.

There was also the problem with the dog. Lou had a brown teacup poodle named Garbo. The name seemed appropriate for a man who hid from the world. He loved the dog; the dog did not love me—which only made what happened next worse.

One day I was supposed to be watching Garbo. She got out and within five minutes was killed by a large dog on the beach. I had no idea this had happened.

"Where's Garbo?" Lou asked when he got home.

"I don't know," I told him. "She must have gotten out while I was in the shower."

I panicked, sensing something really tragic had happened. He went out and found her and brought her home cradled in his hands, dead. It was all my fault. The beach, the ocean waves, and whirring sound of the wind all closed in on me. My ears were ringing and my head pounding. Standing there in front of him as he sobbed, I was consumed with the inauspiciousness of this whole venture: bringing his beloved dog into an ultimately hostile environment where she could and would be attacked—all of it culminating in that sad and empty moment. He was inconsolable and my apologies wore extremely thin. He packed up his small case along with the doggie bed, and drove back to his home in Bel Air.

A week later we were living together again.

38.

Earthquake

In the '60s, my brother Ken had introduced me to an astrologer—a strange young man who approached the future like a time-traveling atomic physicist. After a long pause, he slumped back in his chair as if from the force of gravity and announced that he had seen me sitting on the front steps of a little white house with two children. Daughters, he insisted. I was only nineteen at the time, but I wasn't surprised.

I'd always wanted children, and toward the end of my relationship with Lou, I became pregnant. I went a full trimester before he woke up one morning and told me he didn't want me to have the baby. I was in shock. I made a desperate phone call to my gynecologist and went off in a flood of tears to have an abortion. I had wanted this baby. I had easily gotten off smoking dope and loved being pregnant. I felt womanly and serenely connected with the life inside me.

No one knew that I was pregnant—not my parents, not Aaron Spelling. And now no one would know that I was ending my pregnancy except Lou and my doctor.

After a D&C surgery at 6 A.M., a big earthquake hit L.A. and rocked the hospital. I woke up screaming, "Daddy! Daddy!" but no one came. I was still drugged from the anesthesia but immediately flung myself out of bed and unhooked myself from the IV. Fire extinguishers popped off the walls and out of their glass cases, spewing their yellow guts while various alarms rang and patients cried out from the rooms behind curtains. Nurses, doctors, and orderlies raced through the halls wondering who to attend to first. The older woman in the bed next to me seemed strangely calm. She didn't talk or move or groan or seem afraid.

For a split second I saw the building swerve against the palm tree outside the window. I watched the elderly patient in the next bed. She was calmly taking it all in. I heard myself in a high-pitched shaky voice say, "Aren't you . . . aren't you afraid? God, it's an earthquake!" She turned to me and said, "And that's all it is." I didn't understand her reaction; I needed her to commiserate with me in my terror and tell me it would be over soon. Then I saw the numbers etched into her arm and I was no longer afraid.

I took off from shooting for a few days, saying I had the flu. The show shot around my scenes. I couldn't face Lou and I was angry. I found his lack of loyalty unforgivable. He bought me a kitten. No, that wasn't going to do it. Still, I was relieved to know I wouldn't be having a child by him. I had been saved and once again moved home to my parents. In my distraught state I comforted myself by returning to my old bedroom with its little blue piano and daffodil bedspread. In the previous few months, I'd been drowning as the disasters and pressures kept piling up. I wanted to retreat, to become a little girl again. Being taken care of by my parents was exactly what I needed to feel whole again.

39.

I Hallucinate Vincent Price

Michael and Clarence loved to tease me. Many of our scenes were shot on location—on beaches, in discos, out on the street. We stood around a lot. One morning when we were waiting for the crew to set up a shot in the sweltering heat, I looked up at the sun and said, "Is there shade on the next location?" It was an honest question, but Michael laughed so hard he began to choke. They thought I was being a Jewish princess, and for the next five years, whenever a problem arose on the set, one of them would feign a pout and demand in whiny voice, "Is there shade on the next location?" Even today when they greet me, it's the first thing they say.

We genuinely liked most of the guest stars and directors who came on the show. And then there were our favorites: Earl Bellamy, Gene Nelson, George McGowan,

Sammy Davis Jr., Richard Pryor, Lou Gossett, Ida Lupino, Richard Dreyfuss, Lee Grant, and Lesley Ann Warren, among others. There were also some Academy Award–winning actors on the show: Jo Van Fleet, who won an Oscar for playing James Dean's madam mother in *East of Eden*; Ed Begley Sr., and Robert Duvall.

One of the people I had a special relationship with was Vincent Price. He appeared in an episode called "A Time of Hyacinths," playing an almost mythical beach hermit, a character who seemed close to his own eccentric, lovable self.

During our lunch break we'd go off into a corner of the stage, pull up our chairs and listen to Mr. Price as he talked about the smoky allure of a *fumé blanc* wine, his love of cooking, his passion for painting, and his plan to bring great art to a place where anybody could see and appreciate it—in department stores, for instance, rather than in museums. As he waxed on eloquently I felt the character from the episode had burst through into reality and joined us. The great thing about Vincent Price was that he was a wonderful character himself. His idiosyncratic qualities shined through into any character he played.

Sammy Davis Jr. guest-starred in a couple of episodes. The first morning Sammy came on the set, he arrived with an entourage. There must have been twenty people with him: dressers, hairdressers, gofers, managers, secretaries, and so on. The second time he was on the show, the crew hid Sammy's Rolls-Royce and told him that they'd sold it. He didn't care; he just started laughing.

To attract those kind of people, the show had to be the real deal, and *Mod Squad* was one of the first cop shows that wasn't formulaic. *Dragnet* and other cop shows that came out before *Mod Squad* were extremely predictable: the crime is committed, straight away the cops are in pursuit and then there's the inevitable capture. Every show was the same thing. *Mod Squad*, because of its unique premise, encouraged an unconventional approach to plots—resolution instead of conclusion. The look of the show was always evolving. The latest fashionable clothes, a beautiful musical score, even a trademark freeze-frame at the end of every episode. The camera would pull back and off we'd go with the melancholic theme song behind us, on to the next week's adventure.

The show was beautifully paced. Lots of plain unadulterated space in which people didn't talk over each other, plus *Mod Squad* had some of the best production values on TV. It was a very progressive show for the time: none of us ever carried a gun, we were against the Vietnam war, and we were all for young people protesting about issues they felt were cruel or unfair.

At the end of one episode, Clarence gave me a friendly spontaneous kiss. The executives at ABC wanted it taken out, predicting we would get mountains of hate mail. Aaron fought for that scene and when the episode aired, we didn't get one negative response. The times were ready for it; we were playing to an audience that craved change.

Mod Squad received so many letters that the post office had to assign a special truck to deliver the bags of mail to the studio. One day Aaron summoned us to his office and showed us a letter we received from a sixteen-year-old girl. She was brought up on the streets and had started doing drugs. She then turned to prostitution in order to pay for her habit. She wrote that after watching *Mod Squad* every week she was determined to change her life. She entered a rehab program and successfully kicked her habit. She eventually became a counselor, helping other kids get off drugs. This was as close to a *Mod Squad* episode as you could get.

The teaser for *Mod Squad*—the opening shot—captured our mood exactly. Pete is racing down a tunnel, obviously escaping from someone or something. He runs into Linc. They catch sight of a frail, frightened waif—me. I look like I'm being blown down the tunnel by a gust of wind. They grab me and pull me along with them. We don't know where we're going or what we're running from. Our pasts, our problems. We don't even know each other at this point, but we end up in the same place and have to figure a way out—together. The classic '60s solution.

40.

What Kind of Fool Am I?

seemed to have an intimate relationship with turmoil. But what I'd never been able to figure out is did I attract chaos or was I actually some sort of instrument of it? Was I my own psychic cyclone, whirling through life, tearing the roofs off houses and uprooting trees as I moved off the coast?

I've always had a sixth sense when things are about to go haywire. Probably because I engineered it, opened the door, and let it enter my life. It was at moments like these that I should have probably just gone off by myself and been very still and quiet until the moment passed, but, in the past, I inevitably did the opposite. I jumped in with both feet and ended up making things crazier than they already were.

Here I was, on the run from my very dysfunctional relationship with Lou and trying to be normal. Unfortunately, whatever normal is, you can't decide to *be* it.

Was it normal to be asked by Sammy Davis Jr.—singer, Rat Packer, entertainer extraordinaire, and a man I hardly knew—to lock myself up with him on a two-week cruise? And even more to the point, was it normal to accept? Sammy was extremely talented, a legend, much older, and way out of my league. He'd appeared on a *Mod Squad* episode; I'd been a guest on his ABC variety show, *The Hollywood Palace*. Nothing more. But when Sammy asked me to be his guest on a boat in the Caribbean, I impulsively agreed.

I wasn't sleeping with him. I wasn't even physically attracted to him. But he was courting me. Calling me, sending flowers, and inviting me to come to New York and see him perform at the famed Copacabana. He'd chosen me to go with him on the first true vacation of his entire life: a ten-day cruise with his friends around the Bahamas on a private yacht.

But even I knew that when you go on a cruise with someone, sooner or later, you're going to have to sleep with him. I couldn't get by with, "You're such a fabulous man; let's just be friends." I knew it was going to be a difficult situation, but I wanted to push myself to be more open and flexible, to take chances, to meet new men! I was ready for an adventure—just not this one.

I'd spent a couple of days with Sammy while he was performing in New York. He wasn't exactly the most stable person in the world, but he was funny and attentive. Finally out of the very pressured and heavy relationship with Lou, I thought I could handle Sammy. The truth was, I couldn't.

Sammy was as close to a whirling dervish as I had ever run into. He was more obviously neurotic than almost any man I'd ever known—and that's saying a lot. He was tap-dancing through life as if the ground beneath his feet were made of hot coals. I went to a few shows at the Copa and afterwards went back to his hotel with him. He'd lie in my arms on the sofa laughing, crying, cursing, reminiscing, and then I'd gently get him up and put him to bed.

On the plane down to the Bahamas it all began to dawn on me. "This is not good," I said to myself. "In fact, it's all disastrously wrong."

We were meeting three couples on the boat: Terry McNeely and his girlfriend, Prez; Sidney Poitier and his new girlfriend, Joanna Shimkas; and Quincy Jones and his wife, Ulla. Sidney had chartered a small, very beautiful yacht to go from Paradise Island to some of the smaller islands. Sidney was raised on Cat Island in the Bahamas, so it was to be a very special trip for him.

Sammy and I laughed a lot when we got to the Bahamas. Nervous laughter. I immediately felt very uncomfortable. I had an ominous feeling in my gut. It was as painful as going away to summer camp. I had no idea what this situation with Sammy could evolve into and I didn't want to find out. I desperately wanted off that boat.

Out of the spotlight and nightclub fog, in the clear light of day, Sammy started to look weirder than ever to me. Stepping onto the boat, he had at least four heavy Nikon cameras strung around his neck, and there were way too many Gucci suitcases being loaded onto the deck. Sammy hadn't stopped working since he was three years old, and he was acting like a kid out of control at Disneyland. He had been told lovingly by Sidney that he could bring his camera equipment, music tapes, and all the clothes and games he wanted—but no entourage, just "his lady and himself."

I was embarrassed and frightened. I wasn't his "lady." I didn't know this man well enough to think any of this was cute or charming. It felt anxiety-driven. I was so shy around people, especially strangers, that I almost couldn't stand myself in my own skin. Everyone else there knew each other really well. Above all, they were adults. I was twenty-two but feeling more like a twelve-year-old girl who didn't know how she'd ended up there. Joanna Shimkus was a gorgeous woman. I took one look at her and her fabulous body in a bikini and thought, "Oh no!" In comparison, I was this spaced out, don't-know-what-to-say, gangly flower child.

Once on the boat and settling in for the night, Sidney and Joanna showed Sammy and me to our cabin. I froze as I looked around the tiny room. We were going to be out at sea for seven or eight days. Very scary to be with someone you don't know and at the same time to be so disconnected with yourself. It was all wrong. Everything about it was wrong. I hadn't quite grasped that "adventure" meant being trapped for days on a boat full of strangers, all of them couples—including, presumably, Sammy and me.

Everybody was being very kind, and Sammy was so happy to be starting out on his vacation. I went to the upper deck to sit with him . . . and there was Quincy Jones. They pulled out a very large joint and lit it. All my attention was now focused on Quincy. Good Lord, he was fine. He had dimples, a cute body, and a soft little Afro, and he was completely relaxed with it all. He sat on the bow of the ship with the sun behind him and it was as if he were glowing. At one point I caught him sneaking a long look at me. This wasn't good in any way. He was very much married and his wife was here with him on the trip. After a long moratorium on drugs, I smoked a joint with them, and got way too high, and at that moment realized I didn't want to be on that boat with Sammy Davis Jr. I also began feeling a little too out-of-control attracted to Quincy. Paranoia escalated. I slithered down the staircase to my room and tried to think this out. I felt panicky. What could I do to get out of this trip? How would Sammy react if I left? I could guess and it wasn't a pretty thought. I didn't feel strong enough to make it happen yet. I closed my eyes and prayed I would be left alone. Sammy was partying on the upper deck. He called down for me to come up and join everybody.

"We're all going over to the Paradise Island casino to gamble and have dinner," Sammy announced.

At that moment it sounded positively menacing to me and I declined the invitation. But the way Sammy had said it, I knew it wasn't exactly an invitation. It was more like a command.

"No, I'm not going," I said grimly, as if I were reacting to a death sentence.

They were stunned at my reaction. Nobody could understand it. *Why is she trying to flake out on the first night?* Intuitively I could feel that some crunch was coming down. I could sense it, but didn't know what it would be.

"Come on, Peggy, it'll be fun," they pleaded with me.

"I'm sorry," I said, "I have a headache." I would have said anything to avoid going with them all. Sammy looked flustered, embarrassed, and generally peeved.

I looked at myself in the mirror of the cabin's bathroom. "There's no way you can go on this cruise," I said to myself. "You have to get out of it. You're scared shitless, and you haven't even left port."

Quincy went to the casino with everybody else. He was having fun, drinking, and playing roulette, when all of a sudden there was an agitated man at his side, asking, "Where's Peggy? Where's Peggy?" It was Lou Adler.

"Who? Peggy Lee?" asked Quincy. He had no idea who this Peggy was. To him I was just the white hippie chick with Sammy.

The joyous group came back from the casino, but Sammy was in a rage. He'd been drinking and something had happened. He ranted on as I tried to feign sleep.

"I saw your boyfriend tonight," he said.

"Who? What are you talking about?"

"Your boyfriend, your lover, Lou Adler. He was at the casino tonight looking for you."

What had possessed Lou to follow me there? Jealousy, I guess, but in my state I confused it with something else. I was now in a pressure cooker and had to stave Sammy off when he tried to get into bed with me. Running into Lou Adler in the casino had not improved Sammy's mood. He was furious and alarmingly hostile. Shit. When he tried to get into bed with me, I panicked. What the hell was I going to do? Luckily, he passed out.

It was 8 A.M. and they were hauling up anchor to push off for our trip when someone called me on the ship to shore phone. It was Lou.

"I'm in the park at the end of the dock and I have to see you," he said. I went to the park. Lou sat there without looking at me and spit out the words, "I love you." In all the time I'd known him, he'd never said that.

"I want you to be with me," he said. "Please don't go on this trip."

I was stunned. I walked in a trance back to the boat and started to pack my things. I told Sammy I was leaving. I think I blanked out a lot of the angry expletives that Sammy threw around because it was all getting too chaotic. He lost it. His temper, his decorum, his cool. He knew where I was going. That's why he had been so angry the night before.

"What am I going to tell people?" he screamed.

His ego was being clobbered. He would have to face everyone and tell them his "lady" was leaving. We thought of a plan. We would tell them that my costar Michael Cole had asked me to come back to Los Angeles, where he was recuperating from a car accident. Michael really had been in a crash. He was doing okay, and he was now at home with his wife. I hated to use this as an excuse, but I was desperate. I needed to get out of there and Sammy reluctantly agreed it would be a believable explanation. When we got on deck he blurted it out. I couldn't speak. He didn't want me to say a word, anything that might compromise him. He needed to have control of that moment. And after that, he didn't want to see or talk to me ever again. I had let him down, and he felt completely betrayed.

I had to drag my luggage up the little path to the park by myself. Sammy didn't lift a finger. Did I really expect him to? Lou picked me up and took me away. I told myself he'd rescued me out of love. We'd start all over again fresh. At the Ocean Club where we spent the night, we went to bed. Sex at these times seemed to be at its most passionate and revelatory. Given my addled romantic state of mind, I imagined I was the fair maiden who had been kidnapped from my castle chamber by a devious knave but that my knight in shining armor (Lou!) had come to my rescue. Looking over at Lou, I could see he didn't easily fit into the chivalric role I'd created, but such was my careening fantasy life that I managed to keep the illusion going.

After we made love, he was silent. He'd reverted to his old uncommunicative self. Without warning he opened the closet door and with one violent move jerked the hanging bar out of the wall and pulled all the clothes and suitcases to the floor. He looked at the mess. He was stone-faced. He never raised his voice, never said a word. He just stared at the pile of clothing on the floor. This was Lou angry.

I traveled back to L.A. with him. Everything went back to what it had been. If anything, he was even more sullen. By now he'd had a huge hit record with Carole King's *Tapestry* and was producing his first movie, *Brewster McCloud*, directed by Robert Altman. While we had been in L.A.,

I had composed the title song for the movie, and Altman had liked it and agreed to use it.

Lou was nervous about starting. We went back to the little beach house. The night before he was to leave for the first day of filming, someone baked some very strong hashish brownies. We didn't realize their potency. We both ate them, but Lou got very high and quite paranoid. He spent an hour walking the tiny perimeter of the house bumping into walls and doors. He wouldn't stop until I ran a bath for him and he reluctantly got in. It was now 3 A.M. on a Saturday morning. I called his doctor but couldn't get through. Finally I got ahold of a friend who said he would make the forty-five-minute trip down to Malibu to help.

While I was on the phone I suddenly realized I had left the water running in the bath with Lou in it. I ran into the bathroom and there he was passed out with the water a millimeter from his nose. I quickly drained the tub. A half hour later Lou's friend arrived and helped me dry him off and get him into bed. When he finally came to, he was furious. He blamed me for his missing his plane that morning to the film's location in Houston and for not telling him how lethal the hashish brownies were. But how could I have known? I hadn't eaten as many of them as he had, and that was the only reason I could pull myself together enough to make the phone calls and revive him. Another disaster averted. He hadn't died in the tub or put his head through a window or walked out alone under a hashish spell into the Pacific Ocean.

But that was it. I'd had enough. I wanted out of this relationship—permanently. I left him for the last time and found a house all my own in a deep L.A. canyon. Here, I told myself, I would finally find peace and, in bucolic tranquility, become truly focused on eliminating chaos from my life for good. Dream on.

I didn't know it then but the aftermath of my two days on the boat had upset everyone. Sammy fully raged after I left. He felt I had used him and deserted him. He called Altovese, the lead dancer in his Copacabana show, and she flew to meet him. Hearing that Altovese had joined him relieved some of my guilt. Quincy later told me that he and everyone else on board thought I was the biggest flake. They saw me as a young girl in the throes of fame without much experience in the world. In Sidney Poitier's first book, *This Life*, he tells a story about the hippie with long blond hair who almost turned the boat topsy-turvy. It was a twist of fate for most of us. Sidney and Joanna, just getting to know each other, went on to marry and spend their lives together. Altovese and Sammy got married. Quincy would eventually divorce Ulla and marry me. I had fallen in love with Quincy Jones just by being with him those few moments when the sun lit him up from behind. The long look he gave me wasn't anything more than amused curiosity on his part. But Cupid had shot his arrow, and on that day, on the fateful boat trip I never took, it had pierced my heart.

41.

The Pains-in-the-Neck Fight Back

In the beginning Aaron Spelling wrote and produced everything on *Mod Squad*; he was completely hands on. By the third year, however, he began to farm out the writing and, eventually, the producing. And that's when the problems began.

I saw an interview not long ago on the TV show *Where Are They Now?* One of our producers, Harve Bennett, talked about how impossible the three of us were. He said that we were the biggest pains in the ass he'd ever worked with. That we were like children. That we didn't concentrate. That we just fooled around all the time and antagonized him and so on. Well, yeah, we did fool around when we felt like it. We had to. What else were we going to do? Take everyone's shit and opinions and insecurities out on ourselves? Harve is an intelligent man and he did some good writing on the show, but we couldn't stand him as a producer. He didn't know one iota more than we did about our characters, and that was just the beginning of the problems. Aaron's dropping out of his relationship with us left a gap and Harve Bennett couldn't fill it. No one should have been expected to. Harve must have dreaded coming to the set knowing we'd contradict almost any reason he gave us for saying lines we thought were clichéd and inane. We saw ourselves as little angels. We bonded so closely. If we felt something was not right or somebody was getting in our face, there was nothing they could do—they'd hit a brick wall.

Harve complained in his interview that we were never on time, that we gossiped and laughed at him. He was right; we could be pains in the ass. We were young and had a hit show—and Pete, Linc, and Julie *were* the show. We kept the fires burning for the audience, we pulled in the advertising dollars, and we had thousands of fans writing us weekly. Yet the show was basically a cohesive unit. We were creative people; we all wanted to contribute our ideas. After the fourth year, the powers that be wanted to control us, and by that point we were no longer controllable. We were considered brats and troublemakers, and it became a struggle. We always loved the crew and most of our directors, but by then we weren't going to take shit from anyone.

The changes they were insisting on were almost covert. They came disguised in our script as long expositions. Pete, Linc, and Julie going on and on about things they would never talk about—in language they would never use. Logistics about police work, how police laboratories were breaking down clues, describing other characters' entire life histories. These were all writing devices for lazy writers to get information into the story. Our characters would never say half these things. The power of our characters was that they lived in the moment. If the three of us were talking together, we'd always speak from our hearts. These new lumbering explications were bad for the show. We tried to fix the problems and did the best we could, but we were tired of fighting.

In the beginning, *Mod Squad* had a core story about fusing two apparently diametrically opposed groups of people—hippies and cops. It combined elements that you'd think would never work, which when they did is exactly what made it great. But by the early 1970s, the cops-versus-hippies thing was basically over, and at that point the show became a drama about being cops who couldn't say they were cops. Once we lost the tension between the authority figures and the freedom-loving hippies, the spark was gone. Our ratings remained high, but the show was losing its edge.

LEFT: My mother and father.

BELOW: Voluptuous Rita in Santa Monica, 1933.

LEFT: Aunt Pearl.

BELOW: My mother changed my name on my birth certificate. "Peggy" probably didn't sound sophisticated enough for her. She changed my name *seven* years after I was born.

My seventh birthday party. Our dining room looks so luxe in this
photo, but wasn't compared to the other houses on our block.

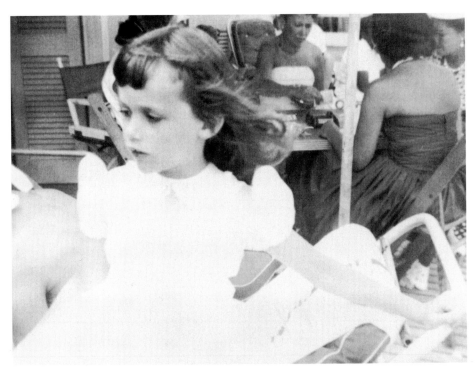

The beginnings of a sad childhood.

My brother Bob's bar mitzvah; he and Kenny are at the right.

No matter what else, my parents
were a gorgeous couple.

ABOVE LEFT: At thirteen, I needed help with the "hair issue."

LEFT AND ABOVE: In the summers, I was always tan, and at fifteen I finally figured out my hair.

ABOVE: Clairol Deb Star of the Year.

RIGHT: My best friend, Jill, at sixteen. I would have followed her anywhere (and did).

RIGHT: Do I look triumphant? Meeting my idol, wearing my mother's Pucci.

BELOW: "The Beatles' Love Lives in America." I still have this clip about my meeting Paul.

The 'Beatles' Love Lives in America

The Girl Paul Kept Hidden for 48 Hours

Paul's Story: house where they were staying, there were guards at the iron gates, and down the street there was a crowd of girls held back by police. But since my name was on the invitation list, I was permitted inside.

"My heart was hammering as I walked into the house. There were several people there, sitting around quietly, and there didn't seem to be much of a party going on. But things picked up when I felt a hand clasp mine and a voice, with a charming English accent, say, 'What a pleasure to see you again.' Paul! With that adorable smile on his face. I was so thrilled that for a moment I could hardly speak.

"He took me by the arm and introduced me to the other B's. I remember the impression I had about each one; they all have different personalities, you know. I found John rather strange, really; he was wearing dark sun glasses, even though it was evening and we were indoors, where the room was (Continued on page 59) home—how do you feel about it, Peg?" I

Beatles

continued from page 24

o. Do you think MIN n't ver play mo, be w s styl nce er. He lou i n und

tim s ha out, e. I polo t ca

Paul's Story: Peggy Lipton, a long-haired blonde who had just turned 18 on the weekend that The Beatles were in Hollywood, smiled pensively. She certainly had good reason to smile because she had just spent two fabulous days as Paul McCartney's date!

"I met The Beatles by chance," she explained. "Through a friend I learned I could be invited to the garden party that was given by the Hemophilia Foundation in their honor. When I got there, I stood in line along with hundreds of guests, mainly teenagers like myself, to meet The Beatles and shake their hands.

"Well, something just happened when I was presented to Paul. I could sense that we clicked. He smiled at me and said how nice it was to meet me and then I passed on, floating on a cloud. I couldn't get him out of my mind, but I never dreamed that he would remember me. But when I got home there was a phone call for me! The Beatles—Paul, it was—would like to invite me to a party they were having that night. Me—out of 500 people they'd met at the party. I was delirious, really spinning.

"As I drove up to the big, white Mediterranean style *Stories continue on page 54*

rican teen-agers nade some ham- d them on the the den, turned d ate our ham- y." ences, these two the globe—this ger who lives utiful home with Estates, one of ighborhoods in this time, had n girls. Peggy's nd she was in- ground—how his mother had died when

As he saw her to her car, Paul held Peggy's hand. What he couldn't say in words was clearly visible in his eyes. "Will we ever see each other again?" Paul asked.

Peggy knows that their work will take them all over the world. But there is a possibility that she will be going to an English university next year. Maybe there will be another time. . . .

"I got into my car," says Peggy, "and waved goodbye to Paul—maybe for the last time or maybe until we meet again. But whatever—my date with Paul is a memory I'll cherish all my life. I'll be telling my children about it."

PEGGY LIPTON
AS TOLD TO ROY ANDERSON

ABOVE: Me as the California girl, an early modeling shot.

ABOVE LEFT: With my beloved younger brother Kenny, 1967.

LEFT: Me with my oh-so-handsome brother Bob, 1968.

Julie, Pete, and Linc in something other than the standard "Squad" pose.

Our first season together.

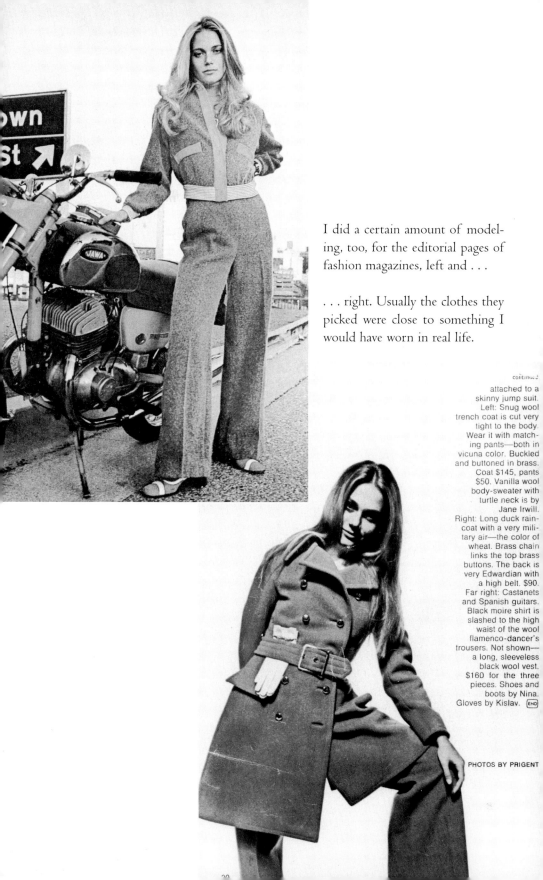

I did a certain amount of modeling, too, for the editorial pages of
fashion magazines, left and . . .

. . . right. Usually the clothes they
picked were close to something I
would have worn in real life.

continued

attached to a
skinny jump suit.
Left: Snug wool
trench coat is cut very
tight to the body.
Wear it with match-
ing pants—both in
vicuna color. Buckled
and buttoned in brass.
Coat $145, pants
$50. Vanilla wool
body-sweater with
turtle neck is by
Jane Irwill.
Right: Long duck rain-
coat with a very mili-
tary air—the color of
wheat. Brass chain
links the top brass
buttons. The back is
very Edwardian with
a high belt. $90.
Far right: Castanets
and Spanish guitars.
Black moire shirt is
slashed to the high
waist of the wool
flamenco-dancer's
trousers. Not shown—
a long, sleeveless
black wool vest.
$160 for the three
pieces. Shoes and
boots by Nina.
Gloves by Kislav. (END)

PHOTOS BY PRIGENT

On the set of the movie *Blue*. I probably look unhappy because Terence is saying, "Look, luv, you're fun to hang out with, but . . ." *(Larry Schiller)*

With Sammy Davis, Jr., on *The Hollywood Palace*. I *do* look interested. *(ABC)*

With Lou Adler. Thank God we weren't at our own wedding.

LEFT: My mother was a superb artist. Here she is in her studio, 1970.

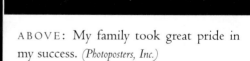

ABOVE: My family took great pride in my success. *(Photoposters, Inc.)*

LEFT: One of the many glamour photos taken at the height of my television popularity. *(Guy Webster)*

ABOVE: A quintessential photo. We were so in love, we were even wearing the same sweater!

LEFT: Quincy and me—in love.

Quincy's mother, Sarah Jones.
A force to be reckoned with.

With Kidada (above); with
Rashida (right). Mother-hood
changed me completely.

RIGHT: Even happier as three than we had been as a couple, 1975.

BELOW: Kidada and Rashie always had a great relationship; they still do.

BELOW RIGHT: Kidada and Rashida with Quincy III (Snoopy) and Tina, the Christmas we were all alone without Quincy but all together.

ABOVE LEFT: With Stephen Spielberg and my husband during the long process of making *The Color Purple*, which Quincy produced.

ABOVE: I hadn't been seen in public in ten years when this photo was taken, but I was a good corporate wife and showed up for this award ceremony.

LEFT: As Norma Jennings in David Lynch's *Twin Peaks*. The role wasn't written for me, but it might as well have been. *(ABC)*

My girls all grown up.
They have become more fantastic than even I could have imagined.

42.

Julie Gets
Suspended

My last year on *Mod Squad*, I decided I wanted to look after myself financially; I was counting on the fact that they couldn't continue the show without the Julie Barnes character. All of us had started off in 1969 at $750 a week and by the fourth season we were making quite a bit more. But after five years of high ratings, I felt we deserved some serious money.

"Everybody is making more money than we are," I said to my costars. "The show is worth millions; we should get what we deserve. We've got to ask for $10,000 a show." I talked to Clarence and Michael for a long time telling them how I thought we could get the raise we deserved. "If we all stick together," I told them, "we will get the money, no question about it."

We didn't stick together. Michael loved

the show and didn't want to rock the boat; Clarence was disillusioned with the series and just wanted off. So it was me—on my own. I wasn't afraid at that point. My father was upset, though, and he advised me not to do it.

"Sorry, Dad," I told him. "I don't care what anybody says, it's only fair for us to get this money. We've worked our asses off for these producers and have too little to show for it."

The producers had never let us own any piece of the show, and residual monies when the show went into syndication were the Screen Actors Guild minimum and only lasted a few years. Even though we had put our guts into making it a hit, they'd given us no deal. I wanted $10,000 a show. If they wanted to let me go, then so be it.

Still, I was upset. *Mod Squad* had been a great vehicle for me and I didn't want to leave the show like this in its last year. After all, I'd been given the opportunity to create a character I loved and got a bunch of awards for doing it (including a Golden Globe and four Emmy nominations). However, when I wouldn't back down on my demands, Barry Diller, the head of ABC, called me at home. We had always liked each other, so there was no hostility.

"I'm going to have to suspend you, Peggy," he announced.

"Okay," I said. "Do what you have to do. But you know we deserve it and I know you can afford it." Within a week we were all back to work at $10,000 a show.

43.

The King and I

t was 1971, right in the middle of my rapaciously romantic period, that I met Elvis Presley. I ended up spending three long weekends with him. Two in Lake Tahoe and one in Las Vegas. People who heard about my fling with him assumed I must have met him at some Hollywood gathering. But you couldn't really meet Elvis socially because Elvis lived in his own bubble and he never left it. He was a rock-and-roll hermit who surrounded himself with people who adjusted their lives to his reality. To meet him you had to enter his bubble.

I had two very smart girlfriends (Janet and Shelly) who were both actresses and seeing Elvis at the time. I would listen to their stories about him. I was fascinated by what they told me and became mildly curious. Janet insisted that I meet him. I really didn't understand why.

It seemed to bode trouble somehow—how could I possibly have anything in common with Elvis Presley?

"I've been talking to Elvis about you, and I really want you to come to Lake Tahoe to meet him," Janet insisted. Later on, of course, she wanted to kill me. But what did she expect?

Both of these girls were crazy about Elvis; they were also my very good friends. Shelly had had the longer affair with him and then moved on to the next thing. They adored Elvis but they also agreed he was a piece of work—by which they meant that fragile, outsized, damaged ego of his. Still, despite all his problems and weirdness, everyone fell in love with him.

Of course, I was intrigued by the idea of meeting him—this was Elvis, after all, the sacred monster of rock 'n' roll, but still I resisted. Finally at Janet's insistence, I gave my phone number over and in doing so a short, strange destiny unfolded for Elvis and me. Joe Esposito, Elvis's right-hand man, called me frequently. At first I wouldn't take the calls. Not playing hard to get, just sensing that for me it would be one more disaster.

"Elvis would like to talk to you," Joe said when I finally picked up. A moment later, Elvis got on the phone. His voice affected me right away. It was deep and glue-like—with a thick Tennessee drawl that had a built-in echo. He talked the way he sang. I heard his words as if he were in the middle of a song. An *Elvis* song, for God's sake. I had no choice. Think about it. The next thing I knew, he'd invited me to come to Tahoe, and I had said yes.

Elvis had his people call me to say he would be sending a car to take me to the airport. I took a little overnight bag. I was a kid. Maybe not sexually innocent, but still young. I was going to spend a weekend with the supposedly sexiest, most sensual celebrity of my time. My ego, curiosity, and need for conquest was taking over—as it inevitably did.

Still, I felt unnerved and frightened. I was afraid he was going to overwhelm me. I was already overwhelmed by the mere *notion* of Elvis. Like millions of others when we were growing up, I had idolized him. His persona was phantasmagorical; he didn't even seem real. But soon Elvis would become more real than I could possibly have imagined.

44.

The Emperor's New Clothes

When I was nine years old, my best friend, Penny, and I had danced in her bedroom in Lawrence, N.Y., to "Don't Be Cruel" over and over—trying to divine the essence of this sexual, gyrating being and summon him into ours. All very natural, very normal.

When I saw his plane sitting on the runway, I wasn't sure how "natural and normal" any of this was. Climbing up the steps, I was excited, queasy, and apprehensive.

Suddenly, I was on the plane. And there he was, sitting in the cabin in full white regalia complete with sunglasses, rings, and rows of gold chains. Not exactly what you would call casual. Elvis looked like an action figure of himself. The clash of our lifestyles hit me like a ton of bricks. I suddenly felt embarrassed and panicky. I wanted to get off the plane immediately. It didn't feel quite as claustrophobic as the boat in the Bahamas with Sammy Davis, but it was still upsetting. When he looked into my eyes, he suddenly became shy and I liked that.

I had dressed for the occasion. A slinky T-shirt, tight bell-bottoms, and boots. And, oh yeah, I was already a TV star and supposedly being pursued by multitudes of fans—I had it all going on, baby. But somewhere gnawing at me was the image of the stammering pimply faced girl from the Five Towns. On some subtle level I was meeting my match. In my own way, I was putting up as much of a front as he was. We both seemed to be reveling in the fanfare of a Venetian masquerade. At that point, however, he had pursued and had won the first rally of the game.

"Hello, darlin'," he said. His voice was sexy and inviting—and spookily familiar. His eyes danced. He was sitting at a small table and it was from there that, like some oriental potentate, he offered me jewelry. I said no thank you to the blue suede cases he opened and offered as gifts to me, even before the plane left the tarmac. His gesture was so immediate I knew he had offered similar tokens before to others. Was it a way of bonding, or gaining some control over the situation? I didn't care. It was probably his way of saying welcome to my world. In the end, I said okay to one square ring with tiny diamonds, rubies, and sapphires that you could move around to form any letter. When he handed it to me I saw it was a "P." For Presley or Peggy. It didn't matter. I accepted it graciously and later put it away.

I sat across from him in his ridiculous outfit. He was funny and wry and very charming. He had a wicked sense of humor. I knew that he was smart and considerably savvy, despite his hillbilly ways.

I'd seen photographs, one or two movies, but the reality of meeting Elvis was still a shock to me. It had a strange, theatrical quality to it—the startling unreality of a fairy tale, as when Belle first sees the wolf-headed Beast. Elvis seemed that otherworldly to me, and in his presence my lips locked, my mind raced, my heart flew around my body, the plane flew to Tahoe, and off I went on another unknown adventure.

I'd brought along a stash of cocaine that someone had given me a few weeks before. I didn't think I could deal with him or the coming events without it. I needed my confidence—*faux* as it was. With coke, I told myself, I could forge a safe distance between us until I could figure myself out in this precarious situation. I couldn't look at Elvis for longer than a few seconds but in those brief glimpses we began to connect. By the time we got to the hotel, he had relaxed and I had softened. To my amazement, and despite all the weirdness on both sides, we seemed to actually like each other.

We started kissing right away. He must have loved to kiss because he was quite good at it. And that face pressed against mine was very handsome indeed. Surprisingly so. Little by little, I found myself becoming attracted to him. Yes, he was overweight, with a paunch, and his skin was kind of pasty, but damn he was good-looking, with his beautiful blue eyes, classic nose, and pouty mouth. We kept on kissing and then went straight into the bedroom. Elvis had the same sort of one-pointed passion that turned me on.

He was a great kisser, but that was about it. We went to bed. He smelled good and kissed like a god. Very warm, wet, and passionate. I lost myself briefly and wanted him never to stop kissing me. We were so different, but I could make him laugh.

We talked a little about his movie career. Elvis was elusive about his past but you knew without a doubt that he loved performing. He said he didn't want to do those movies anymore—"travelogues," as he called them.

"You know," I said, "you could really pursue some great roles and get them. Why don't you take acting lessons?" A glimmer of what could be lit up his face and he danced a karate dance for me. For a moment, he was happy. Just the thought of testing his own limits made him positively glow. But by the end of that first weekend I realized none of that was going to happen; his kingdom was sealed. And when I felt that door close, I wasn't sure I could stay another minute. But I did, and I went back for more.

He sat there silently for a few minutes with the TV droning on in the background. Then his dark cloud vanished as quickly as it had formed and he was his disarming self again. A heavy make-out and petting session with a teenage boy ensued—that's the way I would describe it. He didn't feel like a man next to me—more like a boy who'd never matured. The petting went on for quite a while. And then we made love. Or tried to. Elvis knew he was sexy; he just wasn't up to sex. Not that he wasn't built, but with me, at least, he was virtually impotent. Then again, who could get it up with all those drugs in him? When it came time to actually have sex and he couldn't consummate it, he became embarrassed and went into the bathroom. I knew he felt badly, because he left me a poem scrawled on a torn-off scrap of paper on my pillow.

He disappeared into the bathroom for hours. What *was* he doing in there? I sat in the bedroom in a daze. Waiting for him to emerge and forever hopeful that we could try again to make love.

At some point I looked at the torn piece of cardboard on which he had scribbled the poem. It was part of a traditional Irish blessing. "Peg," he had written:

May the road rise to meet you
May the wind be always at your back
The sun shine warm upon your face

For that moment Elvis had made an effort to communicate. He had been touched, he had wanted to connect. Nothing was said about the lack of sex. Conversation by now had shut down. I didn't know what Elvis was feeling. I didn't even know what he was doing for such a long time in the bathroom. Waiting in bed, I was beginning to feel trapped. I couldn't just amble out into the next room to get a breath because all his guys were in the front of the suite gearing up for show time. I could hear their piercing laughter and loud voices against the background of the blaring TV.

Elvis finally came out. He was in full ceremonial dress: pancake makeup and slicked-back, blackened hair. It was as if he had unpacked his old self and changed into someone else. Two hours earlier, I had seen him naked with his pale, nearly transparent skin. Now his belly was gone. Elvis had probably wrapped himself in some kind of girdle to bring in his waist. His blue eyes were outstandingly lined in kohl and mascara. He'd morphed. Along with his appearance, his personality changed radically. By the time he came out of the bathroom, he was King Elvis, and there was nothing to talk about.

Before I got ready to meet him at the show downstairs, I went into the bathroom and found his huge makeup kit filled with mascara, makeup, black hair dye, and pills.

When I went down to the theater where he was performing, the Memphis Mafia walked me to my seat. Elvis always had his people on you. From two to five bodyguards wherever you went. Still, it was exciting watching the show and knowing you were going home with him when every other woman there was screaming and yelling, wishing they were in your place.

Even though Elvis was past his classic period, he put on a great show. I was beginning to realize that Elvis had to be high. He must have taken drugs just to get up on stage. You could feel the energy build. That, of course, was part of his charm. He'd clown around on stage, joking with his musicians and singers, but when it came to singing, he was totally focused. It was as if the songs, the most ephemeral things that there are, were his stone reality—perhaps the only one. Given his state of mind and the drugs, I don't know how he got through a show. He would sweat profusely during the performance. A number of times during the show one of the band members would walk across the stage and tie a small silk scarf around Elvis's neck. Once it was filled with his divine sweat, he would throw it off into the audience and the women would go wild. They'd scream his name and tears would pour from their eyes.

During some of his performances I stayed back in the room and slept. I had to catch up somehow. After the first couple of shows, I really didn't want to go anymore. By the second weekend in Tahoe, my desire to captivate him and alter his perspective on life was beginning to wane, too. A few nights I waited up for him. Elvis would come back from the show and go through hours and hours of winding down, and I'd sit with him and his "boys" until the morning. It was as if he had the bends and had to readjust his entire organism, joking and reviewing what funny incidents had taken place on stage. And then he'd sing, and though it wasn't my kind of music, watching him sit at the piano playing and singing his Presleyesque versions of gospel music made me smile. I had grown up on what I knew to be real rhythm and blues and I was a total, all-knowing snob in that area. But this was Elvis, after all, and who could resist his delivery?

Finally, feeling relieved, pleased with himself after a good show, and fairly relaxed, he'd eat a huge meal of bacon, fried eggs, and grits with wads of butter and pancakes with sausages—his way of coming down. Elvis ate like there was no tomorrow.

"Peg, eat something, darlin'," he'd say. "You're too skinny, baby. The wind gonna blow you away if you don't put some meat on your bones."

They'd all laugh under his encouragement. Meanwhile I was thinking, "Come on, let's play house, let's just go to bed and kiss and hug awhile and forget the world." All I wanted him to do was hold me in his arms and make love. I just wanted that closeness. We tried it again that first night after the show, but after that we gave up.

Perhaps trying to postpone the inevitable attempt at intimacy, Elvis would prolong the evening with the guys. He'd sing more songs; he'd make more jokes. Everyone would laugh as if it were the first time they'd heard them. And on and on the night went. It was a big fun game to them. There wasn't one serious thing said, but there was an undercurrent that I didn't get at first. After a couple of replays of the same situation, I began to pick up on a disturbing vibe. There was an edge of violence to these post-show sessions. As if they could have chewed up anybody and spit them out. Periodically Elvis would get aroused by the menace around him, and in between showing off his karate moves, he would take out a gun and wave it around.

Every now and again, the mischievous boy would shine through. I saw a fun-loving teenager who wanted to prank his band members with practical jokes. Whether it was a whoopie cushion placed on one of the guys' chairs or dried red peppers poured on someone's eggs, there was always a prank ready to be played.

Elvis had to have people around him at all times. He needed an audience. When he was alone he became morose and elusive. One on one, he hid. Of his entourage, Joe Esposito seemed like the most stable and grounded. Joe was his guy and the only one who seemed to have any common sense. The rest of them were just Elvis lackeys and hangers-on. Joe was also the one who called you and made the arrangements. He was someone I felt I could rely on.

Every day at about six or seven in the morning, Elvis would want a shot, and Dr. Feelgood would come to his suite with his bag of goodies. A real M.D., or at least he portrayed himself as such. Good bedside manner, an authentic black leather doctor's bag in hand. After he had his shot, Elvis came up behind me and wrapped his arms across my back.

"Peg, let the doctor give you a shot now," he said sweetly. "It'll make you feel real good." He was persuasive and of course his holding me helped fuel the possibilities of a night in bed with him. He said it would make me sleep, and I hadn't slept since I'd been there. But that night and other nights my response to his offer was always the same: no thanks. Elvis got upset. His voice was strained and his jaw tight. He became adamant that I take the shot. As if he wouldn't have anything to do with me if I didn't—or would try to force me in some way.

Eventually Elvis got so insistent about the doctor thing, I started to get paranoid. While he was off laughing with his boys I slipped into another bedroom, one with all red walls. The walls began to close in on me and I shut my eyes and prayed to get out alive and back home. I'm Dorothy, I thought, desperately wanting to get out of Oz and back to my safety net. Elvis was shouting through the door about how I had to take one of those shots. I pretended that I'd already taken something, at which point he backed off. Maybe he'd come to his senses and realized he didn't want me to overdose in his hotel suite. I didn't want to fight with him. He had a strong, persuasive energy, and he didn't give up easily.

Had I taken the shot, I'm sure I would have either died or passed out for days. These were heavy chemical cocktails, and Elvis was seriously into them. It was beginning to dawn on me that the prerequisite for being with Elvis was to get as fucked up as he was. I wanted to run as far away as possible.

One night, Elvis finally wound down after his show and dinner and shots—and while we were in bed together he fell off into a heavy-breathing stupor. After an hour he suddenly woke up and started choking. I pulled his upper body to a sitting position. I had to drag him up with all my strength because he was like a dead weight and still passed out. Once in an upright position, he continued to choke. He coughed and spit and then started violently gagging. Oh my God, I thought, he's going to choke to death. I punched him firmly on the back and he made a final heave. I frantically turned on the light. He was white as a sheet but still breathing. In his lap, all over his silk pajamas, was vomit filled with pills and capsules. Maybe fifty or seventy-five capsules and pills of every description. Some whole, others half open—along with the contents of last night's meal. He could easily have died, not only from ingesting a near-fatal dose of pills, but also from choking on his own vomit. At the moment of crisis, he called for his mother. He sat there like a baby wailing for her. I cleaned him up and held him until he fell back to sleep. I stroked his head until I fell asleep, too, while the sun tried desperately to enter the curtained and darkened bedroom.

By the third weekend I was feeling more confused than ever. I cared for him and I knew he was in pain but I felt pissed that he wasn't doing anything about it. My feelings were being fueled by extreme dislocation, not to mention my constant chipping away at what little cocaine I had left. Sometimes I didn't know where I was. In a hotel somewhere, either Vegas or Tahoe. It was hard to tell which was which—life lived indoors with the curtains drawn. I lay there in the gloomy light, just waiting in bed for him to wake up. Elvis kept vampire's hours, a surreal existence of perpetual twilight.

On the plane with him that first weekend we flew to Lake Tahoe, there was a moment I felt impossibly hopeful and expansive about the time we might spend together. I watched him as he stared out the window. "Wouldn't it be great to just take off and go to Europe?" I asked.

"I've already been," he answered. I looked at him quizzically.

"To Germany," he said, "when I was in the Army." As if that were enough. I was dumbfounded.

Ultimately, I found I couldn't see Elvis again. He called over and over again, but I didn't take the calls. There was nothing to say. His way of life scared me. I didn't want to go that far ever again. The people around him, the drugs, the claustrophobia, the insanity before and after his performances—combined with my own obsessive use of cocaine— had all been disorienting and disturbing. A mistake. In my mind the weekends blurred together into a series of distorted and scary images. I didn't care about any of it. The only thing I cared about was his beautiful soul, but I wasn't going to be able to save him—nobody was. Besides, I had problems of my own. Who was I to save anybody?

45.

Lady Bug, Lady Bug, Fly Away Home

As *Mod Squad* was winding up, I met yet another married man. I happened to go to a dinner party at his house. He and his wife had a gorgeous home, and a couple of children. He was a film producer. Later that night I told the friend who brought me, "I like this guy." He said, "Why don't you just call him up?" Hmm, that seemed like a good idea. But was this a man who would be open to dating me? Of course, I had to find out. I called him while he was on a business trip to New York and said, "Hi, this is Peggy, I was at your house for dinner last week, remember...." He was pleasant on the phone, but I knew from his delivery that there was something there.

"Of course I remember," he said. "Why don't we get together when I get home?"

I was having trouble sleeping. Lying awake, I began to think about him. Brazenly, I called him at home. I told him this terrible lie—"I'm really having trouble with the network," I said. "It's got me so upset I can't work, and I was wondering if you could give me some advice." He acquiesced to coming over like any friend would do. It was genuine on his part but not on mine. By the time he got there, I had refreshed my resolve with a snort of cocaine and a snifter of brandy. As long as I was going to watch myself try to seduce him, I wanted to be high.

"So, tell me what's happening over at ABC?" he asked, concerned. We were sitting on the couch. I made up some tearful stories and then just put my hand on his leg. He was quite surprised. His eyebrows went straight up and his mouth made a funny round "O" shape. "Peggy, is this . . . ?" I could easily have finished his sentence: "What I think it is?" But by then I was kissing him and his resistance was melting. Our relationship soon became extremely problematic. And why wouldn't it? This was a last-ditch effort for me to prove my attractiveness and my ability to conquer the unconquerable. So many men had disappointed. A crescendo was building and there was a desperate quality in my character rearing its ugly head. I had been looking around my world and asking myself where I was going with all these seduction dramas and lies. Why couldn't I get to the essence of what was bothering me and deal with it? I couldn't come up with any good answers and there was no one to whom I could admit my destructive tendencies, not a single person I could tell the whole truth to.

This new man—I'll call him Brad—was a steep step down even from Lou in terms of communication. The sex was hot but there would be no willingness to share feelings. The first month, Brad wouldn't actually sleep with me. It must have been a twisted guilt thing, where he thought, "If I don't have actual intercourse, it's okay to have an affair outside my marriage." We did everything else, though, and the more he withheld the more I found myself wanting him. I would come home from work for lunch break and we'd meet at my house, carry on for an hour, then pull ourselves together and go back to our respective jobs. I'd go to his office and we'd fondle each other on his massive black desk anticipating his secretary walking in at any moment. Exciting. At times he'd make his way to the

Mod Squad set driving his sexy car, disguised in dark glasses and a hat, and we'd fool around in my tiny dressing room trailer. This was the stuff of great fantasy, but since he was very married he was always running back to his wife.

Brad and I went to New York together in the hopes of having a real go around and a better time away from L.A. where we might be recognized. We stayed in "not the finest" hotel. I found out early in the game he wasn't going to be lavishing me with gifts or luxuries. It's not that I've ever been into elaborate presents; they embarrass me, but when you're lovers, somewhere along the way you'd like some token of affection: a book, a bauble, a poem—*something*—if only to mark the moment in time and to know that your lover is hoping to please you. Good or bad. Brad was an extremely wealthy man with a showcase house in Beverly Hills, yet he checked every bill when I was with him, down to the last penny. We finally left the hotel one night and went with some of his shady friends to a restaurant in New Jersey. Here we were accepted as a couple, and it made me feel good. No questions asked. I liked that. I liked the feeling of mingling with these unsavory types and seeing him laugh and converse freely and openly with me at his side.

We finally made love during that New York weekend. But actually spending the night with him was unbearable. I couldn't sleep and when he woke up in the morning, he was filled with neurosis and guilt. I wanted to run. Facing a married man the morning after is never fun. You're looking at no future in the bed next to you and it's not a pretty picture.

I was relieved to be back in Los Angeles, and took a week's break from the affair. I decided to throw my first real dinner party. I invited some friends and cooked a good meal served up with brandy and, of course, a little cocaine for dessert. The music was blaring—the O'Jays and Miles Davis—when I got a phone call from my married man. He had broken his leg while racing a fancy car and was in the hospital. In the middle of my own dinner party, I excused myself and left.

I sped down to the hospital at 11 P.M., saw that he was okay, and lay down in the bed next to him. We had sex. The nurse came in and out of the room. He was in a cast, and we were hiding everything under the sheets. It was exciting, but unfortunately back at my dinner party a candle I had lit set a bookcase on fire. My cocaine-fueled guests were having a good time partying and didn't notice. When I got back home, the fire department was dousing my bookcase and my beloved burning books with water and telling me I was lucky my whole house didn't burn down. The party was over.

The Story of Q

46.

The Dream Goes Sour

What was I thinking? Well, clearly I *wasn't* thinking. I hadn't thought things through, as my daughter Kidada is always telling me I should. It was the 1960s—okay, by now it was 1972—but for those of us besotted with the adrenaline rush of the '60s, the new decade had barely begun. I was on my wobbly path, repeatedly blundering into bad relationships like some imprinted bird whose irrational behavior has become the subject of scientific study. Birds that fly into buildings, build their nests on industrial vents, or fly in the wrong direction. At least someone was looking into *their* behavior.

What exactly was I doing with my life? As far as the fan magazines were concerned, my life was either bliss—or a disaster. Depending on the week you flipped through them, I was with Warren or Jack, in peril, about to marry Frank Sinatra (whom I'd never met), abducted by aliens, resolute on destroying my young life by being a hippie, or madly in love with Ryan O'Neal.

I was a success, at least according to the American dream of celebrity. Young girls tried to emulate my character, copy my clothes, my attitude, trying to imbibe the best qualities of the girl I portrayed: Julie Barnes. All over the country little "Odd Squads" formed: two guys and a girl would bond, seeing themselves as cool outsiders, while young boys and grown men were devoting themselves to me under the covers at night. But my real life was a disaster. I involved myself with men who were selfish or just terminally unavailable, and a few—*very* few—brilliant, talented ones . . . who were attached to someone else.

Linking myself with these unavailable men almost guaranteed that I would get hurt. I told myself it was a survival mechanism. By being the mistress, I commanded a certain place in the man's life that didn't change too much, a place in which the boundaries were as clearly defined as they could be. I wanted to always know where I stood. That he cared for me in a certain way, namely sexually. That was easy for me to give; I could control it. And I could employ my nurturing qualities, like being available if he and his wife argued or if he needed to rant or cry. There was always a wife, of course; sometimes a wife *and* another mistress.

The one saving grace in my life, *Mod Squad,* was becoming for me a dispiriting formula show further marred by endless internecine bickering with the producers—so that even my escape hatch, my fantasy life as Julie, had become a disappointment. I no longer wanted to be the waif or the canary with a broken wing. The whole thing, in any case, would soon be coming to an end, and for once Michael and Clarence wouldn't be there to rescue me.

47.

I Meet Quincy

In the meantime, as long as I could work and come home, play with my beloved puppy, Daisy, read my Anaïs Nin and P. D. Ouspensky and find some peace in that, I was okay. I had already given up using cocaine and marijuana as my crutches. I was renting a place not too far from 20th Century Fox studios, which is where we ended up shooting the last two seasons of *Mod Squad.*

My dear friend Allen would call whenever he had an interesting prospect for me, or somewhere new to go.

"Get over here, babe," he would say. "There's a gorgeous guy at my house and you might want to get it on with him." I'd immediately get in my car and drive over there to check the guy out—what else are friends for?

One day Allen called me and said,

"There's a beautiful girl at my house, and she's the daughter of someone I think you like. Come over, now."

The beautiful girl was Jolie Jones, Quincy Jones's daughter from his first marriage. I walked into Allen's house and looked at her. I had never seen anyone more stunning. As a teenager she'd been the first black model to appear on the cover of *Mademoiselle*. She was an intoxicating beauty with coffee skin and almond-shaped green eyes. She was sixteen. There was no doubt as I observed her that she was tough and streetwise—and that she was checking me out. We hit it off right away.

"I really liked your dad when I met him a couple of years ago in the Bahamas," I told her. I had to be cautious as I sensed she was quite possessive of him. "And how is the formidable Mr. Quincy Jones?" I asked.

"Well, you know he's broken up with his wife. It's been two weeks since she moved out—it's o-ver."

With her response, I felt a golden egg drop on my head. First the crack of it opening, then the thick yolk running like liquid gold down my face. I was tasting something delicious.

"My god, it's too good to be true; he's free!" I could hear my mind silently exulting, but I didn't say anything. Eventually, I fished for more.

"Is he dating?"

"Well, you know my dad. He is starting to see other people but you'd definitely be in the top ten."

Top ten? What the hell did that mean? Well, for one thing it meant Quincy Jones was popular, and he was playing now after seven years of marriage. Fine, I could let it go. He'd been out of his relationship for only two weeks, which meant he could reconcile at any time, and I was definitely over the married man thing. But just thinking of Quincy evoked a different kind of feeling in me. It was intense, and emanated this time from my gut. I went home and immediately called Allen.

"Please, can you ask Jolie if Quincy would ever go for me?"

It seemed Quincy really did have a list and Jolie was the proprietor. Candice Bergen was at the top. No, I'm not competing with that kind of beauty and sophistication, I thought to myself. I'll pass on Quincy Jones. For several weeks, I forgot all about it. No men. No dating. No heartache.

Then I got a call from the one who seemed able to make it happen.

"Hi," she said. "This is Jolie Jones calling. What are you doing? Would you like to go out to dinner?"

Jolie was lovely and high-spirited, but I couldn't see myself going out to dinner with her. I didn't know how much I would have in common with a sixteen-year-old, and I wasn't feeling at all sociable.

"Sorry, I can't," I said.

"Well, my dad is coming."

"Oh, I'd love to go," I replied without missing a beat.

I got dressed in a frantic wave of anticipation. I wanted to look sweet for Quincy, but I was so excited I just threw on an outfit without thinking. I do remember the gold platform shoes, though (not exactly sweet). We laughed about it later, for his eyes were glued to them when he saw me standing under the porch light as he drove up.

We went to a restaurant in Santa Monica owned by a friend of mine. It was nondescript—except for the fact that it's where Quincy took me on our first date. When they didn't have champagne, he said, "I'll go to the liquor store and buy a bottle."

Quincy didn't drive, but conveniently there was a store on the corner. Jolie tried to engage me in conversation, but my eyes, my mind, and my heart went with Quincy. I watched him through the window. He was *running*. He was as thrilled as I was. He came back with pink champagne, and after dinner we got in the car and I kissed him in the front seat of their old rattletrap Buick station wagon. With that kiss I could feel something shift. Like the old me was melting.

In the sheer exhilaration of the moment, I ignored the fact that being with this man in any serious way could lead me down a road I knew nothing about. He already had three children. He was older, newly separated, and black.

And, of course, I still had to break up with Brad, the married man I'd been seeing. It wasn't hard. When I met Quincy, every other person fell away like a house of cards. Nothing else mattered. Even the memories of Paul McCartney evaporated. *This* was the man I'd been waiting for. A man who was open, affectionate, loving, funny, smart, and willing to truly give of himself.

At the beginning of our romance, we stayed at my house. We were enjoying ourselves, getting to know each other. I became "Bear" to him, my nickname for being cuddly. I was getting used to him and doing all I could to make him feel wanted and comfortable—but I was no cook. The first time Quincy opened my refrigerator he was confronted with a tub of cottage cheese and one hard-boiled egg. He couldn't believe it. How could someone live like this?

"I want you to come to my house and I'll cook one of my specialties for you," he said, but I resisted.

"No, honey," I'd say. "Let's not tempt fate. I don't want to go back there with you—it's her house. It'll make me feel uneasy." Quincy's wife, Ulla, had gone back to Sweden after living with him for seven years, taking the two babies with her. But the thought of staying over at Quincy's made me nervous.

"I'm going to make you dinner at my house," he insisted, "so don't even bother arguing with me. I'm going to cook you the most delicious meal you've ever had."

I went to his house, and he started with the lamb chops. Loin lamb chops no less. I was a vegetarian and had been since I was eighteen. I hadn't eaten meat in six years, and this was going to be a seriously carnivorous event. I had to brace myself. My food beliefs were flying out the kitchen window. Living on nuts, cheese, vegetables, and air was fine for the hippie I had been, but that wasn't going to cut it tonight. It was between the meat and Quincy. I chose Quincy.

I watched him. He was a joyous cook. Singing to himself and meticulously chopping and cleaning as he went along. He was at ease in the kitchen. A good meal to Quincy was an important part of living well. Having been impoverished as a child, then eating on the run for so many years as he toured with bands, had made him extremely appreciative of the gastronomical arts. He just loved to eat, and he was fun to watch. Buttering his bread for minutes on both sides was like watching Picasso paint with a palette knife. That night he had an apron on, and he whipped up our bacchanal at a built-in barbeque that had been put in the kitchen for just these kinds of barbaric feasts. I was standing back smelling the chops sizzle and

observing him as he conducted his culinary symphony. I smiled inside. I was
gleeful. *Well, of course, Peggy, you vegetarian fool. You will be eating meat
tonight and for however long he wants you to share that part of himself.*

The meal was delicious but I didn't feel comfortable in the house. I
knew Quincy wanted me to spend the night, and I didn't want to let him
down. We got into the bed that he had shared with his wife, and we made
love. I just kept thinking, *Okay I'll stay over this once but in the morning we're going back to my house where it's safe.* But nothing could diminish these ominous
feelings. Quincy dozed off while I remained wide awake. I counted the
hours until dawn.

We were both startled when we heard something in the front room.
Somebody moving around. Quincy quite nervously got up and took out a
gun. I cringed. *What does he have a gun for?* I wondered. It was a side to
Quincy that I wasn't exactly expecting . . . and, shit, there actually *was*
somebody in the front room. I could hear them moving around.

"Oh, don't do that," I said, looking at the gun. "It's so scary. Let's
just—"

"Don't worry," said Quincy. "I'll take care of it." This might have
sounded reassuring, except that Quincy arming himself with a gun was so
incongruous—and dangerous for all concerned. He was all about "peace
and love, baby" and all of a sudden here he was waving a gun around. The
scene would have been funny if it hadn't been happening to us. I was sitting
up in his bed frozen with fear when I heard an hysterical woman's voice.

"I knew you were with somebody else. I knew it." Ulla had come back
and slipped into the house. It wasn't, by the way, as if he had been cheat-
ing all along—he'd never cheated on her during their marriage. I heard
him calling her by her nickname.

"Puss, what are you doing here? Calm down!" They started to have a
very heated argument, but I couldn't make out what they were saying. My
ears had closed. My mouth had gone completely dry. I didn't know what
to do or where to go. I got up and threw on a little black robe of Quincy's
that barely covered my ass. I hid in the bathroom.

I could hear them yelling, and their voices were coming closer and
closer. *This is really bad,* I thought. He has a gun and she probably has one,

too. I cowered behind the door where she wouldn't see me. They came closer and closer. With an unearthly force, Ulla burst into the bathroom with Quincy behind her. *Did he know where I was?* They carried on shrieking at each other a few feet from me. Finally she turned to go and I was so relieved I felt like passing out. But a split second was all it took for her to glance in the mirror and spot me behind the door. The blood drained from my face and I felt the world turn inside out. She screamed and I felt my relationship with Quincy Jones slipping from my grasp.

Having met me two years before on the boat, she recognized me.

"Peggy! I don't believe it's you," she said. I had no defense. I had nothing to explain or offer. If my heart hadn't been beating so wildly I would have thought I had died and was now entering purgatory. I tried to apologize in my timid voice, but it was absurd trying to explain this.

"Really . . . Ulla . . . we just stopped by to pick up some of Quincy's things and . . ." As soon as I said it, I knew it sounded ridiculous.

"In Quincy's *bathrobe*?"

Two women fighting over one man; a moment frozen in time. I saw her devastation and wanted to cry, but I couldn't let my guard down. I didn't know what she was capable of at that moment.

Then fortunately for me and my predicament, she turned on Quincy again and off they went, ranting and raving through the house. I had to think fast and put aside the fears of being somehow demolished by her. This—combined with the distinct possibility that the relationship with the man I had fallen in love with had come darkly and abruptly to an end—was immobilizing me. Even though Ulla might be thinking of killing me tonight, my overwhelming fear was that I would lose Quincy. Now I forced my quaking body to move.

It was totally dark in the bedroom, except for one candle by the bed. I knew I had to find a way out. As far as I could determine in my panic, the only way out of the house was through the living room. Through the eye of the cyclone, the center of their drama. Wait a minute; I discovered a sliding door in the bedroom. I tried to open it, but it was stuck—and by now they were heading back my way.

"Oh my God, please let this door open," I thought to myself.

"Please God," I prayed. "Let me get out." But no matter how much I manipulated the handle, it wouldn't open. Then their voices moved to the living room again. Gathering my clothes in my arms, I took a huge reinforcing breath and slipped by them, out the front door. They were so involved in their own drama, they didn't even see me. I was still alive. I threw on my clothes and drove home.

Hysterical, I waited for Quincy to call. To tell me he was all right and that we were all right. He didn't. I was crumbling, going out of my mind with worry and shame. And I was feeling so bad for Ulla. I tried putting myself in her head, but that felt too terrible.

When I had cried all the tears I could, my blessing came in the form of . . . Quincy. He arrived at my house in a taxi with a rose—at five in the morning. A year later, Ulla told Quincy that what hurt her the most that night was him going to the garden and picking the rose for me. That's when she knew their marriage was over.

When we went back to pack up his stuff after Ulla left for Sweden, I went over to open the sliding door in the bedroom, trying to figure out why it hadn't opened that night. I pushed it with all my might and it finally moved. I looked out and saw that there was no ledge, just a five-foot drop straight down onto a cement ravine below. Because it was pitch black I would never have seen the drop; I would have stepped right out into thin air.

"Baby," I said, "Look at this." Quincy was shaking.

"Jesus, Bear, you could have killed yourself." At that point, after all the drama and grief, all we could do was hold each other.

Within a few weeks, Quincy moved in. My tiny house embraced us and did its best to expand and meet the needs of two people. It was about twice the size of a studio apartment. We were a little cramped there, with all the clothes and music scores piled high on the bed, but I loved it, loved being with him. We lived there until I finished *Mod Squad*. It was cozy and romantic. For the first time, living with a man was sweet. I had a brass double bed; I painted the walls purple and stocked the refrigerator. And I played Laura Nyro and Carole King so loudly that even his studio ears couldn't take it.

"Bear," he'd say. "*Why?*" And we'd giggle and listen to the radio instead.

48.

Fade Out

By 1973, I'd been doing *Mod Squad* for five years. They wanted us to go on, but by that time the thrill was gone—and, of course, I had met Quincy. I knew I wasn't going to do the show for another year, never mind two or three years. Clarence didn't want to go on, either. The only one who wanted to continue was Michael, but all of us had problems with where the show was going: the story lines, the way they were portraying life on the street. Maybe we should have been more gracious in the end, but after 125 shows, the intensity had peaked and personalities were clashing.

Clarence and I would look at each other in the morning and say, "This has *got* to be our last year." It was a little like being in the same grade in high school for five years. We couldn't wait to get out; we were going to graduate in 1973 and that was it.

We were also pushing the age limit as far as the believability of our characters was concerned. Clarence and Michael were hitting their thirties. We couldn't be playing kids anymore. And yet there was never any inkling from our bosses that it wasn't going to go on and on. The ratings were good. It still had legs.

"Why are you giving it up?" everybody asked me. "Do it a few more years and you'll end up millionaires." Well, that was never going to happen. The way the money negotiations had gone, it was clear we were never going to hit that bracket. And I really felt if it went on any longer, our characters—and the essence of the show—would be seriously compromised. It seemed a long way from the early, ecstatic days after the first episode aired, when there was a silhouette of us in an ad in the *Los Angeles Times,* which read: "If you see these three people in an alley, don't run— they're cops." With its originality and heart, *Mod Squad* had captured the imaginations of millions of viewers, but it was time to put it to rest.

We were all very sad when the last day came, but I cut it short. I just couldn't go through all the prolonged good-byes. With the exception of the cast and crew, there were people on the show who hadn't exactly been on our side, so on that last day none of us was ready for sentimental farewells.

After they called the final wrap, I went to my dressing room and stripped it of anything that had meant something to me. I'd lived there for two years; it was more my home than my house was. Production got pissed that I took a plate and a painting. They must have seen it as a hostile act, which it may well have been, because when I got them home I didn't really want them anymore and gave them to a fan. For me, it was definitely time to go. And as it turned out, I had quite a lot of ground to cover.

49.

Rita

My mother was completely unnerved when I started dating Quincy, and it only got worse when I became pregnant during the last year of *Mod Squad*. She called and had her own private conversation with him. I found this odd. As a parent she hadn't interfered with any of my boyfriends—not even the abusive ones. Yet all of a sudden she decided to become involved in my life. More than anything, it seemed she did not want me to have a child with Quincy.

Of course, Quincy was upset about this, but my mother was a force to be reckoned with, especially when you went against her wishes. She judged everything and everyone. Sometimes from a deeply ingrained fear—a fear that almost consumed her. When she didn't get what she wanted, her mouth would lock, her teeth would clamp down and nothing could stop her. When she felt she was losing control, she became explosive. Her objection, she told Quincy, was that I was too young to have a child. I was, of course, twenty-six years old, but Rita hadn't started a family until her early thirties.

But all this was really a cover-up for her fear of my marrying a black man, and Quincy knew it. She called him when she knew I wouldn't be there, and Quincy told me what she'd said.

"My daughter is too young to have a child; she's a child herself."

What was she talking about? What right did she have to give advice? I felt my mother barely knew me. And yet . . . despite my success and despite our differences, I loved her dearly and I remained emotionally tied to her. I'm sorry to say that I went ahead and had the abortion. I was incredibly sad to lose our baby. We both were. That pain cut very deep. And, of course, the sadness never really goes away.

When we moved into the bigger house in Brentwood, my mother became more adamant in her crusade to have Quincy and me rethink our future together. It's not as if she ever said directly that she didn't want me to be with a black man, but it was so far from the future she had imagined for me that it didn't matter. She thought I was going to be with a white prince charming or some great Jewish king. She couldn't envision my life with a black man and mixed-race babies.

My dad was quite the opposite. "Whatever makes you happy, I'm with you," he said, and he meant it with all his heart. He was completely behind me. I decided I couldn't let this go on with my mother. I was being torn in two. One morning, I woke up and made the call.

"You know what, Mom?" I said, and this took everything I could muster. "I don't want to speak to you until you accept Quincy."

No response.

"I won't put up with this," I finally blurted out. It was the strongest move I had ever made in my life.

About a month later, she came to her senses. She called and came over, and after that she became quite the permanent fixture in our lives. She made a 180-degree turn. She came back with a vengeance because she fell in love with Quincy's character and loving goodness. She couldn't get enough of him. For years, Mom and Dad came over at least once or twice a week for dinner. They were great company. We often vacationed with them in Europe, Aspen, Hawaii. We took so many vacations together that Kidada at five years old busted out with, "Mommy, do Gramma and Grandpa have to come with us again?" In front of them, no less. They took it with great humor. Quincy had a dynamic relationship with my mother. He was drawn to her wit and intelligence, but he never really got over her initial rejection of him.

And even though she eventually accepted our love for each other, she'd still say over and over again to my dad or to Quincy or anyone who would listen: "I don't know what it's going to be like for you to have black children." No matter how liberal my mother's views were on integration and equality, her Jewish middle-class background didn't include the reality of her daughter having black children. Maybe she had genuine concerns about her grandchildren fitting into two different cultures. Maybe she thought I was naive, an attitude I found extremely irritating. Didn't she realize that I already knew none of it was going to be easy? It hadn't been so far. But I couldn't live in her fear. I had every intention of getting pregnant again—and this time keeping my treasure.

50.

Black and White

Prejudice and jealousy were hurdles we confronted daily, but facing them, hurtling through them with Quincy turned out to be the most loving period of my whole life. After *Mod Squad,* we moved into a larger house, with room to spread out. Quincy's schedule was erratic. I was sure I'd never see him if I committed to another acting job, so I turned everything down. Besides, all I wanted was babies. Babies...babies...babies.

Almost as soon as we started living together, we began getting threatening notes...and a few stalkers. One very strange, forlorn, unstable man told us his name was Jesus. Yes, Jesus. He would come to our house, jump over our gate and be waiting for us when we came home.

"Hi. How are you?" he'd say. "Have a nice evening?" We had to hire a guard, and we met with Gavin DeBecker, a high-profile security consultant, to help us decipher warning signs and put a plan into action. Jesus eventually disappeared, but we remained hyper-vigilant. Instead of creating a split between us, these challenges were beginning to solidify our bond.

Despite all the craziness in his family, Quincy had succeeded in stabilizing himself. He got out when he was fourteen. He found a trumpet and walked into the wide, wide world outside. He wasn't militant and he wasn't on drugs, which is how blacks were stereotyped in the 1970s. He wasn't any of that. He was a black man, and along with other black musicians and singers, he had to play the game on a white playing field. He became a record executive at Mercury, where there were no black employees at all. He was the only black composer in the movie industry for a long time, and he had to fight for that, too.

We had a wonderful array of friends. Musicians, writers, animators, singers—our mixed-couple friends: that's what we called them. Herbie and Gigi Hancock, Minnie Riperton, and Dick Rudolph. Being a biracial couple wasn't common by any means in those years. We sought out our friends and gravitated to them. Joanna Shimkus and Sidney Poitier were our close cohorts. She was an extraordinary Canadian beauty and an international movie star at twenty. Sidney was, of course, the impeccable Sidney Poitier. Though for her it was love at first sight, they had connected much the same way that Quincy and I had—with difficulty. Sidney had four daughters from another marriage, and the divorce wasn't going to be easy. Meeting Sidney, Joanna forfeited her career and devoted her time to making their lives together work.

When Joanna and Sidney finally married after being together for years, Harry Belafonte made the wedding toast.

"This woman was black when Sidney met her," he said, "and she had to wait so long to marry him that she turned white." When Joanna started seeing Sidney, she was engaged to someone else. She didn't care if she ever worked again. And she wanted babies. A story like my own.

As time went on, Quincy and I became easy with each other, but there were still troubling aspects to being black and white together, and not all of them came from the outside. However much I tried to get into his psychic space, to imagine what it felt like to be black, I knew there were things that I would never be able to understand. And even when I thought I understood it, I didn't. One day out of frustration he turned to me and said, "You'll never understand what it is to be black."

I was about to say, "Yes, I can. I'm married to a black man." But then I thought, "Shut up, Peggy. You can't. Just because you have black children and married a black man, you still don't know and, lady, you never will."

I knew Quincy and I were together for the long haul, but I didn't want to go out in front of the press and talk about it. I hated being photographed wherever we went. I felt judged, although *Ebony* and *Jet* magazines, both black-run publications, featured us often and had only the best things to say. In fact, we were never battered or ragged on in any publications. It was just something I felt inside, an instinct telling me that all might not be quite as benign as it seemed. I was now seeing the world through the eyes of a black man, and this only exacerbated my lifelong paranoia.

After all, only a short decade before, blacks and whites couldn't stay at the same hotel or eat side by side at a lunch counter in the South. And blacks and whites still didn't get married, especially publicly. Can you imagine if we'd gone down South on tour with one of Quincy's bands? We would talk about that a lot. I asked Quincy if, when he had toured in the South as a young man, he had seen the worst of all possible sights— a lynching. He had. I couldn't bear knowing any more. The pain of witnessing something like that must tear a person apart. Quincy never talked about it again.

When Quincy wasn't touring or performing somewhere, we led a somewhat insular life; we rarely took in a movie or went for dinner in a restaurant we didn't frequent regularly. It was a hard world at the time. Eyes were on us wherever we went, and it didn't feel good. If strangers greeted us with warmth, without bias, we trusted that and dropped our protective walls, but we always lived with a certain paranoia. The White

Citizens Council's newsletter, *The Thunderbolt*, had run a front-page photo of Quincy and Ulla, his ex-wife, along with their two children, whom it denounced as "mongrels." The police would often stop us, convinced that any white woman riding in a car with a black man had to be a prostitute. Once when we were pulled over, the cop held my license and asked Quincy to prove that he knew my middle name before letting us go.

51 .

A Tangled Tale

Quincy loved his family, but he wasn't speaking to his closest brother, Lloyd. They had some kind of a rift that had gone on for a few years before I met him. I couldn't understand it because they obviously loved each other. I remember saying to Quincy, "Let's go up to Seattle and see Lloyd. You'll spend time with him and work it out." In many ways this was the most important man in Quincy's life and vice versa, but they had a belated sibling rivalry going on between them. Somehow I knew that's all it was.

As children they had been very close. Quincy had taken care of Lloyd—they had taken care of each other. They had been shipped off to a grandmother's house in Louisiana and lived there without electricity, eating rats they had to catch from the river for dinner. Many nights they would just hold on to each other, shaking in their bed when they were left alone to wait out the thunderstorms in the dark. I kept asking him about Lloyd, probably because the idea of there being someone so similar to Quincy in the world was pretty intriguing. Then we heard Lloyd had contracted Hodgkin's disease. Before we had time to think about it, we were on a plane to Seattle and their relationship began anew. They became again what they had been when they were growing up together. Kids.

During our first week in Seattle, we drove to Bremerton, Washington, where Quincy had moved as a young child with his family from Chicago. Nothing was left of the projects erected right after World War II to house the naval yard workers. Nothing. Not a foundation or any indication whatsoever that it had ever existed. Just an empty field with some tall grass blowing in the wind. I felt Quincy's profound disappointment.

That evening, after the devastating visit to Bremerton, Quincy's closest sister, Teresa, threw us a party at her house—essentially for me to meet Quincy's family and friends. I was the only white person there. I arrived in full Peggy Lipton regalia: miniskirt, long blond hair, and beads. Quincy and I were in love and it was obvious. Nevertheless, I was extremely nervous. My mind was racing. Was I going to be accepted—the little white girl who was now living with their famous brother? Teresa gave me the warmest hug imaginable. She showed us our room, which turned out to be her bedroom—she'd vacated it for the big weekend reunion. I still was afraid I wouldn't be included, or even liked, until she started introducing me to people at the party as "my sister Peggy."

We stayed up much of the night laughing and going over the day in our heads: the people we'd met and the way they reacted to our newly evolving relationship. Quincy's family knew that breaking off with Ulla would be difficult; we had their support. The next morning Quincy showed me a house he had shared with his brother Lloyd for a time growing up, before his father remarried. Then he proudly brought me to meet Miss Mary, a surrogate mother to him when his own mother wasn't able to function. Miss Mary had lived in this house for forty years. To welcome me, Miss Mary had made black-eyed peas cooked with ham hocks.

A sure Southern source of good luck. I'd never had soul food in my life, and I thought I'd died and gone to heaven. I had never tasted anything so delicious. Unfortunately, black-eyed peas are like beans in that they tend to expand in your stomach. I ate so many of them that they had to lay me on Miss Mary's front lawn. They were splitting their sides laughing at me. I was in an agony of bliss.

I never got to meet Quincy's father, Quincy Sr. He was a carpenter and although at times his life was complicated by his marriages and trying to make enough money to support his growing family, he nourished his son's soul and always encouraged him. He died right before Quincy and I met. But on that trip to Seattle, I met all of Quincy's brothers and sisters: Lloyd, Richard, Teresa, Janet, Waymond, and Margie. There were stepbrothers, stepsisters, half-brothers, half-sisters. Coming from a family like mine, I was elated by this loving concoction. It was all mixed up with Korean, white, black, Japanese, and Hawaiian husbands and wives and children. Quincy called it a United Nations meeting, and this huge family all accepted me in the most beautiful way. We ended up staying with Lloyd and his wife Gloria many, many times with our children. They became the children's godparents. They lovingly took us in. We, in turn, helped to take care of Lloyd when he got sick.

Quincy and Lloyd were best friends within a day of reconciling. It was as if they had never been apart. They were two little boys inhaling each other's jokes and tales. Little boys, too, in the way they tried to deal with their mentally unstable mother. When she would come to visit, they'd run to a closet and smoke weed to get up the nerve to deal with her for just an hour. Their mother, Sarah: brilliant, erratic, and totally unpredictable. They would talk about her bizarre behavior and all the strange things they'd been through together. I could just go on and on listening to their stories. She was always the topic of conversation, and they had a lot to catch up on. That kind of trading of childhood tales is something I could never do. I had too many secrets. I never talked about myself. But here in Seattle, with all of us converging on a 1920s wood frame house overlooking the exquisite lake, I found deep contentment with a caring family.

Though for them it was totally natural to welcome me, I found it a noble and sweeping gesture of love and acceptance. We would laugh, play music, eat, love our children, and just live.

Quincy now awakened a new strain of passion in me. His affection was always forthcoming and almost addictive. I had to let myself experience that. It was something I rarely had growing up. I think I sat on his lap for three years. No matter where we went, we couldn't sit apart from each other for long. Those years are the longest stretch of sustained bliss that I have ever known.

52.

Sparks Fly

Quincy was scoring *The Getaway*, director Sam Peckinpah's last movie, starring Ali McGraw and Steve McQueen. Eventually Quincy moved his Moviola (a hand-cranked editing machine used for film scoring) into the second bedroom, which was slightly larger than a closet. In the days before computers, composers scored films on these little contraptions. We didn't want to be away from each other so he brought it home. I was fascinated by the process. Quincy asked me to pick all the source music for the film. I found old rock-and-roll records and some country-and-western tunes, and when I wasn't working I'd sit with him and watch how he synced them to the scenes. Quincy wrote an amazing score for the film. Eerie and beautiful at the same time. He had already scored many, many films. Alan and Marilyn Bergman, Hollywood's finest lyricists, wrote "Far Away Forever," the title track for which Quincy wrote the music. Quincy and I went in the studio and recorded the demo. We were in love, so how bad could a love song sung by us be? Bad. I couldn't get on top of a note to save my life and he sang like the charming trumpet player he was: flat.

Ali McGraw and Steve McQueen fell so passionately and dangerously in love on the set of *The Getaway* that she left her husband, Robert Evans. Ali and Steve couldn't keep their hands off each other, and at this point neither could we. The four of us spent time together on the postproduction of the film. McQueen was uneducated, rough, and very sexy. Ali was cultured and elegant, but that's what made their sparks fly. The story was that she had asked her husband to come down and be on the set with her because she and Steve were already feeling a connection and the intensity was building for both of them during rehearsals. She was afraid something would happen, but Evans never showed up. Quincy always used to bring that up.

"See? Bob Evans didn't come down, and look what happened." He couldn't get over the fact that Ali's husband hadn't come to see her. She had gone away on location and fallen in love with the star.

Quincy never wanted me to work. He always felt that something could happen on the set—and, as we know, it does. Location is a hotbed for affairs. After that first year together, I wouldn't work again until the late 1980s.

53.

Food
Adventures

never wanted to be away from him, but when money got tight—which happened fairly frequently—Quincy would go on what he called a B-flat gig. His first record for A&M Records, *Smackwater Jack*, was becoming a hit in Japan. He needed to take his band there and get a little tour going. Without him, I began to experience panic attacks. These would get increasingly worse once I had the babies. The second time he went on tour, I went with him. But I didn't want to just stand backstage and watch; I wanted to participate, so he put me in the band as a backup singer. This meant I had to rehearse with singers that included the very talented Patti Austin and James Ingram. Rod Temperton, the virtuoso of pop songwriting and harmonies, wrote the vocals. I felt privileged to be part of this ongoing creative experience. Until then, I hadn't realized how much I missed working.

We toured through a number of towns and cities in Japan. I rode the bus with the Quincy Jones Band, with all his great musicians, and got to hear them play every night. We celebrated the success of the tour at its conclusion in Hong Kong, where the Japanese tour promoters treated us to a lavish Chinese feast. First came the familiar dishes, then slowly we got into the more exotic ones. It was a major dinner and they were trying to impress us. We had what were called "hundred-year-old eggs" that had been buried or covered—not for a hundred years but for a very long time—and were now completely black and shriveled. This was considered a delicacy and tasted surprisingly good, almost like a truffle. The dishes grew progressively more complicated and strange until we finally got to one we couldn't recognize at all. They took the top off of a silver platter and everyone looked at the awful stuff on the plate and went, shit! We were all repulsed by the hideous-looking dish. What the hell was it? The meat was thick and gray, one huge grey loaf, with soft little horns, like those of tiny dragons cured in formaldehyde. No thanks, we said. But whatever we felt about it was beside the point; our hosts wouldn't let up.

"This is most desired food of Chinese cuisine. Good for sex life." Everything was good for sex life, and of course upon hearing this all the musicians' eyes lit up.

"Well, okay, man, if you put it that way," they said and started cutting off pieces. Nobody really wanted to eat it. It looked like . . . okay, I'm going to tell you what the horns looked like: tiny gray penises with antennae. We were stalling for time as we scrutinized it carefully, but none of us could figure out what it was. Our hosts were waiting. It had gotten to the point where it would've been insulting if we hadn't tried it. I got out of it, but the guys had to taste it. They kept telling young Benny Powell, the jazz trombone master, "Good for sex life. Lasting long time."

"What the hell," Benny said. "I'll give it a try." He took a bite—and gagged.

Two hours later we got in the hotel elevator with Benny, who was still chewing that same piece of whatever it was, probably because it had the consistency of rubber. He was afraid to swallow it.

"Damn, if this thing don't taste like King Tut's thumb," he said. We found out later what it was: a sea slug. A thing—and there is no other way to explain it—that when taken from the ocean swells up to ten times its normal size. It certainly was interesting being on the road with Quincy Jones.

I had managed to resist eating the sea slug, but I wasn't so lucky with chitterlings—or "chitlins" as they're called by those who actually eat them. Chitlins are pig intestines. When slaves worked the plantations in the South, they were forced to eat what their owners threw out in the garbage: the pig's knuckles, feet, snouts, and innards. This was pure soul food. After years of hearing Quincy and Billy Eckstine rave about chitlins, I decided to try them. It happened years later when the author Alex Haley came to stay with us. He was an excellent cook, and he made us up a pot as a special treat for me. A barnyard smell permeated the whole house. I visited Alex as he spent the day cooking in our kitchen and I smiled, praying that there was no way that chitlins could taste as bad as they smelled. At dinner, Quincy and Billy dug in with gusto, and all three men watched my face as I forced a piece into my mouth. I was stunned. Who could take this odor? This texture? Watching me try to hold my breath while swallowing, they all laughed, and I had to laugh myself as I lay down my fork in defeat. Chitlins were one pleasure I was never going to share with my husband.

54.

I Become the Wicked Stepmother

was twenty-six when Quincy's children moved in. Why not? I said to myself. It was before I had children of my own but it never occurred to me not to accept them into our lives. If I loved Quincy, I would also love his children. I plunged into the water with all my clothes on, not quite thinking it through! It never even occurred to me that I had a choice. These were Quincy's kids, and they needed us—that's all I knew.

"Don't do it," my mother warned me. "It's too much. What do you know about raising children?" Considering the responsibility that was now looming, her advice only aggravated my situation.

Tina and Quincy III were incredibly sweet, and their little lives were suddenly in our hands. Tina came first and settled in.

She was filled with bubbly laughter and a personality all her own. We called her a love bug. She loved giving and getting affection. With her blond curly mop of hair and beautiful green eyes, she always seemed to be on the verge of having a laughing or crying fit. Tina was six when she moved in and happily didn't leave until she graduated from high school. Her mother cursed me through weekly letters. And who could blame her—she felt she was losing her daughter.

Quincy III—or Snoopy, as we called him—arrived later on, and didn't adjust well to his new home. He came to Los Angeles when he was four years old, by himself, carrying a cardboard box containing all his belongings. When we picked him up at the airport he was a bewildered child grasping his baby blanket and sucking his two fingers. Quincy was so happy to have him close, but we both missed cues. I, for one, found myself somewhat at a loss. Ulla had been angry with Quincy when she shipped Snoopy off, but nevertheless this was her baby—and he was still very tied to his mother. Snoopy was naturally suspicious of my role as surrogate mother, and the truth is I didn't do a very good job of it.

About a year after they broke up, Ulla, as a gesture of reconciliation, wanted us to come to her house for Christmas, so Quincy could spend it with their children. That was the last thing I wanted to do. I was frightened to even be around her. I shook. I ground my teeth and seemed to have a stomachache for days. But I did go, although I knew she thought of me as the woman who took Quincy away from her. Had I? I had to question that over and over again. I knew they were finished by the time Quincy and I got together, but I was deeply sorry for both of them. I was miserable at the thought of seeing her, but I did it. It was as if everything that I was most afraid of, I pushed myself to do. For me, it was never a case of, "Oh, I can handle this." It was always, "I could disintegrate from this, but I have to do it."

Snoopy was shuffled back and forth between Sweden and L.A. amidst recriminations on both sides. He eventually moved back to Sweden and spent most of his adolescence there. I feel sorry to this day that I wasn't able to be more of a comfort to Snoopy when he needed it. Let's face it, Quincy's only son had selfish adults around him.

55.

Happy Birthday, Quincy

I loved Sarah Jones despite her sometimes psychotic behavior and downright meanness. I tried to always remember that she was Quincy's mother and for that reason alone deserved my respect.

She was an interesting and intelligent woman. She had graduated from Boston University and had been an honorary member of the only black sorority there.

She'd type long confessional letters, some of which were deep and moving. Her mental acumen could at times be astounding, so I'd find myself once again letting down my guard. Then she would flip on me and the most vile accusations would pour from her mouth. *You're a bitch, a white whore, get out of my son's life.*

Sarah had been diagnosed with dementia praecox, also called schizophrenia. She spent much of her younger life in mental hospitals, emerging every few years to track down her sons. When Quincy was a boy, his father had taken him and his brother Lloyd to see Sarah in the state hospital in Chicago, where she had been committed to the psychiatric ward. They were only four and five years old. Quincy remembers going into a large room filled with inmates and seeing an ugly old witch of a woman violently out of control. She ran frantically around the ward in front of them waving a pie tin high above her head. The two boys clung to their father, their little knees shaking and teeth chattering. There was excrement running from the tin and the smell was overwhelming. The woman was screaming at everyone, "Let them eat cake. Let them eat cake." Quincy never could get this out of his mind. A child's indelible vision of the macabre and destructive nature of humans, it gave him nightmares. He talked about it all the time, but it wasn't until he wrote his autobiography that he remembered that the insane woman screaming was his mother, Sarah.

Quincy, a great food lover, never turned down a good morsel, but there was one thing he had a ferocious aversion to and that was coconut. You couldn't show him coconut in any shape or form.

"Promise me you won't put any of that in the curry or anything else you cook," he'd say, not even wanting to mention the word *coconut*. As a kid growing up poor, he'd make a meal out of whatever was around. Lorna Doone cookies with salami inside and pickles impaled on peppermint sticks—so it wasn't as if he were a picky eater. But if I brought out something with coconut, his hair would stand on end.

Then one evening a year into our marriage, I was on the phone with his mother, listening to one of her long, endless rants. It wasn't as if you could tune her out, either. You had to listen and pay attention. She would ask you questions about what she'd just told you—and you'd better know the answers. I wanted to stay on her good side so she wouldn't make life difficult for Quincy, but it was draining. Sarah would talk about anything and everything: her school days at Boston University or how Elvera, Quincy's stepmother, had stolen Quincy's dad from her. She'd quote the Bible, and rag on Quincy's ex-wives and girlfriends. Much of what she had to say was hard to take because, while her observations were frequently keen, they were often scathing and cruel. And every once in a while she would say something that was so funny it would just rock you and make you burst with laughter. In the middle of that evening's rant, she stopped talking for a moment.

"Yeah," she said out of the blue. "I baked him the most beautiful coconut pie." She began to wind down and I could hear the emotion cracking her voice. Tears were coming full force; she seemed to be on the verge of hysteria. "The most beautiful coconut pie you ever saw.

"I was trying to be normal and give my son a birthday party the way other mothers do," she said. "All his friends were there and everybody was coming in and out of the screen door, in and out, in and out, coming on the porch. Those kids were banging on the porch door and every time they opened it and came in, that screen door would slam. It started to get on my nerves, so I took the coconut birthday cake and threw it over the porch railing." In front of Quincy and all his friends, his coconut cake flew out and smashed to the ground. Quincy must have been so mortified by Sarah's behavior, he'd managed to forget it ever happened.

"It's okay, Sarah," I said. I hung up and immediately told Quincy. This was why even the thought of coconut made him sick. It was interesting and alarming and I guess satisfying to discover the real reason for his over-the-top aversion. But at this point in his life he'd become numb; he just wanted to tune Sarah out. I would get pissed off at her, and then feel sorry and want to make it up to her by listening to her rants and consoling her. Most of the time I managed to tolerate and even soften her wrath, but it was work.

56.

A Storm in the Brain

J oy of joys. We found out I was pregnant and my world became illuminated from the inside out. Nothing I had ever experienced had meant this much to me. My pregnancy was easy and I felt alive and loved. I read every one of Dr. Spock's books I could find. Quincy and I took Lamaze classes together. Nothing could feel this good, I told myself and it was true. My health, my heart, my belly were as full as they could be. Kidada Ann Jones was born on March 22, 1974. It was a fourteen-hour labor. She also had jaundice, and we stayed in the hospital six days so she could be treated under the light of the bilirubin machine—but my joy overcame everything. "Daddy," as I would call Quincy from then on, was equally joyous. We took Kidada home, Quincy kissing her on the top of her head for the whole car ride. My mom and dad and our dog, Daisy, were there to greet us. Slightly yellow from the jaundice, with her long straight black hair, impossibly thick eyelashes and freshly minted dimples, Kidada became the focus of our love.

And then one morning, when Kidada was just a few months old, everything changed. It was a Sunday, beautiful and sunny. I had packed Kidada's clothes and diapers for a day at the beach with my parents. She was in the living room with my aunt Pearl. All set to go. Quincy wanted me to get in bed with him before I left. We made love. Those were the last moments, the last I would remember clearly for a long time. Quincy rolled over to the other side of the bed in what I thought was the bliss of sexual satisfaction. I, too, was feeling the same and didn't want to rush off right away. "Hmm, Sweet, I love you," I whispered. He didn't respond, which was odd. Quincy always responded to displays of affection. His eyes were closed and his breathing was erratic.

"Daddy," I said, and kissed his lips. He didn't move. If he were asleep I'd be able to wake him, I thought, as I nudged his body and squeezed his hand. Nothing. I started pumping his chest. He just wasn't there. I flung myself over him and dialed 911. Then I took Quincy's face in my hands.

"Daddy, do you know who I am?" I asked. There was a long silence and my heart fell.

"You're . . . you're Bear," he finally whispered. I was very panicky on the inside, but still focused. I knew I had to keep him conscious; I couldn't let him slip away.

Within five minutes an ambulance arrived. There hadn't been time to tell my aunt, so when she saw the paramedics coming in she quickly put Kidada in her crib and asked what had happened. I told her I didn't know and watched as the paramedics worked on him for a few minutes. "His heart is strong," they told me.

Quincy's eyes opened, but they were clouded over, as if he had gone someplace far away. He was disoriented but breathing more normally now. Once his vital signs were stable, the paramedics left our house. Quincy wasn't fully alert but asked, "What happened?" My heart was caught in my throat and my hands were sweating.

"It's okay," I reassured him and then called our internist, Dr. Elsie

Giorgi. She drove over and the next thing I remember we were putting Quincy in her car—and my aunt, Dr. Giorgi, and I were driving him to Cedars-Sinai Emergency Center. I just sat in the back seat and held him; I didn't know what else to do.

It had all happened in an instant, a flash. Life as we knew it had altered irrevocably; we were now in the throes of something terrifying and unstoppable. In the car, Dr. Giorgi told me that it was possible that Quincy had had a brain seizure.

"It could be an aneurysm," she said. An aneurysm, she explained, was the ballooning of a blood vessel that then bursts and floods the brain with blood.

I was crying now. This can't be happening, I thought. Less than an hour ago our lives were normal and moving in real time. We were in love. We had a baby. We had a world of goodness to look forward to.

Emergency nurses were getting Quincy out of the car. Dr. Giorgi had everything under control but I could tell she was scared. I couldn't bear knowing that Quincy might be in pain as he lay helpless in my arms. My man, my stability, whose heart was deep enough to contain all the love I had to give, whose goodness chased my demons away—my Quincy—was ill. Very ill. Dr. Marshall Grode, a neurosurgeon, met us in the emergency room as Quincy lay barely conscious on a hospital gurney. He was about to be wheeled into emergency surgery, but first the doctor wanted to do a spinal tap. Within minutes he came out and quietly said to me, "I'm sorry, my dear, to tell you this, but he has a fifty-fifty chance of making it." My knees buckled, everything went dim, and I collapsed in Dr. Giorgi's arms.

Quincy's surgery the next day took nine hours. The surgeons had clipped the aneurysm with a metal piece called the Heifitz clip and would have to wait to see if it stopped the ballooning and the blood flow to the brain. In the hospital, I paced back and forth between the waiting room and the fire escape. Now there was nothing to do but wait to find out if any part of Quincy's brain had been affected.

They let me see him in the intensive-care unit. His head was wrapped in thick bandages; needles and I.V.s were stuck into his hands and arms.

I could hardly breathe as I watched him. He was so vulnerable lying there with a half dozen monitors beeping and buzzing around him. Doctors and specialists were in and out constantly. The hospital smell was acrid and medicinal, and the room was chillingly cold. I watched his chest move up and down and synchronized my breathing with his. I leaned down and kissed his hands. I talked to him, though he wasn't conscious.

"I love you, I love you," I told him over and over. I was afraid; doubts entered my head. Would he wake up and be all right? Would he even wake up? Would he know me and the baby? Would he be able to see, talk? Would he be robbed of his most precious gift: the ability to hear music? I prayed in the room. I couldn't stop praying. Quincy and I were together in that moment fighting for his life.

My mother and aunt took me home. I had to leave the hospital to nurse Kidada. After nursing and cuddling her, I lay on my bed. I could hardly move, and I couldn't stop crying. Rita and Pearl sat on my bed consoling me, trying bravely not to imagine the worst.

"He'll be all right, darling Pegs, he'll be all right," they kept repeating. I just wanted to sleep, to wake up in the morning and find Quincy loving and perfect in bed next to me.

For two days we had been surrounded by doctors and family. Now, by myself, I had to accept reality. In the bathroom washing my face, I looked at myself in the mirror and said, "Peggy, you have to face it. He could die." There, I had said it. I had let the fear push through the adrenaline rush of the last thirty-six hours.

Quincy had survived brain surgery, but he still might not make it through the night. Everything, every obstacle and opening that had come our way, every joy-filled or gut-wrenching moment we had endured—his career, his music, our baby, our lives, my pregnancy, our families—all this had been manageable. Our love would overcome all—whatever obstacles confronted us, we would get through them. But I couldn't imagine a world without Quincy.

And yet talking to myself in the mirror that night, I forced myself to look into the abyss. I was alone. No mommy, daddy, or child could take away this feeling. This was between me and God. I asked for grace and blessings. And I made a pact to go on with my life, no matter what happened.

Quincy recuperated over many weeks at home. His doctors agreed he was a living miracle. He was swollen and in pain and groggy, but he was alive with no side affects from the aneurysm. He had round-the-clock nurses who couldn't get over his energy, humor, and determination. None of us could. He was an inspiration to everyone. He'd laugh, kiss, and hug his children, and plead for just one meal of baby-back short ribs and some music. All signs were good. I sobbed in his arms. I now had him near me, home and recovering, but I was terrified it might all happen again.

The one thing that I couldn't get out of my head was the memory of that terrifying moment. Could overstimulation cause the blood vessel to burst again? Could too many people visiting, worrying about when he could work—or making love—cause the worst to happen again?

And Quincy still had another aneurysm that needed to be operated on; there was no way he could have sustained having both blood vessels sealed off in one surgery. As it was, they had drilled open his head and inserted metal plates behind his forehead to hold the skull in place. This would all have to be done again; Quincy would have to go back in for another surgery.

The night before the second surgery, I sat on the bed with my mom and my aunt. I remember I had just finished nursing Kidada. Now was the time to tell them something I had hidden from them my whole life. I just blurted it out. There was no way to get around the truth anymore.

"Aunt Pearl, there's something I need to tell you about your husband." I took a deep breath. "Your husband abused me . . . sexually . . . for years."

"No!" they screamed in unison. I tried to give the details. The attic, his late-night work at the bakery, my brother Kenny asleep in the next bed. Incredibly, the horror of that realization made them both sit there in disbelief. They couldn't accept it as truth, and to this day I don't know if they ever did. I guess they didn't want to believe I had suffered through something like that. Maybe they felt guilty. I know how shocking the truth must have been for them, but in that moment I felt abandoned. Almost like the child who had wanted to reach out way back then—for the comfort she deserved but couldn't ask for.

But now I had to deal with an immediate crisis: Quincy's second operation was looming. Before his first surgery, on the afternoon he had been admitted to the hospital, Quincy's family flew down from Seattle. The next of kin had to sign papers directing the hospital about what to do with his remains should he die during surgery. It was a chaotic scene. I watched them all cry and huddle together and sign on the dotted line. But I couldn't be a part of it; I was the outsider because we weren't legally together. I was determined that this not happen again. I had a baby; Quincy was the father. I needed to know we were protected. If it came to that point again, with Quincy teetering on the brink between life and death, I would be the one to sign the papers.

"No man will ever love you like this," I said to myself, and I knew it was time to do it. On September 14, 1974, when Quincy's divorce had been final for just one day, a judge married us at my parents' home—with Quincy in between his operations and me nursing Kidada. I was now Mrs. Quincy Jones. I couldn't think of anything better.

I had never wanted to get married, even after having a child. Marriage hadn't even occurred to me. I wanted to know I was free and that love would be the bond that held us together, not a certificate. Even though my parents had had a wonderful forty-year marriage, I'd always felt a deep-seeded restlessness and fear of commitment. Being with men who were already married had temporarily solved that problem. As for having been abused—at the heart of all of this—I'd managed to keep it well hidden, even from myself. But when I told my mother and aunt the truth, the abuse suddenly became real. It had happened. I couldn't change it, but it was time to stop running.

I survived it. I understand it. You can't take it back. You can't blame yourself. If you can, you help others, and that's it. It's good to breathe out.

57.

"Help Me, Bear"

While Quincy was recovering from his second surgery, we decided to let his mother come to visit. She was frantic to see him, claiming that I was keeping her away from her son. He didn't even want to tell her about the surgery, but how could he keep it from her? After all, the whole world knew. Finally, Quincy told me Sarah could come down from Seattle, but only if I strictly limited her access to him. He lay in bed, his brain cut open and steel plates in his forehead, looking like a swollen pumpkin.

"Bear," he whispered, "just keep her away from me."

At first, she was on her best behavior, tiptoeing around Quincy, talking nonstop, and trying to get along with his nurse, who was totally irking her. She didn't like anything the nurse was doing for Quincy, but she kept herself in check. At first. She played with Kidada and Tina. I was vigilant, watching her behavior with the kids and making sure she was fairly calm when she went into our bedroom to see Quincy. But by the second night Sarah could no longer control the demons within.

The baby's bath is too hot, she'd scream. *Don't give Tina ice cream for dessert. The cook is poisoning Quincy.* It escalated to, "You're not a good wife. You made this happen with sex and too much pressure on my son."

That was fucking *it*. It was the most natural feeling of anger rising and then being put into action. No one had thought I would be strong enough to deal with Sarah Jones. I surprised myself. Instinctively I knew I couldn't call my own mother or even ask Quincy what to do. I stared straight into her face.

"You've got to go," I said. "Get out."

"What!" she said. "I don't leave my son's house; this is *my* son. You're nobody. *You caused this.*"

She was out the door in twenty minutes: bags packed and in a cab to the bus station. I cried in Quincy's bed. He didn't know how it came about, but he was glad she was gone. She called.

"I can't believe you did this to me, Peggy."

"Believe it," I said, and a peace settled over the house.

Our relationship sustained over the years—even after the divorce, and right up until the day she died. I went to Seattle often to spend time with Sarah. It was never easy, but my children asked to see her and grew to love her. She was gentle with them. When we visited her in her apartment, we'd sometimes find her in the bath asleep, dried up like a brown fig. "Grandma Sarah," Kidada and Rashida would ask, "why do you fall asleep in the bathtub?"

"Little children," she'd say, "it's quiet here and I can pray knowing God is with me."

58.

The Little Studio That Could

Quincy always needed a separate space to work in. We had a one-room guest house in the back of our yard in Brentwood, and when he was working, he'd stay in this "studio" for days, never sleeping, breaking only when I brought him his dinner or I came in to nurse Kidada and we could both play with her. Most nights during this time I slept alone in our bedroom. Quincy would write in a sea of paper. Before we moved him to the makeshift studio, he would lay out his music charts, orchestrations in his own hand notations, on the carpeted floor in front of our bed. I still hold that image of Quincy enveloped in his score paper. When he'd get frustrated, he'd crumple pages and throw them in the trash. I would go out and retrieve them the next morning.

I thought someday he might remember he wrote something amazing and want them back.

As brilliant as he was, Quincy could also be very hard on himself about his writing. He would work feverishly for three or four days without sleeping and sometimes all there would be were two notes on the score paper. My heart would hurt for him when he came up against those blocks. There were so many nights when he would be on the verge of tears because he couldn't get what he wanted. Then all of a sudden, it would come to him. He always attributed this to God—his ultimate muse—coming in and taking over.

If you share a home with a musical genius, your life will inevitably revolve around his creative rhythms. After the surgery, Quincy went at his work full throttle, wondering, perhaps, how long he might have to live. As exhilarating as all this creative mania was, I started to miss sharing a normal life with Quincy. His schedule was erratic, to say the least. He was either constantly working or else hibernating. He'd be up for days and then fall asleep in the middle of eating or talking. When something that he considered worthwhile had finally been achieved, he'd take off a few days and fall into a deep, dreamless sleep. It was becoming increasingly difficult to get the time with him I wanted, and it started to bother me. Still, when Quincy was writing music, he was tapped into his essence, and it was through his music that we formed a profound bond. He'd play me pieces of a score or song he was writing on the electric piano and I felt our souls fuse through the music.

Sometimes he'd ask me to get more actively involved in his work, and I was thrilled. We would write together. Quincy liked that I had an ear for music. Nobody in my family was musical, so I don't know where it came from, but I could hear music and play anything on the piano without reading a note. As a child, I had seriously studied piano. I even gave a concert playing a duet and solo at Little Carnegie Recital Hall in New York City, but I never learned to read music. The piano teacher assumed I was reading the notes, but I faked it. I was impatient; I wanted the sounds to all come together *now*, so I went ahead and memorized every piece by ear.

During my early years with Quincy, there were great musicians streaming through our house: jazz and pop geniuses. I'd be nursing or in the kitchen or putting the girls to sleep. I'd stay and socialize for a few minutes and then leave Quincy and the others to their work. I was quite in awe of each of them, but there was no one more beautiful and composed than Lena Horne.

I don't believe Ms. Horne was by nature a social creature. I got the feeling she didn't like being around many people. I met her when I sat in on her recording sessions with Quincy for her Broadway show album *Lena*. On her day off she came to visit us in the home we were renting in East Hampton, Long Island. She played and laughed with the kids. A few months later Quincy and I took her to lunch back in L.A. I was fascinated by her serenity; the way she walked and spoke. Her life had been a difficult one. Even with all her talent and beauty, racism in the 1930s and '40s in this country had deeply affected her life. During more recent years, she had moved to Northern California.

"Why did you leave Los Angeles?" I asked her.

"Because living in L.A.," she told me, "means spending the whole day looking for the perfect avocado."

The funny thing about this is I eventually turned into "that person," a homemaker in L.A., spending my whole morning looking for the perfect avocado.

Every imaginable talent passed through our house, from the suave George Benson to the rough and handsome Bruce Springsteen to the hilarious Richard Pryor and the debonair Mr. Billy Eckstine, or "B" as Quincy called him. This man could charm the pants off anyone, and I'm sure he did. He was a famously cool ladies' man. He talked dirty and I hear he fought dirty, too. I knew he had a real street side that could get nasty. But B and Quincy would go on a roll for hours: laughing, eating, drinking, and reminiscing about the old days—the music, the characters they had known along the way, the women, the adventures of touring. During these prolific and creative years, Quincy produced his own albums and others featuring Patti Austin, James Ingram, the Brothers Johnson, and jazz greats like Ray Brown and J.J. Johnson. He also produced albums for women artists like Lena Horne, Chaka Kahn,

Miriam Makeba, Donna Summer, Aretha Franklin, and Sarah Vaughn. They'd come write and vocalize with him in his little studio at home. If you can imagine a cartoon image of a small house bursting at the seams with musical notes pouring out from the doors and windows, that was our home.

Down the road, Quincy and I would write together. One of those songs was called "L.A. Is My Lady," which became a hit for Frank Sinatra. I was beside myself at the recording session—Frank Sinatra was singing a song I had cowritten. This was the highlight of my very slight musical career. Frank exuded charisma. You knew you were in the presence of a legend. You didn't have to take it on faith—he proved it by being courteous and the consummate professional. Quincy had produced and arranged a number of albums for Frank. They seemed to have a special rapport and great respect for each other's musical talents. Frank was so on that by the time half an hour had flown by, the session was over.

"Hey, Q, was that good, man?" he asked.

"Yeah, Frank, it was terrific." They hugged and thanked each other and Frank was out the door.

When Sinatra was performing in Las Vegas, Quincy and I went backstage and found Frank, ten minutes before curtain time, stuffing himself with pasta.

"Sit down, kids, eat," he offered, but we declined, amazed that he could sing on a full stomach. For the show we sat at a table close to the stage, and when Frank came out, he walked over, looked down at us with those piercing blue eyes, smiled at Quincy, and blew me a kiss. I was so surprised, I felt giddy. It was a small gesture but it was Frank Sinatra including us in his dazzling universe for an instant. At the time, when few white stars—never mind stars of Sinatra's caliber—would work with a black composer, arranger, or producer, Frank put his faith in Quincy Jones, and it always paid off.

My life was once again filled with joy when I became pregnant in 1975. I called Quincy from my doctor's office with the news. I waddled and ate and grew wide, gaining fifty-five pounds. I had lost most of the weight I had put on with Kidada by nursing her and just running around trying to keep up with her energetic self. By now Kidada was a year and a half old, and so cute with her little front teeth coming in. She was smart and entertaining and I couldn't get enough of her. Motherhood was everything I'd hoped it would be; unadulterated joy and wonder and a chance to heal some of my own childhood wounds, through love. Now my heart was open and anxious to have another baby. Rashida Leah came in the early morning hours on February 25, 1976. I had stayed at home until the contractions were a few minutes apart. I was confident with this second pregnancy, and Rashie was coming into the world *fast*. Labor this time was only three and a half hours. She weighed more than Kidada and her birth was infinitely more relaxed. There were no complications. We had her by the modified Leboyer method: the overhead lighting was dimmed, the voices of the nurses and staff were lowered, and she was gently coaxed through the birth canal and put in a warm bath with the umbilical cord still attached. There she was submerged until her crying subsided, then put at my breast to nurse. All this was taking place in an operating room at a great big hospital! It was how I had imagined it when I first read the book by French physician Frederic Leboyer, and it had proven to be a gentler, more humane way to have a new life enter the world. My life was complete.

It was around this time that Alex Haley first entered our lives. Haley had first gained fame as the coauthor of *The Autobiography of Malcolm X*, but what really brought him to prominence as a writer was *Roots*, a fact-based novel tracing the story of his own family back to Africa. There was tremendous excitement around the idea of this book. No one could ever have dreamed that this man would be able to go back to Africa and find out who his ancestors were. No black man had ever explored this, at least not as exhaustively as Alex had. He had spent so long researching *Roots* that he virtually ran out of money. As he was writing the end of the book, he came and lived with us. He was a great cook, having acquired his culinary skills in the Navy. Cooking was his way of thanking us: baby-back short ribs, sautéed cabbage, and sweet potato pie were this ex-naval officer's specialty.

Quincy and Alex were friends before Quincy was hired to do the score for the *Roots* miniseries—one of the biggest television events of all time.

The first two-hour episode of *Roots* was a disturbing look at the African slave trade. Quincy wanted to pour his entire being into this work and spent months researching African music. He listened and experimented with every known ancient and modern African instrument: from a myriad assortment of drums, koras, and mbiras to vocal sounds, field calls, and chanting in dialects. He gathered together the crème de la crème of African-American musicians and singers to bring his score to life. The music emanating from Quincy's tiny studio was otherworldly and filled with the incessant pulse of a man who'd now been given a second lease on life. There he stayed, engrossed and exhausted until he finished.

Shortly before *Roots* started filming, Alex came into the studio and rolled out a large blueprint. From all across the African continent, thousands of people were pulled from their families and transported by the English and Dutch in the cargo holds of large ships. These were sketches of men, woman, and children lying shoulder to shoulder, body upon body, manacled, starved, and infested with disease. We had tears in our eyes as the three of us looked at the blueprint, but none of us could say a word.

Quincy wrote one of his most beautiful scores for *Roots*, but after the first episode he was replaced by Hollywood executives who found his music too provocative (read "evocative"). They had no idea that the series was going to be as successful as it was; their only interest was in rushing it out. They started saying, "Hurry up, we need it yesterday." Quincy just ran out of steam fighting with the producers. *Roots* was an eight-episode series, and they needed scores banged out to fit their schedule. That wasn't Quincy's way.

He never scored another TV show. His heart and guts had gone into *Roots* and he couldn't take another disappointment like that again. I felt for him. This project had meant so much, but eventually for Quincy it was, "Let's forget it and move on." That was his way of dealing with professional frustration. I knew it bothered him deeply but he wanted to put it behind him. Although he ended up scoring only the two-hour pilot episode of *Roots*, Quincy's *Roots* CD is one of the deepest, most elegant, and ingenious scores ever written for a TV series. In 1977, he won an Emmy for it and was nominated for three Grammy Awards.

59.

Thriller

The following year Quincy began working with Michael Jackson. Michael was a handsome fresh-faced bundle of musical genius. Quincy had helped cast him as the scarecrow in the film *The Wiz*. I imagine the whole time he worked with Michael, Quincy was observing Michael's talent and devising a way to produce his first solo album and make him a superstar. Working together on Michael's first album, *Off the Wall*, was the beginning of Michael opening up and tapping into his own brilliance, away from his family and the unerring hold they'd always had on him. Quincy was the captain of the boat that set sail that year: the mastermind. They were close while they worked together; pretty much consumed with the project. Michael spent a lot of time at our house. He was a shy and cunning young man yet still acted like a child.

The day the 1983 Grammy nominations were to be announced we decided we just had to get out of the house and try to calm down. Finally, just the two of us! There we were, waiting to hear something, anything, and also trying to concentrate on eating shrimp salad at a little Swedish restaurant in Beverly Hills. We had no appetite and kept looking from the old clock on the wall to our wilting salads. We couldn't eat. We just kept beaming at each other, hoping there would be some nod of acknowledgment for his work, but never ever anticipating what was to come. Two or three times Quincy got up and scrunched himself into the restaurant's tiny phone booth.

"Does anyone know anything yet?" he kept asking. On his last trip to the phone booth, he walked back to the table looking like he was floating two feet off the ground. And then we screamed. He'd been nominated for seven Grammys, including Record of the Year (Michael Jackson's "Beat It"); Album of the Year (Michael Jackson's *Thriller*); Best Recording for Children (*E.T. the Extra-Terrestrial*); and, amazingly, Producer of the Year—all of which he ended up winning. This was the recognition Quincy had been wanting and the confirmation he needed to know he'd made the leap. He'd successfully fused his jazz roots into pop music. It had taken years, but he'd been determined in that very Quincy Jones fashion.

Soon he would become a master of this genre, but on this very auspicious afternoon we shared the news more like children being told we had the run of the candy store with a hundred pennies in our pockets. We leapt into each other's arms and thanked God for giving Quincy back his health so we could fully relish this moment. In some ways this was the high point for me. Not yet filled with people and their phony congratulations, their shiny awards or back-slapping compliments. I felt the deepest joy for Quincy's accomplishments and his life, but I would never reach this height again. In the future, all the accolades that would be bestowed on Quincy would come with a price. And I'd always be looking over my shoulder, waiting to see who would latch on—who was sincere and who the takers were. I wasn't cynical quite yet, just cautious. And to my dismay our loving moments alone would become fewer as our lives became bigger and our options wider.

60.

"Do You Really Want to Hurt Me?"

My daughter Kidada never responded to authority. The fact that she was dyslexic but never diagnosed with it only added to her problems in school. In those days dyslexia wasn't recognized. Teachers believed children who had trouble reading just weren't smart enough to learn. Consequently, Kidada attended a multitude of schools. I think I had her in seven different schools. She couldn't sit still and more often than not was asked to leave the classroom. The frustration grew over the years. Teachers had me in for conferences at least once a week from the day she started school. One of the problems was that Kidada was impossibly clever and aware and usually had a way of outsmarting the teacher. Instead of being seen for the child she was, Kidada was labeled as a child unwilling to concentrate and take orders. During her entire school career, only two teachers took the time to really understand what she might be going through. Kidada was looking for a true heart and an authentic person in a teacher. She seemed to see through the ones who didn't care enough or just chose to give up on her. She could smell their lack of interest. But Kidada always knew she was different, and, of course, her problems were compounded by the fact that her first school was mostly white.

Kidada had a special effect on Quincy. She was our first child and her resemblance to Quincy's mother, Sarah, was undeniable. For one thing, Kidada was feisty in the same way. When we'd try to cuddle her, she'd push us both away coyly telling us, "No." But when she did give us kisses or hugs, it was like getting to an oasis in the desert and drinking all the sweet water one could. Kidada loved to paint and played creatively with dolls, puzzles and costumes. She would make up entire scenarios with her friends. In those games, her dolls would play out all her feelings of love, caring, and frustration. I tried not to be the obnoxious mother hovering over her, but despite my best intentions I often found myself in her room, just watching her play; this was the only way I could enter the world of Kidada. She always made me laugh, with her witty observations and out-right quirkiness.

Once when she was eight, I grounded her. She retreated to her room in a huff and emerged . . . as Boy George! Made up with cat eyes, an all-black suit, scarf, and the black fedora, she took a toy microphone and announced she had something to ask me. She turned on her tape deck and proceeded to lip-sync: "Do you really want to hurt me?"

Come on, how could anyone resist that? I laughed and melted and let her go to her sleepover. Unbelievably imaginative, Kidada would stir it up when things were going along a little too smoothly—quite a bit like her grandmother Sarah Jones. If little girls were running around somewhere at a party or school, with no rhyme or reason, she'd terrify them by telling scary stories. They'd burst into tears and want to go home. You had to have stamina and courage to be around Kidada. No wusses allowed. You had to be able to survive her scrutiny. She never settled for the status quo and tweaked everything to her own comfort zone, where she had the greatest amount of control. She was always the leader and kids followed her, mesmerized by the challenges she set for them. We always had a houseful of her schoolmates. They were a quirky lot and very much hand-picked by her. She'd come home from one school or another with some raggedy friend and they'd build a veritable mountain of dolls and clothes and dollhouses and talk endlessly like little old ladies.

61.

55 Causeway Road

At a particularly raw time in my life, when the children were small and I was taking care of Quincy's children as well, we rented a house in East Hampton for the summer. Sounds like fun. It wasn't. Quincy was scoring the film *The Wiz* in Manhattan day in and day out. He'd come home once a week too tired to talk. Into the bargain, the killer Son of Sam was out there somewhere on the loose. I needed all the comfort I could get! The mounting activities and responsibilities with the children made me yearn for Quincy to be there. One day while we were driving into the city for a night alone together, I felt this dull ache. I wanted to go home, not to L.A. but to my two-story brick house with the honeysuckle bush and the Swedish Elm tree that my mother had planted in the front yard. To 55 Causeway Road. I wanted the smell of damp oak leaves after we had raked and piled them on the lawn. I wanted lamb chops and roasted potatoes cooking in the kitchen. I wanted home.

When I could speak after holding in alligator-size tears, I asked Quincy, "Daddy? Can you buy us that house if they would consider selling it, and can we all move in?" I was deadly serious. He didn't truly understand what I was working myself up to or why. Neither he nor I realized what might come of opening the door to my past; now I just wanted to be a child again, feeling and imbibing the familiar smells and sights. Unbelievably, he said, "Yes, Bear, we could probably do that." Quincy was an incurable romantic, and after all this was a thoroughly romantic and slightly skewed notion—to try to recapture myself as a little girl in the house in which I grew up. I wanted to relive some long-ago fleeting essence of childhood as if I had never ventured away. Or, who knows, maybe I wanted to return to the past in order to *change* it, to undo the things that had happened to me. In any case, Quincy had an all-encompassing need to love me and give me what I wanted, and his saying yes was a grand gesture for me. It was never going to happen, of course. You really can't go back; only your dreams can take you there.

62.

The First Female Jewish Black President

Rashida, our second daughter, was peaceful, calm, and, as I once was, the "good girl" of the family. Even her name, Rashida, means "rightly guided on the true path." Rashida was the baby, at least until the birth of Quincy's last daughter, Kenya. She was coddled, it's true, and she relished it. School came easily to her, and her ear for music and a photographic memory gave her a special bond with Quincy. From the age of five, she studied piano and became a polished pianist giving classical concerts and winning awards. She would curl up next to Quincy and watch him write music, sometimes well into the night. Like him, she was a night owl on the prowl. No matter what time I put her to bed she'd remain awake reading under her covers with a flashlight. She would sometimes sleepwalk and end up absorbed in some project in her closet or another quiet room in the house. When I'd bring her to bed she'd be in that somnambulist state, eyes glazed over and not fully aware of where she was. We never pushed her to become the musician she turned out to be: a gifted singer and composer. As a child, she aimed even higher. "I want to become the first female, Jewish, black President of the United States," she announced, as serious and determined as a ten-year-old could be. She achieved many honors at school. She won the Senior Drama Award for all-around best play performances, and the President's award for Model United Nations for her debating skills. She was head of student government and a three-varsity athelete. She thrived scholastically and personally in the same school from kindergarten to graduation.

We could all see her talent for acting and musicals when she was still tiny. Rashida had watched all the Rodgers and Hammerstein musicals on video, the very ones I had loved when I saw them on Broadway as a young girl. *The King and I, The Sound of Music, Carousel, Oklahoma.* She was already showing a talent for singing and dancing, had the utmost confidence, and was—unlike Kidada and me—highly coordinated. By eighth grade this child would come home with homework from school that was so over my head I'd feel idiotic. At some point in her education she no longer needed my help. She had it covered, from biology to math to literature.

Kidada and Rashida almost always got along when they played with each other. They would make up dialogue for their dolls and imaginary companions. Unselfconsciously, they would slide in and out of two cultural dialects. Together, their imaginations took off. Ultimately, my daughters thrived on all their mingled roots. They were Jewish, black, and white. Quincy's mother had converted to Judaism and so had my stepdaughter, Tina. To do that, Tina studied Hebrew and then had to have a Mikvah, a ritual bath. I encouraged her and ended up at the ceremony representing her mother. My visions of this ritual must have been a little off. It took place on a very sunny afternoon in the rabbi's kidney-shaped swimming pool. I don't know what I was expecting, but it wasn't that. Only in L.A.

We celebrated Passover with my parents and our Jewish friends and went to Temple for the holidays. For Yom Kippur we went to Chabad House, an Orthodox sanctuary filled with singing, davening, and prayer. All three girls loved the religious observances, but Kidada and Rashida felt conspicuously black and out of place in Jewish Sunday school where there seemed to be only little fair-skinned white girls. That was hardest for Kidada, who had darker skin. And being ethnically Jewish and half-white left her somewhat alienated from her African-American friends. It was difficult for me to watch her struggle with such painful questions of identity, which inevitably stoked the fierceness in her personality. But it was that ferocity that let me know Kidada would always find her own place in the world.

For Rashida, the struggle appeared less dramatic. She was light-skinned with green eyes and straight blond hair. She was always taken for something other than what she was. Hispanic, Middle Eastern, South American. When new acquaintances would try to guess her origins she would always tell them with pride that she was black. The three of us would watch Miss America pageants together much as my mom and I had, but we were all too aware of the conspicuous absence of black contestants.

"Mommy, why is everyone white?" they'd ask. They couldn't see anyone who looked like them.

"One day the world will look like you," I told them. "You are the color of the future." I knew it and I meant it. Now you see it everywhere: on TV, at the movies, and in magazines—the boundaries identifying beauty through race or ethnicity are becoming blurred. I always knew my girls were extraordinary beauties. Anyone could see that. But today, for themselves and their children, they will have their unique diversity mirrored back to them.

63.

Travolta

was giving Kidada and Rashie lunch in the kitchen, a favorite time for me. I loved seeing them enjoy their food. They were great eaters, testing and trying everything. These were the years I got to pick and choose their food: organic chicken, fruits and vegetables, and healthy snacks. I packed their school lunches and took way too much pride in the fact that they only ate health food. They told me years later, in the sparkling way children do to get back at the adults who dictated every move they made, that they always switched their sack lunches with their friends so they could ingest as much junk food as possible before they came home.

The only star I ever saw Kidada and Rashida get shy around was John Travolta. He'd gotten into a minor car accident with a woman who was on her way to work at our house. She stood at the front door, her face mortifyingly red. Behind her stood John Travolta, handsome, tall and wearing—what else?—a leather jacket. He trailed her into the house, apologizing profusely.

When Kidada and Rashida saw him, they tried to hide their delight and shock. John Travolta had appeared out of nowhere and was standing in their kitchen. They were so hooked on the movie *Grease,* they must have thought they had materialized him. He had simply walked out of the television set and into our house. John Travolta! John Travolta! They blushed, but ended up having a relatively adult conversation with him, while asking him a million questions and giggling.

"So, where's Sandy now?" and "How did you learn to dance?" He was sweet and so natural with them, answering all their questions, but it was his turn to be utterly surprised when out strolled Quincy Jones and Travolta realized whose house he'd walked into. We all sat down for an unexpected lunch together. Afterward, Kidada and Rashie both claimed that I was more excited than they were. They were clever and tried to nail me. They were too cool to ever want to show their hand when it came to celebrities, but with John Travolta they could barely contain themselves. They ran to their rooms giggling and whispered about him for the rest of the night.

64.

Breaking Up

Being with Quincy had transformed me in some fundamental way. Even physically. I was no longer the anorexic-looking girl whose identity—and obsession—rested on her appearance and need for acceptance. If I never felt glamorous again after I had my two babies, I didn't care. I'd wanted to stop working and raise a family. I could stay in the house all day and just be with them and that's what satisfied and fulfilled me. I felt no need to go out. I was content to stay home and never attend another awards dinner or ceremony. This hurt Quincy, who loved being around people.

Since I was a kid, I'd always felt that I was too much for anybody to handle: too much passion, too much neediness. But in Quincy's eyes, I wasn't too much. He loved me unconditionally; it was I who couldn't sustain the intimacy between us. What I hadn't been able to face for twenty years was the dark secret from my past that began to surface just as everything in my life was working out. The abuse I'd suffered as a child was bound to erupt at some point, and I was about to find out that telling my aunt was just the beginning.

In some ways Quincy was as needy as I was. This was one of the reasons we locked together so tightly, but it was those same forces that ultimately split us apart. Quincy, too, was emotionally bereft. In his case, because of the mother he'd always yearned for but never had.

"She left a hole that I can't fill," he told me more than once.

It's a metaphor, but no less real. Like black holes in space, those voids have terrifying negative power, sucking in everything in a desperate need to be filled. For Quincy, it was a very visceral want. His overwhelming need came out of the terrible vacuum of his childhood. His more lasting relationships were a quest for the family he hadn't had. He thought I had come from a close-knit family and that in some way with me at his side he would be able to reconstitute his own.

My family did seem ideal. Quincy and my brothers, Bob and Ken, loved each other. My father was Quincy's staunchest supporter. Eventually, Quincy even grew to love my mother with her strident opinions and personality. It seemed as if I came out of a vibrant group of loving people. But the more I thought about it, the more I began to realize I was letting him believe a fairytale of my childhood. At first I didn't try to dissuade him. I wanted him to see only the good. But as I revealed little bits and pieces about my childhood, he came to realize that I, too, had had a very dysfunctional family.

Quincy was that rare and sensitive kind of man who is in touch with his heart. I had never had that kind of real affection in my life—the kind that I'd wanted so much from my parents and my lovers. You wouldn't, for instance, have called my mother nurturing. She didn't know how to be, something I was unable to admit to myself until I went into therapy years later. My grandparents, though I hardly knew them, weren't exactly open with their feelings either. Aunt Pearl was the only one who would hug and kiss me. This lack of physical affection ran in my family. My aunt would tell me that when she was young she would crave affection from her mother (my grandmother).

"Just a hug and a kiss, Mummy," she'd say, and her mother would always reply, "I'm too ashamed, darling." She was a proper Englishwoman and displays of emotion were hidden away from family and, ultimately, the outside world.

English or not, there were flaws in both our family trees. Because of his own schizophrenic mother, Quincy hadn't had a real family. So when he met me, it was as if this missing piece of his history had been restored to him. He thought he had met someone from a fully developed family and could count on them to comfort him. When he began realizing how dysfunctional my family was, the illusion evaporated. My parents loved me dearly, it's true, but when he started seeing the ungluing of what he wanted to believe was the ideal family unit, it seemed to unravel him.

We were in love. We never said a bad word to each other. We never had an argument, not in all the years we were together, but some time late in 1984, I started to have a breakdown. Quincy, not understanding what was at the root of my malaise, projected the problems back onto my romantic past.

65.

Breakdown

Quincy began asking me about my old lovers. I told him about my alcoholic, abusive boyfriend and I know it disturbed him. He would bring up his name. And when he began to ask me about the uncle who had sexually molested me, I became disturbed and unresponsive. I had blanked it out almost completely. I couldn't confront the shame. Quincy would try to get me to talk about it, which made me feel violated and uncomfortable. His probing made me uneasy, as if he were trying to get inside me. I kept thinking I was fine and it would all evaporate if I didn't pay attention to it. There began to be so much charge on these feelings that I would sometimes pray that the bomb would just explode so I could get it over with. The complete disintegration and deconstruction of my life as I knew it was not far off.

Quincy began to feel that I had given more of myself to other men in my life than I was giving to him, that I might be holding back some unrealized passion. Sometimes when we'd talk about my past I began to sense an undercurrent of anger. Though I had always trusted him implicitly, I began feeling that he was going to use my past against me at some point. I became fearful; I closed down. I was afraid that he might persist in trying to coerce confessions from me—a terrifying prospect. An alarm bell went off in my head: if I exposed anything, I could once again be bait for a predator.

But none of these feelings, real or imagined, could be blamed on Quincy. The problem was mine. I was incapable of opening up. Everything was on lockdown inside me. I wanted the way I was treated as a child to stay as far away as possible from my current reality and the raising of my children. It had to be buried so deep that there would be no chance it would ever rear its ugly head again and wreck my life.

In what I believe was a haunting twist of fate, Quincy pulled an old boyfriend back into my life—my teenage love, Paul McCartney. All of a sudden Quincy was producing a single with Paul and Michael Jackson. It seemed to come out of nowhere.

"You've got to come to the sessions," he'd say.

"Why would I want to do that?" I'd answer. I had no interest in seeing Paul again.

Eighteen years had gone by. There was nothing to assume except that I was over him. In the interim, I'd had a career, lovers, met my husband, and had babies. Why was Quincy doing a record with Michael Jackson and Paul McCartney anyway? I don't think Quincy had ever been a dedicated Beatles fan. Michael and Paul were big stars—and who would dismiss such an opportunity?—but something didn't bode right with me about the whole situation. The thought of having to see Paul working with Quincy was striking a raw, dissonant chord, a feeling that Quincy might be worried I hadn't gotten over Paul.

Quincy went to Arizona where Linda and Paul had a house and a recording studio. He was very fond of Linda.

"They want you to come down here. Linda, especially, wants to meet you," he'd say, and kept pressing it.

The idea of going to Arizona and staying in the same house with Paul and Linda was overwhelming. Hmm, maybe I wasn't exactly over it; I was resisting too much. I became vehement in my refusal to show my face at the McCartney residence or in the studio. I made as many excuses as I could think of not to go. One night at a recording studio in Los Angeles, they were putting the last touches on the Paul and Michael single, "The Girl Is Mine."

Quincy called me at home and said, "Bear, if you don't come in tonight, they're going to think something is wrong." I thought, *Who the fuck cares?* I smoked a joint for the first time in years. I'd hidden it for some very stressful occasion, which had, unfortunately, arrived. I sighed, and I went.

I got to the studio and stood paralyzed in front of the door. I couldn't open it. My hands refused to grip the knob. I must have stood outside the door for fifteen minutes trying to think of what it was going to be like when I opened it. Inside it was dark and smoky, but right away I spotted Paul at the control panel. For an instant, I didn't know where I was. My heart was beating so fast I could barely think. Paul looked up and said, "Oh, hello, Mrs. Jones," as upbeat as ever. "Oh, hello," I replied and we gave each other a peck on the cheek.

I was moving in slow motion because everything was painfully p-r-o-t-r-a-c-t-e-d. I spotted Quincy and Linda standing at the end of the console. I went over to meet her, anticipating Quincy's reaction. Then I moved toward the two figures in the dark. I was introduced.

"Bear," Quincy said. "This is Linda." I thought, *Is he talking in a slow drone and is she moving to shake my hand as if she's underwater?*

"Niiiice to seeeeeeeeee you, Linda," I said, feeling the words expand as I spoke.

She looked at me through the haze and said, "Nice to seeeeee you . . . again!"

Again? Shit. Did that mean she remembered our encounter eighteen years before at the Beverly Hills Hotel—the morning she and Paul ran away from me and into the waiting limousine?

I went home that night and cried. So many years had come full circle and I needed to mourn the end of the adolescent in me, the ultrasensitive kid who had given her whole heart to her teenage love. During the next week, Linda and Paul spent a lot of time at our house. I babysat for their children, taking them along with mine when we went shopping for toys and trinkets. I wanted to please them and Quincy—and also to prove to all parties involved that I had no feelings left for Paul.

During those few days I was around Linda McCartney, I grew to like her. She was honest about things that dismayed her; like Paul's marijuana bust in Japan and the short jail sentence that followed. She also adored her children. That was easy to see. She seemed to always listen to them and give of her time and love. But Quincy wasn't really acting like himself that week. I think he had been waiting to see if I would crack under the pressure of seeing Paul again. If only we could have talked about it. If only I hadn't been a secret-keeper all my life.

What I was going through, however, had little to do with Paul or any other old boyfriend.

66.

Breakup

By 1985, Quincy had received countless accolades. His health was good and he was in high demand. He wanted to build a studio in our home and convert a beautiful outdoor brick patio with its 100-year-old oak tree into a large living room—tree included. We hired an architect. I resisted the whole process. I had no wish to see things change; if anything I wanted to go back to our original simple lifestyle. But his laser-like determination burned through all my objections and I didn't have the will to fight with him, so we went ahead with plans to add 9,000 square feet to our house.

I found a rental house for us to live in up the street. In the meantime I fell ill with pneumonia and then contracted Epstein-Barr, an insidious and debilitating illness. Epstein-Barr's symptoms are hidden from the outside. There are no obvious symptoms, and after the pneumonia I stopped coughing. No real fever to speak of, although I always felt like I was burning up. I had a constant metallic taste in my mouth, and I couldn't keep my eyes open for more than an hour. My appetite fell away completely. People think you're all right be-cause you don't look that bad, but in fact you're critically fatigued, achy all over, and in general useless. There's no medication for it—just homeo-pathic treatments and sleep. It lasted almost a year and a half, and I don't think Quincy ever quite understood what was going on. I had no strength, and I resented having to do anything I wasn't up to. I couldn't face going out to dinner or to award shows, even the ones honoring Quincy. That, coupled with a feeling that no one understood my condition, made me want to stay under the bed covers and not come out. Luckily the children were busy at school, so they were out most of the day and wouldn't see all that much of my worsening condition. But I remember that first July when I'd stop the car after dropping them off at day camp and just cry and cry.

Despite my lack of energy, I felt strangely restless. I didn't want to be living in a strange house while everything I loved about my real home was being torn apart and rebuilt. The estimates for remodeling were getting outrageously high, but I didn't have the energy or desire to walk the half mile down the street to check on the workers. I was pissed at Quincy. He was the one I wanted to take my anger out on, but instead of confronting him, I didn't say a word.

Quincy was away much of that year working on the film *The Color Purple*. Producing it, helping cast it. Working closely with the director Steven Spielberg was a dream come true for Quincy. He knew the story was profound and that the locations were crucial, and spent months in North Carolina on the film.

Quincy, too, was waiting to move back into our real home and wasn't too delighted with the rental house we were staying in (and we ended up staying there for more than a year). I had no choice. I had to make it my own so the children wouldn't feel too out of place, but I was in no shape to participate in the usual activities and attend conferences at their school. The kids missed their father terribly. Snoopy, Tina, Kidada, and Rashida were all in different schools, and the sense of dislocation was clearly affecting them. We spent Christmas together—just the five of us. Snoopy had moved back with us for the year and Tina was struggling with being sixteen. We were all trying to make the best of it.

Most days I felt too sick to get out of bed for any length of time. Our nanny, Ana, who had worked for us for eleven years, became a sister to me, helping with everything. I was living in my own little world, waking up, getting the kids ready for school, and then going straight back to bed. I'd get up, have lunch and then go back to bed again, waiting until they came home on their different buses, helping them with homework, having dinner with them, and then reading them to sleep. When I wasn't with them, all I wanted was to be left alone. Quincy was missing from my life and I felt lost. Unreasonably perhaps, I was irritated by his need to prove himself again—to get *The Color Purple* under his belt and into his award-winning repertoire. Without realizing it, I was starting to fall into a deep depression.

Unaccountable feelings of grief were beginning to weave themselves into my sweat-filled afternoon naps. I found myself sobbing in my dreams and reaching out in bed for an absent Quincy. At night I would tiptoe into the girls' room, go under the blankets and hold them. During the day I'd close my door and dive headlong into melancholy music, Russian novels of despair or mystic poetry written by the saints. The more I withdrew from the world, the more I wanted to know how the saints found inner peace. I consulted Kabir, Rumi, Hafiz, Milarepa, Baba Muktananda. I'd close my eyes after reading their works and pray to be transformed into something else: someone free and detached from this earth.

Watching any old black-and-white film on TV in the afternoon became a form of solace, a way of escaping into the dreamy world of 1940s movies. Their idyllic locations and passionate plots reminded me of my parents and I began to fantasize about what their lives might have been like before and during the war. I had abandoned my own life and now was living the wistful lives of the women in *Since You Went Away*, *The Ghost and Mrs. Muir*, and *Mrs. Miniver*.

Later, *The Color Purple* was nominated for ten Academy Awards. At the ceremony I sat between Quincy and Alice Walker, its Pulitzer

Prize—winning author. Each time an award was announced, a sigh of disappointment would escape from Alice's throat. I could sense her heart dropping. By the time the last three awards were announced—Best Screenplay, Best Director, Best Picture—the long evening, with its failure to produce a single award, had eroded all our high hopes. Later, at Spago, Alice Walker sat dejected, fuming at the way Hollywood had treated the movie. Never again would she put herself in that position. Everyone who worked on the film seemed shocked. In our minds this was an obvious snub: Whoopi Goldberg, Oprah Winfrey, Margaret Avery, Danny Glover, Quincy Jones—all ignored. And for the director, Steven Spielberg, another miss at the Oscar.

My mother was the best friend I had while I was ill, but she was beginning to get sick herself—very sick. She had been diagnosed with cancer a year earlier but now there was a recurrence. God, what would I do without her? How would I go on?

The signs of an impending meltdown were already evident. My marriage was on the rocks, my mother's serious illness loomed before me, I was having difficulty raising my stepchildren, we were building a new home I sensed we were never going to live in, and on top of everything my depression was deepening.

In my state, fantasies started to arise. I wanted Quincy to come home and walk through the little white picket fence like the one that surrounded the house we had first lived in fourteen years before, when life was newly ours and filled with light and the possibility of starting over. I wanted to fall in love with him again and to experience the same needs for comfort and attention that I had when I was twenty-six, before fame and growing up interrupted my daydreams.

A brief liaison took place with a woman around this time. Our relationship of push and pull went on for a while as I tried to sort things out in my head. It was the first and last time I went down that road. When it was over and Quincy and I separated, I didn't want anything more to do with relationships and abstained from sex for the next nine years.

67.

Gurumayi

My agent sent me out on my first audition in years. It was there, I met the consummate actor and all around interesting guy, Peter Falk. We did a scene together and then talked. He asked me who I was studying with now that I was going back into acting. I wasn't really going back. It had taken every ounce of *faux* confidence to even get myself to the audition. But I listened when he gave me the name Sandra Seacat. She was his teacher and he said I would like her class and the way she worked. I wrote her name down in my book. It was 1985 and I was recovering from pneumonia. Each day I'd stare at the name *Sandra Seacat* scrawled in my appointment book. The name itself felt magical, I thought, but I'll never be able to call her: she's a stranger and it might mean I would have to go to a strange class with strange people. I wasn't up to it—physically *or* mentally. I hadn't socialized for years. Quincy was working nonstop as usual, and the girls were in school full-time. One afternoon, after staring at the name *Sandra Seacat* for ten minutes, I picked up the phone. My voice was so timid, she must have thought I was half-dead. I stuttered and stammered when I introduced myself and told her Peter Falk had recommended I call. She calmly said "Why don't you come over and we'll meet?" "Okay," I said, as I flipped through my empty appointment book for a day in the far-off future. That way I could eventually cancel. "When would be good for you?" I asked. "Right now," she said. "Come right now." For some unknown reason, it felt like I was being drawn to the light of a flame.

As I entered Sandra's apartment, I spotted something that would soon transform my life. It was a large photograph propped on a chair. I said a quick hello to Sandra but couldn't keep my eyes off the picture. "Who is that?" I asked. "That's my spiritual teacher, Gurumayi Chidvilasananda."

Gurumayi was very beautiful: an Indian woman with cropped black hair, sitting comfortably on a stone ledge in front of a green tree. An enigmatic smile played on her lips and her hands, with her long fingers relaxed and open. She wore orange robes and a delicate shawl around her shoulders. I stared and stared into her eyes. There's something here, I thought. I felt cautious about even admitting this to myself, but her eyes were boring a hole in me. As I looked into them, time disappeared. An energy began to move through my heart like a dart, radiating heat and fire. I remembered as a teenager visiting Jerusalem and the Wailing Wall (or Western Wall); a huge sacred structure still standing from the days of the second Holy Temple. The stones are as big as your body, and as I faced it I noticed its crevices were crammed with thousands and thousands of notes from pilgrims asking for blessings. I grabbed a pen and a small scrap of paper, and inscribed it with my deepest wish. I folded it tightly and found just the right crack. I pushed it gently in. A peace descended over me. My prayer was a simple one: "Dear God, Please let me find a spiritual teacher."

Now, standing in front of the picture of Gurumayi, this same peace was sweeping in along with an excitement that I was doing my damnedest to conceal. I didn't want to show on my cards to Sandra. But she was way ahead of me, asking if I would like to come to a program to hear Gurumayi speak. I blushed and said "maybe" but knew I would eventually.

I ended up studying with Sandra for the next two months. It all felt so new to me. To avoid having too much interaction with anyone, I sat under a table near the door, just in case I needed to get out. After class, the students would pile into their cars and go to a theater in Santa Monica to hear Gurumayi speak. I was too nervous and proud to ask if I could go along, too. Of course, I didn't need to. Everyone was welcome. But no one gave me a personal invitation. I waited and waited to be asked until I realized it wasn't going to happen. It had everything to do with my own volition. *I* needed to take that first step, and so I did, arranging to meet Sandra at the theater.

When I got there, I saw happy-looking people of all types standing outside. I certainly wasn't feeling happy and I questioned why they were and how could it be real? In fact, I was feeling positively irritated by so much good humor as I took off my shoes to enter the hall. I found Sandra and sat with her before a small stage.

When Gurumayi came out and sat in her chair, I tried to put what I saw into perspective. She was small in frame and dressed in flaming orange robes, I wasn't sure what I was looking at: man, women, child. She spoke softly, quoting passages from the Indian scriptures. Her wonderful sense of humor came as a genuine surprise. For the next six weeks, I went to every program.

I kept to myself most of those nights, not wanting anyone to see or notice what bad shape I was in. But in the spiritually charged atmosphere not much went unnoticed. People I met back then still remember how sad I was. I usually brought Kidada and Rashida with me. We'd listen to Gurumayi speak, then meditate and chant mantras. Kidada and Rashie would lay their little heads in my lap and disappear into their peaceful dreams. Gurumayi was intelligent, witty, disarming, and very real, not what you might expect from an enlightened master. Most of all, I knew she was authentic. I had never encountered anyone like her in my life.

There wasn't a phony gesture or wasted word. Sometimes what she said would sink in so deeply I could feel it enter my heart and pierce it like an arrow.

Slowly, I began to feel better, expanded, with a new energy, but I was cautious. I had tried many avenues to understanding my soul and its purpose in a human body. Nothing had really failed me because I had learned from it all. The drugs, the love of another, the yoga, having children, the loneliness, even my isolation had served a purpose. But being with Gurumayi was different. I knew I didn't have to look anymore. I would just have to meet every inner and outer challenge that arose with courage. There would be many, and it would take a long time to build the fortitude I needed, but it would be done. I had no doubt.

68.

My Mother's Hands

After my mother was diagnosed with cancer in the fall of 1985 the disease went into remission. She wasn't feeling her best, but her *joie de vivre* was ever-present and we were enjoying wonderful times together. She summoned all her courage and flew from California to meet me in New York. The purpose of her trip? To spend time together and to meet Gurumayi.

My mother had questioned my need for a spiritual teacher and my dedication to that relationship. It wasn't how she had been brought up. Not quite understanding any of it, she showed up, nonetheless, and put herself in my hands. I was proud of her. She trusted me and I needed that. More importantly, I wanted her to be in Gurumayi's presence.

We went for a weekend meditation retreat. When Gurumayi entered the hall, I heard my mother take a sharp breath. She grasped my hand like an excited child and whispered, "Oh, Peggy! Now I know why you love her."

My mother and Gurumayi got along famously. There was an instant rapport. They managed in those first few minutes to establish something very special between them. Gurumayi laughed with my mother. She held her hand and dear Rita just melted into a ball.

During a long meditation session, Gurumayi came over and stood before my mother. In the dark, she took a wand of peacock feathers and stroked them lovingly across my mother's face. I could feel the energy sweeping over her. For weeks after that, Rita sailed. She was the happiest I've ever seen her. Each day she'd ask, how was I? How were the children? How was Gurumayi?

The cancer returned. This time its treatment would be more problematic: chemotherapy, radiation, and the general consensus that her prognosis was not good. My heart began to ache and for the next six months it didn't stop. I didn't want to lose her. I couldn't get enough of her. I wanted her with me and the kids as much as possible. The treatments began to weaken her physically, but not her resolve to celebrate every day. She had become my role model, at last. Every action she performed was done with love and the determination to make it count. Halfway through her treatments, we brought a picnic lunch to the park. I had to hold her up while walking, but she let me. We found the perfect bench and I wrapped her favorite shawl around her shoulders. "Pegs" she said, "I need to tell you something." Her hands were frail and boney now as she touched my own. I stared at them. Swirls of color pulsed in my head. I was with her in the basement in my home as a child, and I was seeing those hands dabbing paint onto the canvas with her paintbrushes stuck between her fingers. The artist she was still existed in those hands. She stared at the leaves of a maple tree. She silently watched them as they moved like pointed stars in synergy with the wind. She would soon be a part of that synergy. She said, "At the meditation retreat last September when Gurumayi touched me with the peacock feathers,

I suddenly knew I would be entering this last phase of my life and that I wouldn't live out the year. Up until that moment I hadn't accepted it. Now I can. I have Gurumayi's love. I have my connection with God."

Her eyes filled with tears but a sweet smile made its way across her lips. She took my hand. We were connected now. I was at last . . . my mother's daughter.

She was magnificent in her final surrender and she took me with her those last weeks as her dear companion all the way to the end. Her moment of passing was gentle, resigned. She was finally at ease without pain. The night before Rita died, when I thought she was deep in sleep, I lay my head on her chest and wept. But so like my energetic, ever vigilant mother, she was fully conscious and not asleep at all. She hadn't gone anywhere. She was present. She touched my head lovingly and gifted me forever with her last words. She said, "Don't cry, darling Pegs, I'm going on a great adventure."

My life changed again after that. Nothing would ever be the same. A part of me didn't want to exist anymore, but I knew I had to go on for my children. I didn't know where to turn. It was the beginning of a spiritual crisis brought about by the absolute necessity to face who I was and why I was on earth. The deepest part of my journey was about to begin.

The day of my mother's funeral, Quincy and I gave a magnificent party to celebrate Rita's life. He was deeply saddened and at the same time completely supportive.

By now Quincy, too, was exhausted. He went to Tahiti to think about everything that had happened, and ended up having a serious emotional breakdown while he was there. When he came back two weeks later, he walked up the stairs to the landing where I was waiting and gave me a black Tahitian pearl necklace identical to the one he had around his neck. "Bear," he pleaded, "please let's work this out." I stood there for a moment, then hugged him and said, "I'm sorry, Daddy, I can't."

In the two weeks he'd been away I'd decided that I couldn't go on. The loss of my mother was devastating, and the longer the shame about my past lay hidden, the more I wanted out of the marriage. I needed to examine the dark places lurking in my soul, and this couldn't be done with him or through him. I was stepping out into a void with no safety net and no one to help me.

Quincy wanted to help me through it, to mend what had been broken. I didn't want him to. As simplistic as it sounds, this is what I knew I had to do. But to this day I struggle with the way I handled it. Quincy had always wanted me home and for many years I wanted that, too. Now I needed to go on another path; I needed spiritual guidance from within. That fourteen-year cycle of being together and bringing up our children was over—even though the karmic cord wouldn't be cut for years. All I knew was that whatever was coming I needed to do it on my own now. There was no doubt in my mind about it: I had to end the marriage.

I knew no amount of compromise would help and so I adamantly refused to see a therapist or seek any kind of marriage counseling with Quincy. It wasn't about him or his love for me. I simply sensed there was something I needed to do, that there was something unfinished in my life. When he truly understood that I wasn't willing to work on saving the marriage, he was devastated and eventually moved out.

The house we were building became a white elephant of disastrous proportions. We had now sunk more than a million dollars into the building of the large family room, studio, bathroom, and pool cabana. It was Quincy's very big dream, but now I knew I could never help him fulfill it. I lived in the new house we built with Tina, Kidada, and Rashida for just two months before it was sold. I hid by the phone in the kitchen door, cowering in the cavernous space. I went out and bought another house and moved everyone in there. I lived close to Quincy but we couldn't talk about any of it and really didn't see much of each other. For Quincy and me, it would take nearly twenty years to unravel the cause and deal with the disappointment that surrounded our breakup, but eventually we would both come to accept it and make our peace.

After the breakup, Kidada would say to me, "Dear God, please don't let my life be like my mother's." Now she tells me she hopes to be just like me. When I told my own mother before she died that Quincy and I were having problems, she said to me with all her heart, "Please don't break up with him." She must have seen that my life beyond that would be very difficult. Even though she was dying, I couldn't make that promise to her.

After my mother passed away I went back to her apartment to clean out her things, and standing there, I realized I'd broken the cycle. My mother adored my father, but in doing so she'd stifled herself. She compromised her life as an artist to stay happily married. I understood why she'd done it, but I knew that I couldn't repeat that for myself. So whenever my daughter said she prayed not to live a life like mine, I said, "You'll learn as you go on that you don't have to follow in your parents' path. It's up to you to see the gaps and the links and the reasons you are connected. If you need to change them, change them. That will push you through and allow you to live the life you want." It's okay to break the cycle.

Being Momma

69.

Being Momma

was being the best mom I could to Tina, Kidada, and Rashida. My worst moments came if they heard or caught a glimpse of me during one of my crying spells. There were many. I hadn't lived alone for fourteen years. I'd wait until the girls went off to school, then just walk around my room in circles and get back into bed. I started staying in bed most of the day. I had hurt Quincy. I had three children to raise, and I couldn't fall apart. But I *was* falling apart. I couldn't take a step forward. I didn't have my mother anymore, and friends that had been around throughout most of my marriage weren't there, either. Nor was Quincy's family. I'd lost contact with his brother, Lloyd, who had come to mean so much to me. Both my brothers were busy with their own lives. My dad was struggling just trying to stay afloat without his beloved Rita. After a year, he had started dating. It seemed outrageous. He was in his seventies but he just couldn't make it living on his own. I wanted him to be happy. I didn't want to go back to my marriage, and yet I didn't know how I was going to exist without it. The world felt threatening.

Many times I'd get dressed, wanting to go out, maybe to shop or to meet a friend. I'd spend a long time getting myself excited about leaving the house. Finally I'd walk to the door, open it, see the very beautiful morning, close it, and never step foot outside. Once I stayed in the house for eighteen days. I had developed agoraphobia. A deep fear was holding me back. When you are going through something like this it feels more like a necessity to protect yourself rather than an actual fear. This is the way the mind justifies the behavior. I would curl up in a ball in the closet. Now nothing mattered: the beautiful clothes, the lovely new house on the hill. I stopped wearing anything nice and would forget to wash my hair.

With the girls at school, I began to force myself to go to yoga, which I had practiced on and off for years. I found a good teacher and made an effort to go to class. I felt if I could get this one thing accomplished every day . . . Once again, I became a vegetarian. I didn't want to feel heavy in my body. I couldn't sleep at night as I had slept away large chunks of the day. I didn't take pills. I just tossed and turned and wrote in a journal I kept by my bed. I'd ramble on and on about my pain and grief. But I wrote more about the *sensation* of the feelings rather than what was at their core: the loneliness, the loss of friends and family, the guilt of having ended a fourteen-year marriage, and the futile feeling of still not knowing who I was. As long as I wrote, I didn't have to tell anyone what I was feeling. Staying home, I didn't have to see anyone or have them see the disheveled state I was in. I absorbed myself in spiritual biographies.

I wanted to know how great beings and even ordinary people had dealt with their grief. Being alone all day, I once again started having fantasies about men. I was now free to sleep with anyone I chose, but I didn't act on it. I couldn't. I saw it as wasted, misplaced energy. I chided myself for the years I'd spent catering to my obsessive drives and my forays into indiscriminate love affairs. I abstained from sex. I longed to connect with something greater than myself. At the same time, I had become unduly narcissistic. Every thought, with the exception of those about my children, was about me, and how stuck and miserable I was. This was depression at its worst.

Sometimes I'd have manic bouts. At night, I'd run down a long stretch to the beach until I was sweating so much I had to wring out my T-shirt. Endorphins would kick in and my metabolism would race. In this state, I wrote reams of poetry—and believed I was doing fine. Then I'd crash. I meditated daily and visited Gurumayi's ashram in New York.

I volunteered for social work at the downtown Los Angeles Mission and worked with abused teenaged girls. I saw my dad often. He never asked me what was wrong. I knew he was upset and worried. Yet he was good at hiding his concern—just as I was good at never letting him or anyone else know what I was going through.

70.

Dislocation

When I met Quincy I abandoned my career for motherhood and never looked back. So it was not until the late 1980s, after my marriage unraveled and my daughters were more independent—involved with school and their friends—that I began to look for work again. Having been out of circulation, I had to take small parts in some B-movies. One of them was playing Charles Bronson's wife in *Kinjite: Forbidden Subjects*. It may not have been high art, but it was a start. It's not that I wanted a career, but I felt I should be working and I had to prove that I was serious about starting over, even to get an agent to see me and eventually sign me. This process in itself took almost a year.

The first job I got after I left Quincy was a film called *War Party*. It was going to be a wonderful picture, filmed in Montana. So said my agents. I hadn't worked in fifteen years, and I felt incredibly insecure. But I knew at some point I would have to break the ice and get in front of a camera again.

War Party was a western, centered around the plight of modern-day Native Americans. The location for this misguided epic was a Blackfoot Reservation in Browning, Montana—a desolate, poor, and depleted community on the edge of town. On the way to the location we drove through Glacier National Park. As I looked around at the ancient redwoods, I thought, "Hey maybe this won't be too awful."

After a three-hour drive, we arrived just as the sun was sinking into the horizon. In the car I had been gabby with the driver, asking him about the area just to alleviate my impending panic. *I have to get my head around this,* I repeated silently to myself.

We drove up to a one-story motel on the highway opposite a huge billboard advertising a nearby strip club. I had brought a giant duffle bag for the two-month stay but the hallway was so small I literally could not get it into my room. No matter how we twisted or angled the bag, it wouldn't fit. I had to unpack my clothes and carry them bundle by bundle down the impossibly narrow hall to my room. The driver left, wishing me luck. I sat on the caved-in bed bemoaning my fate. I had no car. There was no phone in my room. There was a pay phone under the train tracks next to a bar frequented by local drunks.

I stayed at the highway motel and two other places before I called Laura Kennedy, the casting director. I told her I was having a little problem dealing with the accommodations. She arrived within the hour, and I was so relieved to see her that I started crying. Time passed. I had been cast to play the part of a TV reporter, but I hadn't worked once during all the time I'd been there. I'd go to the set watching and wondering when I would be used. When I had met with the director in L.A., he had assured me the role would expand. Well, nothing was expanding except my ongoing fear that I would never get home.

It was now fall and what little tourist season there'd been in Browning was over. All the restaurants had closed. One little supermarket remained open that sold packaged food. Laura moved me to a hotel that was straight out of *The Shining.* It would be open for only a week before the season ended but it was, in all its gothic glory, something of a relief. At least there were ghosts here that I could talk to. Yes, there were definitely spirits wandering around. I set up my music, wrapped a wet towel on the overly hot radiator, and tried to settle in.

I did two scenes and waited for more to be written. But it seemed nothing could curb my panic attacks. I ended up living in five different places on location and in every one of them I had a significant break-down. When I say breakdown I mean a complete meltdown; hysterical on-the-floor crying, teeth chattering. And the more isolated I became, well, the more isolated I became. I cut myself off from everyone. Even the beauty of Montana now took on an ominous cast.

Whenever the movie location demon gets its claws into me, I go slightly mad. Isn't it interesting that I chose a profession in which I would constantly be put in that position?

By then the director and producer were fighting vehemently in public. I'd sit for ten days at a time doing nothing but stressing about when I could go home and see my children. I'd see the director on the set.

"Please, let me go home," I'd say. "Just for a few days."

"We may need you tomorrow" was always his response. I felt trapped. I'd be called to the set and still wouldn't work. Sometimes in the midst of the chaotic production the director, Frank Rodham, would see me sitting and waiting and write something quickly to get me on camera. He felt bad for me.

Sometimes I wouldn't speak for days on end. Walking near the woods seemed like a good idea, but black bears had been seen there and had at-tacked and mauled a tourist. Warnings were posted everywhere. Still, I went into the woods. I really didn't care about a bear. I didn't see that as my demise; I figured my mind would eat me up alive way before a bear would.

On a chilly October morning when I was in hair and makeup finally ready to shoot a scene, someone walked up the very long hill to our loca-tion informing us there'd been an earthquake in L.A. Climbing up the hill was the only way they could reach us to give us the news. There weren't any cell phones in those days, just big clunky boxes that could sometimes connect you to the outside world. When I heard about the earthquake, I started to panic about my girls. How were they? Were they on the school bus when it happened? Were they scared? I needed to talk to them. The producer wouldn't let me use the phone and the panic got worse. My mouth went dry and my heart rate sped up. I tried to calm myself. I looked around. No one but me was freaking out. They seemed to be taking everything in stride. I was having a panic attack before I knew what a panic attack was. I'd had them much of my life without realizing what was happening, especially in isolated situations or when I was separated from my children. Once I could speak to the girls, I knew I would be fine. I sat there wringing my hands and saying prayers. Suddenly, adrenaline pulsated through my veins. I was pissed, really pissed.

"Fuck this," I told someone when I couldn't get hold of the producer or his damn phone. "I'm leaving the set, going down the hill, and using anyone's phone I can find to call home. If you need me and I'm not here—tough shit."

I walked the mile to the production office and called the girls. They were fine. This reassurance spurred me to action. I called my agent in L.A. I hadn't yet complained about my situation. I hadn't, in fact, spoken to him once while on location. I still wanted to be the good girl, not causing problems or speaking my mind. I took a gulp of air. What would he say? That I was overreacting? His reaction surprised me: "Peggy, if you have to quit the film— go ahead." I had waited for someone, anyone, to understand my bizarre inner turmoil. I sat in my little motel room and contemplated the situation.

It was twenty-seven miles to the film location. I called the only car rental agency in town. It turned out there was one car available for a few hours. It was a 1970 Buick and it was my vehicle to freedom. I put a beautiful Siddha Yoga chant on. I put a picture of Gurumayi on the dashboard. I asked for her blessings and took off. I knew what I had to do. I drove through such beautiful country with wildflowers everywhere and Montana's big sky engulfing me, but all along the road were small white wooden crosses, hundreds and hundreds of crosses where members of the Blackfoot Nation had died on the highway in car accidents. Children, mothers, fathers. I had seen these gruesome markers while I was being driven back and forth to location for the last month but now the sight began to get to me. While I drove, I thought of the encounters I had had with the Blackfoot people. How gentle they were despite their poverty. How one Native American extra on the film had noticed me and made a sacred medicine bag to go around my neck for protection. How I had been invited to enter one of their tepees far from location on the open range. How I had watched their sun dance ritual performed under the hot summer sun. These thoughts and memories melted into my consciousness. I was on a mission now. I was the leader of my own War Party.

"I can do it, I *can* do it," I repeated to myself as I drove.

I got to the location. The minute I parked my car, three crew members came up to me and asked, "Where have you been? We've missed you! Why don't you come and hang out with us?" *Oh God*, I thought. *Somebody noticed.* After six weeks of isolating myself, I realized all I would have had to do was to reach out. We were all basically in the same situation. They were just making a better time of it.

I started to count my breaths as I spotted the director and walked towards him. I was going to do it. Somehow it felt like being on that walk with my father and trying to tell him what I was feeling in my aching heart.

"Frank, can I speak to you for a minute?" I asked. He was setting up for a scene involving a lot of actors and some complicated stunts.

"Just let me get this shot and then we'll talk," he said.

I waited, my heart racing.

We sat in two chairs facing each other. "Frank, I'm leaving," I finally said. It had taken me a month to prepare for that moment.

"Really?" he said.

"I know that I'm not needed anymore. I've done all of my scenes." At this point he was fully aware that the producer was not in his right mind.

"Okay, Peg. I can write you out," he said. "That's not a problem, but I just want to say something to you. I think you should stay . . . for you. If you stick it out, you'll be doing something for yourself." Words of wisdom coming at the perfect time. I had always stuck it out when it came to work. I had fought every demon in one way or another all my life, and, I always seemed to rise out of the ashes. That night, I drove the 1970 Chevy back, knowing I would stay until I finished my commitment to the film and to myself. Three weeks later, I was home with my children.

71

Kidada Takes Off

At fourteen Kidada said to me, "I want to go to Fairfax High where I can be with my black friends." She became insistent that I take her there to see the campus. Fairfax was basically an all-black high school. At one time it had been a top public school but no longer. Gangs had formed; children were searched for weapons at the door.

"Mommy, I can take care of myself," she would always tell me. I knew this wasn't true on any level, except that intuitively she knew that the black community would accept her completely. It would be where she would feel her most comfortable and creative. She would align herself with their music, clothes, expressions— even with their black mothers and fathers and extended families. Kidada would finally become herself. This would be the beginning of one of the greatest changes in her life. No one trusted it. My friends and family couldn't imagine any good coming of it.

"Aren't you scared?" they would ask me.

"That's what she wants," I'd answer, but I was frightened the whole year she went there. I took her to school the first week. I gave a phony address so she could get in. I tried to check in with the principal—who didn't even know she existed—as much as I could, and I prayed for her safety.

So Kidada went to Fairfax, probably in the last year it was a decent school. I would just pray: *Please let nothing happen, please let nothing happen.* She didn't actually attend school much. This she told me much later on. She and her friends would go to each other's houses for the day and then I would pick her up in the afternoon, never realizing she hadn't been to school. I was in denial—always trying to help her with what looked to be legitimate homework. A math tutor was brought in. Who knew that at school no one cared whether she ever turned it in or not? She started to form friendships with some tough young ladies. Kidada, this chocolate-brown, well-pampered, Bel Air baby was right at home. I drove her everywhere and often picked her up in the L.A. ghettos. From North Hollywood to South Central, I made contact with every single friend she had. One of her friends stole from us. Others were just displaced persons coming from families where no one paid them any attention. She brought each one of her new pals to the house and continued that for years. There were girlfriends, boyfriends, rappers, dancers, babies. She wanted them all to meet me and feel the comforts of home. A three-year-old baby stayed with us, a niece of her girlfriend's, away from her family, for a week. Kidada took care of her: bathing her and playing with her and then tucking her into bed to sleep with her. I was Kidada's best ally. Unless it got threatening, I always allowed her to explore her need for leadership, for consoling others, and for just being a bad-ass adolescent. I'd worry and cry. Friends thought I was out of my mind, but I never gave up on her.

"Mommy," she'd say, "no matter what you think, I will never go too far. I am the best judge of myself." I sweated it often.

I would sometimes check in with Quincy, but our relationship was so strained I couldn't share my deepest concerns. Were there drugs, sex, bad people in her life? Probably. She was a normal teen, I'd tell myself. Just very very smart for her age, a wise old lady in a little body. She'd talk back, mouth off, be surly and obnoxious and then I'd see her being unbearably kind to a stranger in the street or a friend at school who couldn't afford much of their own. She'd give away clothes, toys, and food. She was always available to listen to her friend's tales of woe and give loving advice. She wanted me to let her drive. Not to *teach* her, of course, for she actually thought she knew at fifteen how to do everything. Just to let her get behind the wheel—that's what she wanted. Okay. I let her drive out of the driveway and up the road. When she got in the car, she put the seat back to an almost reclining pitch and stretched her arms way out to reach the steering wheel. Was this how kids drove? She was a little too relaxed. She kept saying she knew what she was doing. Within fifteen seconds of driving, a car came up the road and she sideswiped it. Shit, she wasn't even old enough to have a license much less insurance. She came to a stop a few yards past the car. No one was getting out of the other car. *Oh my God, were they hurt?*

"Quick!" I said. "Change places with me. Just keep praying," I told her.

"Please God," she said, "let everything be all right. I'll never do this again. I promise." The lady came out and was fine and miraculously there wasn't a dent on her car. Grace had intervened, and we both knew it. We let the beating of our hearts subside.

Kidada didn't want to listen to or do anything I said. I realized I was the natural place for her to dump her misgivings and grudges. One afternoon I grounded her for being rude. She looked at me.

"I hate you, Mommy," she said, and she meant it. For me it was the worst possible group of words a child could throw so pointedly at a parent. I walked out of her room and sobbed in mine. The sting was undeniable, but I regrouped, thought about it and decided that she could hate me as long as I was true to her. And that meant going in there and saying, "Hate me, but you're still grounded." This ended up being a tremendous breakthrough for us. A seminal moment. It signified for the future that we would and could hold our own boundaries, say what we feel, and recover with love. Kidada was going to do what Kidada wanted. Kidada had attitude. She was one powerful vortex of energy, and this was her world I was living in.

72.

Rashida
Graduates

Rashida got a dose of prejudice when she went to Harvard. As a freshman, she pledged to an all-black sorority. They rejected her based on the paleness of her skin. She tried to figure it out. Why? She had never judged anyone that way. She felt burned, but in the end she didn't need any sorority to enhance her life there. She graduated from Harvard University, Quincy's first child to graduate college.

Quincy, who had an honorary doctorate from Harvard, gave the keynote address to Rashie's graduating class. We were both so happy for Rashie, but Quincy and I were no longer together and our coming there on her special day made our breakup all the more poignant. Rashie sensed I was feeling bad and came to my room to see what was up. She hadn't been there for more than five minutes when I broke down in tears and asked her to forgive me for breaking up the marriage and not giving her the full life she deserved by staying with her father. She gave me the boost I needed and it came straight from her heart.

"It's all good, Mommy," she said. "And don't worry. If you and Daddy hadn't broken up, I would have never gotten to know each of you as the great individuals you are. That has been your gift to me." Rashida went to college at seventeen. I got into bed for a year after that. I really didn't want to move, life was not the same without her living in the house.

Rashida got the short shrift, I think. Divorce was harder on her, the youngest. The worst moment in my life was the day I had to tell them Daddy and I were breaking up. Nothing devastated me more than the words I uttered that day. Their reactions, especially Rashida's, still haunt me. She screamed once, like a hurt puppy and that was that. Kidada and Rashida pretty much hid their feelings about it all. They tried so hard to manage. I was in awe of them and never let up with my love. I was strict with Rashida in those years partly because I had not been able to control Kidada when she was young and had given her more freedom. It was unfair to Rashie. It placed a tremendous burden on her. She was an amazingly disciplined student and child, yet I overprotected her in every way. We ate all our meals together and each night before she went to sleep I'd go into her room to talk and cuddle. She'd tolerate me being there, but began to feel she was mothering me. I'd break down in her room and then quickly recover by reading her a story or listening to her essays. Then I'd go into my room and sob. It was hurting me to do this to her, and yet I couldn't help needing her so much. She was inspirational and so gentle. At times I just couldn't believe that her fairy-tale life with Mommy and Daddy was over and I was the cause. I gnawed away at myself with guilt. No matter how hard I tried, I couldn't be dispassionate about it. It haunted me.

By now Kidada had moved out. She didn't want to be boxed in anymore. She wanted to move in with her father. She saw the golden opportunity at Quincy's to not have her every move clocked—and she did miss him. Time with her dad was more important than she or I even knew at that time. In the end this served her need to really understand what he was made of; to forgive him and enjoy him at the same time.

73.

India

I went to Gurumayi's ashram in Ganeshpuri, India, in December 1989, four and a half years after meeting her. I took Kidada and Rashida. They were fifteen and thirteen. Kidada had been to Ganeshpuri two years before on a sabbatical from school. Those, she claimed, were the happiest days of her life.

The three of us were met at the airport in Bombay at midnight. We traveled for three hours north by car. We were in great suspense yet we felt intoxicated. We hadn't slept for what felt like days, but the minute we arrived we went to Baba Muktananda's Samadhi shrine, the final resting place of this great saint. Baba, Gurumayi's teacher, had built the ashram and had lived there until his death in 1982. In the shrine, everything exuded the tincture of the sanctity: the aromas, the warm air, the deep silence. It was like the inside of a great white pearl. We moved from there into the courtyard, the center of the ashram. It looked luminous, with candles glowing beneath a full white moon. Watching my daughters take it all in filled my heart with overwhelming gratitude. "Mommy," they whispered, "we can't believe we're here. We love it, Mommy." And they did.

The next day, I saw Gurumayi while I was walking at dusk. She greeted me sweetly and asked how long I planned to stay. All I knew for sure was that the girls had to be back at school by January. Instead, I found myself saying, "Gurumayi, I'm staying until I have a break-through." This provoked a hearty laugh. She said good night and walked on through the twilight gardens. I didn't know exactly why I had said this to her. But somehow I sensed something profound would happen to me.

There was always something for us to do, and the girls and I flourished. We had a little house of our own to take care of. We swept the halls and walkways, washed dishes, and scrubbed huge pots in the kitchen Baba him-self had cooked in. We were offered courses on Eastern philosophy and meditation, and we sang beautiful chants every day. My daughters and I were showered with love as we immersed ourselves in the ashram practices.

After our jet lag had subsided we enrolled in a five-day course. Here we were asked to remain silent as a way of retaining the meditative energy. Some old negativity and rebelliousness started welling up. I knew this was symptomatic of many of my old patterns. After all, I was in a place that was so deeply infused with spirituality, impurities of all types would ultimately need to be flushed out. I wanted to stir things up—some-thing I had indulged in so often in the past. Feeling angry when I slipped into bed after the first day of the course, I woke the girls up and started complaining about everything. "Mommy," they said. "You're not sup-posed to be talking." Then they calmly went back to sleep.

The next day in the courtyard, I watched as monks clad in orange robes walked in a line to greet Gurumayi. It was an Indian holiday cele-brating the sadhus and holy men; the spiritual travelers who crisscross the countryside, each with nothing but a loincloth and a kettle for water. I fo-cused on their cast-iron kettles. I thought how heavy they must be. When I arrived in front of Gurumayi, she looked at me and said, "Peggy, why are you so negative?" Her words weren't cruel, but their impact made me feel I had been hit in the face with one of the iron kettles. I was embarrassed and could feel my face turning red and beginning to ache. I left the courtyard but I couldn't get her words or the image of the kettle out of my head. Why had I been so angry and full of complaints the night before? Were old seeds of rebelliousness still trying to sprout? She had seen right through me. Suddenly the image of the iron kettle became a symbol of my own ego and it was filled to the brim with all my negativity.

In January 1990 the girls were ready to go back to school. "How long will you be staying, Mommy?" they asked in the car on the way to Bombay. I didn't know the answer. I assured them I would keep in touch by mail and telephone. After a tearful good-bye at the airport I made the long journey back to the ashram. Sitting in the back of the bus, I closed my eyes and felt gratitude. My daughters had gotten everything they'd come for: rest, upliftment, and Gurumayi's company. They were ecstatic. Without them I would have to be alone and face myself, and I began wondering how the journey would unfold.

Soon after the girls left, I was given a new duty. I was invited to join Gurumayi in the courtyard while she gave *darshan*, helping to introduce to her the thousands of people who came to see her daily. I asked two of my young Indian friends if they could come and help dress me in a sari. As they wrapped me in folds of brilliantly colored silk, I began to feel like a goddess. I loved sitting close to Gurumayi. As the days went on, I noticed Gurumayi began to correct me more and more, teaching me how to greet people properly. Her comments were practical: how to sit more comfortably for the long hours, improve my posture and not strain my neck, how best to interpret a letter or request, and how to be conscious of the needs of other people. It was quite a wonderful gift to receive this much attention to detail from Gurumayi, like a class in which I was the only student. I followed the instructions, but soon I found them imposing and I started to resent the fact that it seemed like I wasn't doing anything right. In my mind I was already doing the job. Couldn't she see that I was really good at this? I didn't want to be seen as anything less than perfect, and my insecurity began to rear its ugly head.

I kept my job for two weeks. Then in mid-Feburary, as I entered the courtyard one morning, a young Indian boy informed me that my services were no longer needed. My mouth dropped open in disbelief. I'd been fired!

I returned to my house, seething. I looked in the mirror and saw the beautiful mogra flowers that had been laced through my hair. I pulled them out and let them fall. I quickly unraveled the beautiful sari, leaving it twisted on the floor. I wiped what little lipstick I was wearing away. A voice as clear as day seemed to rise from my gut and said, "You have to rebel." I was feeling out of control. Every button was being pushed. I threw on a dreary long top with pants and, satisfied with my downgrade, I made my way back to the courtyard.

The first words Gurumayi said when she saw me were, "Why did you change your clothes?" She hadn't seen me that morning, so how did she know I'd changed? "Why did you change?" she repeated three more times.

I fumbled and stuttered but there wasn't enough time to come up with the answer. Saying I was angry and rejected wasn't going to fly with her.

"Why did you come back to the courtyard, Peggy?"

"I thought I might be needed," I replied. But it wasn't true. I had changed my clothes to look as bad as I could. I had purposely arrived in a stance of defiance with anger written all over my face. Why would she "need" anyone like that?

Then she said, "You only come here when you're *needed*?"

A long deep uncomfortable silence ensued. I felt frozen. I couldn't move to get out of the way of the people who were coming up in droves. Suddenly Gurumayi turned her head and said, "Get away from me! You are so negative!" My eyes locked with hers. They were huge. In that moment I thought my heart would burst with its own pain. "Get away from me!" she repeated. Her voice sounded like thunder. My eyes filled with tears, but an astounding thing began to take place. Two plumes of fire seemed to come from her mouth as she spoke, in burning hot streams of red and orange. They entered my heart, and in that split second I felt something ignite deep inside me.

I stood up on my wobbly legs and made my lonely way out of the courtyard. Everyone had heard the exchange and my every step was like wading through thick hot lava. As I got near my house, I began to shake. My vision became blurred, and the top of my head felt like it was on fire and every second it was getting hotter.

In my room I was hysterical. My tears and instantly swollen eyes were making it difficult for me to see, and my head wouldn't stop burning. "Oh my God," I repeated over and over. What had happened? It was as if I had been struck by lightning. There was a small place in my consciousness where I knew that every word, every action, every intention from a great master, springs from an eternal well of compassion. This serves to ultimately transform and restore a student's heart. I couldn't process it all yet and in the week that followed I found myself becoming morose.

I didn't talk to anyone and remained silent. No one really talked to me after they had seen what had happened in the courtyard. Instinctively they knew this was a time for an inner search to take place. I went back each morning for Gurumayi's *darshan*. I kept thinking of those times as a child I had fallen off my bicycle and gotten back on. I'd leave the courtyard after seeing her with my heart pounding. No words or glances were exchanged. I'd go into Baba Muktananda's shrine and pray for her to speak to me again, to acknowledge me. But she didn't. This went on for weeks. My ego, my heart, and my physical body were all hurting. My arrogance and old ways of doing things were no longer going to serve me and I knew it.

One sleepless night I called on my deceased mother, Rita. I asked her to help me. She came to me in a dream and gently said, "Pegs, everything will be all right."

The next day in the courtyard, while standing halfway hidden behind a pillar, I felt Gurumayi's eyes watching me. I went into Baba's shrine and sat on the marble floor, letting it cool my inner heat. Today my prayer would be different. I realized that the spiritual path wasn't about my personal relationship with my teacher, worrying about how she would perceive me, if I could stave off rejection, or how perfect I could appear. It was about my relationship with myself—and that the recognition I was so desperately seeking on the outside needed to come from within. And with this understanding, a profound feeling of grace and contentment descended on me and found its way into the core of my heart.

An hour before my departure in March, I went into the courtyard for my last *darshan*. There Gurumayi sat—beautiful, serene—while she greeted her guests. Watching her, I felt my heart open with gratitude for all I had experienced on this trip to India. As I said good-bye and thanked her, she looked at me and smiled with so much compassion, I nearly melted at her feet. The love streaming into me from her eyes was undeniable. And it was also undeniable that the seed of my rebelliousness had been removed like a thorn from my being. I was no longer that little girl who had to fight to get her way or the teenager and young woman trying desperately to cover up her insecurities and prove she could handle or manipulate any situation. Now I had the opportunity to become the person that I wanted to be and truly was. My real journey was just beginning. The breakthrough I had come for was mine.

74.

Love from Twin Peaks

My mentor and acting teacher, Sandra Seacat, taught me that any part that comes to you is for a reason. It's something that you need to work out in your personality and spiritual development. You can break down any character—the qualities of motivation and behavior in every script—and there will be an uncanny blueprint of some part of your own life. Choices the character makes will somehow reflect the ones you have or haven't made along the way.

Prior to *Twin Peaks*, I had appeared in TV movies, guest shots on dramas and sitcoms, and a few independent films. But I've never been as possessed by a character as I was by Norma Jennings.

Mark Frost, *Twin Peaks*'s coproducer, remembered me from *The Mod Squad* and recommended me to David Lynch, the show's creator and director. I was called into David's ultramodern office at Propaganda Films, a dimly lit room with no windows. Inside this dark cubicle was a huge shiny black table that David had probably made himself. That was the kind of thing he did when he wasn't working on films—which he always was in his head. He built his entire house, painting and designing everything in it.

He'd not only written the script for *Twin Peaks,* coproduced it, and was going to direct it, he'd designed the very furniture we were sitting on to talk about it. In the middle of his desk was an eight-by-ten photo of me and nothing else.

"What do you think of this?" he asked, referring to the script he held in his hand. "Do you think you'd like this part?"

Having read the script by then, I knew that nothing since *Mod Squad* had touched me quite this way. Like me, Norma Jennings was a woman on the verge. She was smooth and contained on the outside, but running a hot fever inside. She was nurturing but took no one's bullshit. If it hadn't been for her inner strength she would've had a nervous breakdown. She was waiting on a husband serving time in jail, hoping she wouldn't feel attracted and sexually drawn to him when he got out. Meanwhile, she was having an affair with Ed, played by Everett McGill, her old boyfriend from high school. Though he was thoroughly in love with Norma, he was very much married to Nadine, whom they both felt would never let him go. Norma ran the local diner and was serving not only great cherry pie and coffee to a confused and distraught community but serving as a surrogate mother to her young, vulnerable employee Shelley. These details were obviously not part of my personal experience, but Norma's essence was about as close to mine as you could get. And it came at a time in my life when I didn't think I was ever going to work on a great project again.

"Yes," I said, trying to contain my enthusiasm. "I want this part."

I don't know if David knew my work. But somehow, when I came into the office and saw my picture on his desk, it didn't matter. Although he had never met me, his intuitive sense saw me as the character and I felt his total trust in that. Nobody else ever read for that part. "You'll never have to read for me," he said. "You are Norma Jennings."

ABC was less decisive, however, and given its investment in the show insisted that we audition. David was a film director and they didn't know what he was capable of in a TV series. They were also unfamiliar with many of the actors he'd chosen. He wasn't in a position to say, "These are my actors and I want them."

The excitement around this part was building for me because I knew it was something truly out of the ordinary. I was given pages of the pilot with my character in it and worked with the well-known L.A. acting coach Ivana Chubbuck on them.

"Oh, Peggy, this is such an important, quirky, wonderful piece of work—and you are Norma Jennings," she said after we read through it only once.

I did my test with Everett McGill. We went in about three hours before the test and David worked with us on one scene for two hours. He kept apologizing. "I'm sorry you guys have to go through this, but the only way they can cast you is if you test for the network." I was impressed that David worked so patiently on that one scene. He wanted to make those people at ABC want us as much as he did. He approached the screen test as if it were a Shakespearian play, investing in it all his concentration and enthusiasm. Everett and I were cast as Ed and Norma.

In 1989 we shot the pilot for *Twin Peaks*. I flew up to Seattle, where we stayed during the filming. We shot interiors there as well as in Snowqualamie, which became the backdrop for the most eerie scenes of the show. By that point I'd met the other actors. As usual there were dramas already going on—there always are on location. My friend's boyfriend was having an affair with one of the actresses in the film. I had to mediate on that little subplot for a while.

My first sequence was a night scene in which Ed and I are huddling over coffee trying to find ways to be together. The set was a bar filled with rednecks, preppies, and punks. We are sitting in a leather-covered booth facing each other. Over Ed's shoulder, strange stuff is going on. A frail young blond woman is nearly having an orgasm while singing in a provocative drone on a smoky stage wearing a torn black dress and smudged black eye makeup. People are fighting and seething on the dance floor making corrupt and murderous plans—a very Lynchian moment. The camera pans over to us in the booth and we have a conversation about Ed trying to break it off with his wife. In our ardor we are oblivious to the goings-on around us.

After weeks of preparation and days of waiting on location, David was going to direct us. He'd patiently discuss what the scene was about and help us open up to all its possibilities. He'd talk us through in his hypnotic Midwestern voice, which had a way of settling you down and making you go, okay, whatever you think. He gave us the feeling of the scene and let us take as many chances as we wanted. You could freely tell him any and all your opinions, but basically, it was going to go David's way. "Great. Good. Good," he'd say, but at the same time he'd tell you in his own diffident way what to do and you'd go with it.

"Ed is the love of your life and you are the love of his," he told Everett McGill and me. "But you are both in very bad situations. You want to be very tender with him, but you are also afraid for him and you want him to be strong."

David's intuition about the emotional charge that carries a scene is uncanny and his vision flawless. He would offer inventive and practical suggestions and then let solutions arise instinctively.

"What are Norma's needs in that moment? What about her history with Ed? How would fears about her jailed husband affect her behavior?"

Answers to these questions sprung up spontaneously. Like Norma, I wanted to be loved. I felt secure with Ed's love yet I wasn't completely finished with old patterns and habits. I wanted Ed to leave his wife but could foresee tremendous problems for us both. I connected so strongly with my character that it put me in an almost trancelike state. I'd never really transferred my whole being into a character in quite this way. With Julie Barnes in *Mod Squad,* it was more a case of showing up every day and being Julie. The external obligations of the scene were always highlighted. This, on the other hand, was internal.

David talked about the scene, rehearsed it, and shot it. Then we'd talk about it more and shoot it again. For Lynch, any aspect of the film was important enough to spend a lot of time on. If you look at the series, you'll understand why, especially in those early episodes, the ones he directed himself. Even I got chills when I watched the scenes between Ed and Norma, although I never really liked myself on film. As simple as the dialogue was, there was always an underlying tension and desperation between the two of them.

None of the actors really knew the whole story of *Twin Peaks* or where it was going. From the scripts you just picked up on the atmosphere of this small town and its secrets. We could see that it was strange and dark. The murder of a high school beauty in a small congenial town takes on ominous proportions when it is revealed that everyone in mystical Twin Peaks is in some way connected to her and to each other. David was excited about everything and everybody. He was thrilled about every little part of the show no matter how small or big your part was. He had his hand in everything from directing to wardrobe to the production values to Angelo Badalamenti's provocative score.

Within days of my arrival, I could see that every single actor was walking around in a state of exhilaration. We all knew that we were involved in something strange and brilliant.

Many times I didn't know what the other characters were doing, because I was so engrossed in my own little world, Norma's world. I ran the Double R Diner and worked as a waitress there. I was advising a young woman working for me who had an abusive boyfriend. I was having an affair with the nicest guy in town, the wonderful Ed, my childhood sweetheart. He had a crazy wife, Nadine, with a patch on her eye, wild mood swings, a chocolate addiction, and an obsession with the curtains in her house. Norma went back and forth with Hank, her husband, a mean domino-chewing ex-con who was currently in jail. My character's story line—abusive boyfriend, having an affair with a married man—was all too familiar to me, kind of a honky-tonk reenactment of my real life.

Twin Peaks debuted in April 1990, and David became famous almost overnight. He ended up on the cover of *Time* magazine. *Time* pronounced Lynch the "czar of bizarre," calling *Twin Peaks* the best show—ever—on television.

The downside of this was that David stopped directing, became the producer, and began hiring other directors. As time went on he became a little more distant and no longer as involved as he had been. He was becoming a huge star. Suddenly he was a household name.

"Please, David, don't change," I used to say to him.

"Oh, no, Peggy. I'm still just me and everything is fine. We have a wonderful show," he'd say, but things were changing.

Talented directors were hired who went on to become famous, too, and they brought their own distinctive style and pace with them. It was alarming to some of us, though, because we had gotten used to David's way of doing things. I was feeling a little too attached to him as our director, overseer, and guide.

Dissentions began to divide the family. Tensions were running high and even the best of these directors would encounter a certain anarchy on the set. Whenever I'd see my costars, our conversations were now strained. I tried to stay close to Norma and forget the situation on the set.

Diane Keaton directed one of my favorite episodes of *Twin Peaks*. I never got more encouragement than when I was working with Diane. After a well-executed scene, she would scream and yell, and jump up and down. Diane was a veritable bundle of enthusiasm and talent.

The scene Keaton directed was one in which Ed's wife, Nadine, catches us in bed. After making love we hear a small commotion in the living room. Ed reassures me that it's not Nadine.

"Don't worry, darling, she's out buying curtain rods," he says. But when Nadine comes right into the bedroom I fumble, trying to pull the covers over us, and sit there speechless. It was a situation that uncannily paralleled a very real moment in my life. It was more parallel to my first time with Quincy than I could ever have imagined. And sadly comic. Nadine looking right at us, saying, "Look at this. Isn't it amazing? I've got to fix these curtains." Nothing about our being together in bed registered. She didn't get what was going on. "Norma, is that you?" she asked, totally missing the fact that her husband was having sex with his high school sweetheart under the covers of her own bed. Norma didn't want to hurt anyone but love had compelled her to follow her heart. Tears came, unanticipated emotions welled up in my throat and chest. I cried in front of Nadine, even though she was oblivious to it all. But I was crying for myself as well, and the pain I had caused others in my life. Every feeling was on the surface. That, of course, is an actress's ultimate goal.

Within a year, things began to fall apart. David's warm and genuine personality contrasted with his very dark imagination and this is, of course, what fueled the fiery engine of *Twin Peaks*. But now, even though he was still writing some episodes, he had become so popular that he didn't seem able to concentrate on the daily operations of the show anymore. This state of affairs was beginning to echo my experience at the end of *Mod Squad*. I tried to pull back. I didn't want to go through that again. David wasn't as involved on a day-to-day basis and he brought in young producers who cared more about the financial bottom line than the flow of the story. Oh well, it happens.

In the meantime, Norma's longings were overlapping onto my own. I was beginning to learn that being so close to a character might sometimes get me in trouble.

In one episode Norma goes to visit Hank in jail to tell him she wants a divorce. She wants it to be over with Hank. She wants to finally let go of him and break his violent and sexual hold on her. I asked Chris Mulkey, who was terrific as the character Hank, to rehearse the scene with me. He had been open to rehearsal in the past and our scenes together were always highly charged. When I'm working I don't socialize or warm up to someone if it wouldn't be right for the scene, so I didn't talk much to Chris on or off the set. Maybe just a good morning in the makeup trailer. Whether it's an estrangement with a mother, or ex-husband, or villain, I keep my boundaries on the set separate so as not to mix the two realities. People will assume I'm being cold and detached from them personally when in fact I'm quite connected—just observing. If it's a love scene, I will watch silently. Or in ordinary conversation with the actor playing opposite me, I will search for the qualities that could elicit feelings of affection. And when it just isn't there, as often happens, I use substitution, imbuing that actor with the attributes of someone I do feel that way about. It sounds tricky but it's really not. It just requires being in touch with your feelings and having enough confidence to create what isn't there.

One morning we were getting ready to shoot the jail scene sequence with Hank and Norma.

"When you have some time, we can rehearse," I said to Chris.

"I don't want to," was his curt answer.

It was a long tense scene where Norma finally gets up enough nerve to ask him for a divorce. This obviously doesn't sit well with Hank as he's pissed and miserable being in jail and wants her there when he gets out. He tells her no.

"Why can't we rehearse?" I persisted.

"I just don't want to," he responded sullenly. Was this a black mood or was he just staying in character? It puzzled me, because rehearsal, especially in film, is essential. It gives the actors, director, and crew an opportunity to try out the scene a number of different ways. Above all, it allows actors to become familiar enough with the material to be able to forget the lines and leave themselves open to whatever feelings arise. But he was adamant, and I had to acquiesce.

The scene was set up and blocked, but just for the camera and my physical movements. With the cameras rolling, I walk in, my trademark raincoat tied tight against my waist.

He's sitting in the cell, his face and body turned toward the wall. I get closer to him by walking over to the bars.

"I want a divorce, Hank," I tell him. After hearing my proclamation of freedom, he waited a few seconds, then without warning came up to me, twisted his hands through the bars and grabbed the collar of my trench coat. He yanked my face with all his strength *hard* and straight into the bars and held it there as he spewed profanities at me. The scene was perfectly in character for the evil Hank, but it was a frightening trick to spring on another actor not to mention physically bruising—even if it did make for a compelling grand finale. I hadn't anticipated the violence he would use to make the scene work for him, and when we got through the end of the scene, I was outraged. He'd clearly been planning it all along without sharing it with me or the director. I started crying and shaking.

"How dare you, you fucker?" I said under my breath. He heard me and was silent.

I was sure that he'd planned to hurt me, to get the reaction he wanted—all under the guise of making the scene real. That was bullshit. It was crossing a certain line professionally. It's permissible under certain circumstances to surprise the other actor, but it's always done with the consent of the director. Unplanned violence isn't ever acceptable.

"How could you let this happen?" I complained to the director. She said she didn't know anything about it and of course she didn't. Now I had large lumps on my face and I was crying. Thus ended my last episode of *Twin Peaks,* a not-so-happy conclusion to what had been a great experience for me.

Twin Peaks ran for fourteen months and then quite suddenly it was over. We were on hiatus when I read in *The Hollywood Reporter* that *Twin Peaks* had been cancelled. That's how I found out. There was a lamentable lack of communication at the end. I felt let down but relieved to be moving on, away from my fusion with Norma Jennings, her problems, and sad life.

75.

Depression

One evening when I was seventeen, shortly after our move from New York to Los Angeles, I was having dinner with my parents. I suddenly felt so haunted by my own demons I was compelled to tell my parents I was sinking. I was feeling lost and adrift in our new life, having just moved to a new school. I'd looked around at the few people I knew and realized I couldn't really make connections with anyone. In this state of crisis in the middle of dinner, I asked my parents if I could see a psychiatrist. My parents' reaction was totally unexpected. My mother seemed alarmed by my request. I remember her saying, "Why would you need to do that?" How could I explain the confusion and disorientation I felt? I was tied up in knots, and my anxieties were beginning to manifest themselves physically. The year before, while twisting like a crazy teenager with my parents on the dance floor at the Peppermint Lounge in New York City, I suddenly had to be rushed to the emergency room with unbearable stomach pains. When it was all over and I was recovering at home, we laughed.

"Pegs dear, you just twisted too long!" my parents said, feeling relieved that I was better. But later on, I was diagnosed with a spastic colon and given medication for whenever the attacks would come on. I was having nightmares and I would wake up crying. I desperately needed to talk to someone, but my parents wouldn't agree to it. My God, I thought, why would they be so adamantly opposed to my seeking help? Then it struck me. Both my brothers had difficulties growing up, and maybe my parents just couldn't stand the thought of another of their children having problems, especially their perfectly pulled-together daughter.

So without their knowledge I signed myself into the outpatient psychiatric clinic at UCLA. To see if you qualified for treatment, you were asked to draw a picture of yourself. I drew a sad stick-like figure with an aching heart and a brain in turmoil. To this pathetic figure I added small tears dripping down my cheeks. Although it was only a drawing, this was the most I had ever exposed myself emotionally. Still, I kept many things to myself. I saw a doctor at UCLA and later went to a private therapist, but even then I was unable to communicate the source of my unhappiness. I was still unable to talk about the one thing that was causing my anxieties: the sexual abuse I'd suffered as a child. And so at every session I danced around the issue. At that point, and for most of my adult life, the subject was just too humiliating for me to acknowledge.

When I began working full-time at eighteen I started doing drugs to self-medicate, trying to compensate for the depression into which I felt myself slipping. At first, it worked. Marijuana, diet pills, and ultimately, pharmaceutical cocaine relieved my pain and permitted me to function. This approach had the added attraction of making me feel cool. I could hide everything from myself, my parents and the world. I became a self-contained machine.

I had resisted taking medication for so long, truly believing that nothing was ever going to help. In 1992, when I finally started taking low doses of Prozac, an early antidepressant, it was the first time I'd felt normal in almost thirty years. I started seeing an excellent psychiatrist. I let my story unfold. Working together, we came up with thoughtful tools and ways to help me emerge from the dark tunnel. Here was someone willing to listen and stick with me no matter what my issues were. Shame was a big demon to conquer. For all those years it had stopped me from reaching out. I finally learned that being able to ask for help was not a weakness but a strength. That strength would become something I could always rely on.

76.

My Aunt Pearl

When my mother was dying, she asked me to take care of her sister, my aunt Pearl. Little did I know what a responsibility she would be. Aunt Pearl was as neurotic and obsessive as they come, but she was also loads of fun. She cuddled me, listened to my problems, and loved my children. We could kibbitz for hours.

Her husband had been my abuser, something she must have known deep inside—but she lived in denial. Her life had been a hard one. How good could life have been married to this demented man? There must have been some horrible times between them, but like all the adults in my life, she chose not to talk about them. The only indication she gave of how deeply she detested him was to tell me the story of how she had finally gotten rid of him. The day came when she'd had enough, she said. She dropped him off for his habitual morning swim and never came back to pick him up. Strangely, he never tried to return.

Aunt Pearl lived with me off and on for some years. She had nurtured me as a child and I wanted to repay her kindness. I was only too happy to take her on her biweekly trips to the movies and market, and to pay her bills. She cooked for Quincy and me. Quincy was good to her, as was my dad, but the continual watching over her and listening to her troubled memories was difficult for everyone.

Then things took a turn for the worse. One day after she'd made lunch, she announced: "I hate my life." The next sentence was "Where are we?" Not realizing what was happening, I tried to laugh it off. "Aunt Pearl," I teased. "We're here, in your apartment, but in five minutes we can be at the mall. *Shopping!*" Not even that magic word could get her attention. It was the beginning of Alzheimer's. To watch a human mind erode is devastating. How could this witty, energetic woman become so utterly lost?

From that point on, Pearl lived in her own inescapable hell until the day she died. I tried to hold on to every wonderful memory I had of her. How she would lovingly comb my hair into pigtails for school and tie them with two blue satin ribbons, and stash candy for me in her pockets. From time to time, she would even sneak me out of the house on a school night for adventures like bowling and late-night shopping.

Toward the end she was fearful and paranoid. She would turn on me, spewing profanities and cursing the day I was born. I knew she was not herself, but it was still extremely troubling. I hesitated to entrust her to someone else's care. After all, I was the only one she had in the world. Eventually her inner demons became so fierce I had to put her in a home. She was by then in her eighties. I visited her often, but within three months she was dead.

When I was younger I would carry her groceries or take her on long excursions to the beach.

"Darling Pegs," she'd say, "you won't regret this." I never did.

77

Moving Ahead

Sometime in 1994 I met someone who was freshly divorced. He was a gentle and generous man, older than I. He was that odd mixture of being somewhat set in his ways and at the same time, an adventurer. So we took the high road and went on an adventure together. He was my first lover in a very long time. Being with him made me feel renewed with passion. We never wanted to move in together. Sometimes we'd take a three-day holiday to different cities like San Francisco, Chicago, Palm Springs, and even Paris. It seemed to satisfy our need to be together and yet live our lives separately. There were other lovers as well. Sometimes my heart would be captured for that night alone. They would become friends or I would never see them again. It didn't matter in the same way. I was more interested in understanding why I did the things I did. What was the source of my behavior?

Seeing a psychiatrist was like starting over again, and this process began to open me. I could tell him about the abuse, frustration, and the ways I wanted to be loved. I began to see myself more objectively. One of the best things my doctor said to me over the years was, "It's wonderful to have desire, but it doesn't mean you have to always act on it."

My dad met and married a very caring and beautiful woman named Kate. At first I resented it. Not knowing her at all brought up all the memories of my mother not being with me. Over the ten years they were married she became my best friend. For the last two years of their lives together, she and Dad came and stayed with me three days a week, every week. We became a fun trio mostly staying in, cooking, and talking.

My brother Kenny died in 1998. He had a long battle with cancer. With all the loss I'd encountered, nothing hurt as much as this. Losing a sibling is devastating, and it has taken me many years to even let it enter my thoughts. Off and on, along with his two daughters, Justine and Jennifer, I spent that last year with Kenny. I stayed with him in his bed until he passed. I held him and talked to him. A half hour before the end, his eyes opened wide and a giant expectant smile took over his face. "There she is!" he exclaimed, and I knew he had seen our mother Rita waiting for him.

My dad loved his life and continued working until the day he died, at the age of eighty-eight. Our days were filled with laughter and love, mixed with Kate's and my ongoing vigilance over his health. He wanted to live to be a hundred. He thought he could. He died three days before the millennium from heart failure. He was a fighter when it came to his health. He knew how to surpass pain and fear and heal himself.

Without realizing it, I took my cue from him. I always saw my body as a vehicle for consciousness that had the innate and complete ability to heal over and over again, and it all had so much to do with attitude. My dad always had a positive attitude. He hardly showed his sentimental side, but two months before he died he wrote me a note telling me that no matter where he was, he would always be watching over me. I was deeply moved by this, knowing it was true and that it had come from the depths of his heart and his love for me. I had adored him all my life.

78.

Aaliyah

Kidada and Aaliyah Haughton met in 1997 on a photo shoot for the designer Tommy Hilfiger and immediately became fast friends in much the same way Jill and I had some thirty years earlier. (I didn't have Jill in my life anymore—she had died in a car crash in 1982, while living with Marlon Brando.) No matter what they did or where they were Kidada and Aaliyah had the best time together. They played practical jokes on each other, had sleepovers, shopped and traveled, went on adventures, and shared their dreams.

Aaliyah had been performing since she was a little girl, yet all the attention had not spoiled her one wit, even when her hit songs, like "One in a Million," "Are You that Somebody," and "Missing You," catapulted her to stardom. She was on her way to becoming a superstar and was being offered parts in movies. When she was being considered for the lead in the Broadway production of *Aida*, she asked me to help coach her for the audition.

She was so natural and funny that she would always put the biggest smile on my face. I traveled with her to Miami along with Kidada and Rashida and their boyfriends just because I knew it would be a weekend of great laughs. It was. I loved watching Kidada and Aaliyah together. I delighted in their friendship in probably much the same way my mother had with Jill and me. Their favorite times were when they'd indulge themselves in girly rituals like having facials, talking on the phone for hours, or making home videos to show to their friends and families. Nothing could hold these two back. They wanted to fall in love, marry, and have their first children together. They were obviously going to be lifelong friends. It all changed forever on August 25, 2001, when Aaliyah died in a plane crash.

Kidada was so shattered by Aaliyah's death she packed up and moved in with me. It wasn't a question of getting *over* Aaliyah's death, but simply how to go on without her.

79.

Loss

By now I had lost my mother, father, brother, aunt, brother-in law Lloyd, and my daughter's best friend, along with my two beloved fifteen-year-old dogs. It was time for me to acknowledge and accept these losses. I was present when my dad, mom, brother Kenny, and even my dogs passed into the next world; I was a witness to their last breaths. As excruciating as every moment of shared pain was with them, I'd been granted the grace to understand the sacredness of that moment. And for this I have Gurumayi to thank.

80.

Coming Back

Frustrated by made-for-TV movies and small parts in films, I felt the desire to put myself out there and do a play. I wanted to work in the theater. It was what I had been trained for as a young actress, and in 2002 I got to do just that. In February my brother Bob suggested me for the part of a raunchy, over-the-top, washed-up TV actress (well, wasn't that what I was?) in the Donald Margulies comedy *Pitching to the Star.* We put it on at the Lee Strasberg Institute in Los Angeles. Along with Bob playing the part of an obnoxious, self-serving producer, my daughter Rashida joined the cast as his very coy assistant. We genuinely loved being a family and working together. Our rehearsals were a bit bumpy, but we managed to pull together a funny show and our audiences went from six people on opening night to standing room only when we closed six weeks later.

I felt so good about this experience I went on to do Eve Ensler's *The Vagina Monologues* in New York. One day of rehearsal and you were on your own. Well, not literally on your own—the play is about three women telling shocking, sad, and very funny tales about—what else?—the vagina. I was a little reluctant to do this play until I ran into an actress who'd been in a recent production. "Peggy, do it," she told me. "It changed my life." I took her advice and worked with the highly respected Anna Strasberg, who helped me get to the essence of the three monologues I had chosen. We did eight shows a week for six weeks, but I never tired of the play. Each night was more exhilarating than the night before. I began to feel at home on stage.

A month later, in September 2002, I was offered the part of Joan in Anne Nelson's *The Guys,* a true account of Nick, a New York City fire captain who lost twelve of his men on 9/11. With the knowledge that he would be expected to deliver the eulogies at their funerals, he reluctantly agrees to work with a professional writer, Anne Nelson, a veteran journalist and former war correspondent on whom my character was based.

Like so many others after September 11, I wanted to contribute to the healing of this city, so I immediately said yes. *The Guys* is a mostly solemn but occasionally humorous study of two people feeling devastation over the tragic events of that day but expressing their pain in very different ways. There was very little rehearsal time; you just sort of had to take it under your wing. Many talented actors, from Sigourney Weaver to Susan Sarandon, had already performed it. Once again I packed up my things in L.A. I hunkered down in a studio apartment ten minutes from the theater on Church Street, not far from Ground Zero. The play contained six or seven long monologues delivered by my character; each examining the different stages of her involvement, from professional detachment to overwhelming grief. My costar, Dan Luria, was the best thing that could have happened. For the hour and a half we were on stage; we danced, we laughed, we cried, and there wasn't one moment he wasn't connected with the character or me.

One night near the end of the run, I decided to walk home by myself in the subzero snowy weather. Within ten minutes I came upon an old firehouse I had spotted the week before. It was still covered with flowers and photographs of firemen who had been lost during 9/11. I knocked on a small door next to the giant red garage that housed the trucks. I stood there in the freezing cold bundled up in an old down parka, huge wool hat, scarves, mittens, and a giant duffel bag containing my script, makeup, and wardrobe. I looked like I was homeless, desperately wanting to get in from the cold. A handsome young fireman answered the door. When I asked if I could come in he stared at me for a moment, unsure whether he should let me in. He walked me past the huge trucks and equipment into a warm, softly lit den with a big round table in the center being set up for dinner. I introduced myself to the eight firefighters getting ready to sit down for their evening meal. As I peeled off my outer wear and became a little more presentable I stated the reason for my visit. "I'm doing a play called *The Guys* near here, about 9/11, and I needed to be with you tonight." They were slightly astonished and at first didn't know exactly what to expect, then all at once they chimed in with, "Welcome!" and asked me to share their dinner with them.

As they cooked lasagna and served a giant bowl filled with fresh salad I tried to help, but they stated their golden rule: "When someone comes into our firehouse as a guest they are not allowed to cook or clean up." I told them how acting in the play had moved me deeply. They listened and confessed they either hadn't known of its existence or hadn't felt up to seeing a play on a subject that was so emotional for them. They were all clearly still in mourning. Individual pictures of the men they'd lost hung over the bunk beds along with drawings by their children. I felt sad and uplifted at the same time. These men had a commitment that I could feel in my bones. They had a commitment and a bond of brotherhood that was unbreakable. I was in awe and flattered that on this cold wintry night they had let me be their invited guest. I asked the captain if he would do me the honor of coming to see the play with his company. He mused and said only, "We'll see." "It would mean so much to all of us if you could," I persisted, but still got no promise.

During dinner, the fire alarm bell began clanging. It sounded frantic to me but there was no panic. All the firefighters—with the exception of one—moved smoothly and swiftly into their heavy gear and onto the trucks. I caught a whiff of their adrenaline rush, my heart pounding as I watched them pull out of the station. I ended up staying until midnight washing dishes with the rookie, feeling I had to participate in some way. Getting him to let me help clean up was a fun match of wits but I won. And I left there feeling deeply touched.

The next night when I arrived at the theater I was informed that three firefighters including the captain had come to pick up the tickets I had left for them and were sitting in the audience. "They're here," I rejoiced, wanting Dan and I to shine for them. After we took our bows, a group of Columbia University writing students in the audience participated in a talkback session with the playwright, Anne Wilson. I sat on the stage, still immersed in the last scene, in which my character in desperation pleads to be able to roll back the tape of these men's lives so that none of them— or anyone else—would have to perish on 9/11.

When the audience was asked if there were any final comments or observations, the fire captain raised his hand. He was clearly a tough guy who kept his emotions close to the vest so I wondered what he would allow himself to feel at this point. He cleared his throat, and speaking slowly said, "We really didn't know what to expect when we came down here to see this play. For most of us it was just too soon and too painful. But ya know what? You captured something here tonight that was beautiful and authentic; something that we ourselves had no words for. Thank you . . . from all of us. We're honored." And there were tears streaming down his face.

81.

Life Change

There was nothing ordinary about March 26, 2004. At around ten in the morning on a typical sunny Southern California day, my life turned inside out. I was back in Los Angeles doing a guest role for two episodes of *Alias*. For some brief moments I lost myself in the part, a wicked character named Olivia Reed. I had resisted doing guest shots for TV and had turned down many of them, but I liked the show and I was flattered that I'd been offered the part even before they'd finished writing it. About two days into it, I found that I was having difficulty concentrating on my role.

The truth was I hadn't felt well for five months. In August of that year, I had moved to New York City to write and be with my daughter Rashida. I had changed apartments several times until finding a lovely one near Central Park. But within a week of my arrival, Rashida left to do a TV series in London, so I concentrated on writing. Day and night I wrote, keeping crazy hours. I would become exhilarated and then tormented. I stopped going out for dinner and seeing plays. I began to isolate myself as I became immersed in recalling my life. As much as I enjoyed the process of writing, as time went on I found I was feeling ill and nauseous, and had lost my appetite. I knew something was wrong, but when I'd mention it to friends they'd dismiss it as coming from the stress of moving to a new city and writing about my past. And it's true that poignant memories, misgivings, and regrets surfaced along with the blissful recollections of my children when they were small.

My concerns escalated as I sought out the opinions of three different doctors. I had blood tests, ultrasounds, and vitamin shots, but I wasn't feeling any better. For a while I thought I might have given myself an ulcer. I hadn't. I thought I knew my body well and was willing to put up with the unpleasant symptoms for as long as I could. The GI doctor suggested I get a colonoscopy. I was well past the recommended age for having the procedure. I scheduled the test twice, once in New York and once in Los Angeles, but had to cancel them both because I was filming.

Nothing about a colonoscopy is appealing—the drink to clean you out, the surgical center where it takes place, and the thought of being probed and aerated with an instrument that moves through yards of your insides. I was avoiding it in every way I could. But worries persisted. I seemed to be constantly mentioning that my stomach was giving me trouble. Every day I woke up, I felt worse. After I cancelled my colonoscopy in New York, I got a sympathetic but strangely foreboding message on my voice mail. It was from the GI doctor I'd seen a month before. He had no direct findings but said no matter where I was I should schedule a colonoscopy as soon as possible.

I really didn't know what to expect the morning I arrived for the test in L.A., but it certainly wasn't what I anticipated. They'd found a large obstruction in my lower colon. I didn't mind hearing that part because it explained why I was having so much trouble with my stomach. However, the next sentence out of the doctor's mouth stunned me: "We think it's a tumor and it's possibly cancerous." His tone was caring but grave. I just stared at the institutional wallpaper and nodded my head. I got up, got dressed, and was directed to the next room. My body felt numb and a strange and unsettling thought began to dawn on me: I would never be the same person again. I was driven to a colon surgeon at Cedars-Sinai Medical Center and there I had to face the cold hard truth—from a very cool messenger.

"This is almost certainly cancer," the surgeon began, "and it will have to be cut out. Following that, you'll need to have a colon resection. Here's a diagram of your colon," she continued, showing me a chart. "This is where we will cut. You'll experience a little discomfort when you wake up and you'll have boots tied to your legs to stop any blood clots. Your surgery will run between three and four hours, and you'll be in the hospital about seven days. May I caution you that you have a severe obstruction that could cause immediate problems. After another colonoscopy and a CAT scan, you'll have your surgery at the end of the week. We'll schedule you now. After the surgery, you'll need three full months to recover and we will take lymph nodes out wherever we operate to test them for any disease. Recovery from this surgery is an uphill climb and some days you just won't be feeling that good."

All this was thrown at me forty-five minutes after I received my test results. I excused myself and went into the bathroom to cry. What had happened to me? How had it gone from what seemed like minor stomach problems to a tumor in my colon? I had to think quickly. I had managed to live this long without ever having had a major disease or surgery. Who was I? I asked myself silently. How was I different? There were no immediate answers. I took a deep breath and scheduled my follow-up tests and impending surgery. Then I returned home alone and fell into a deep state of meditation lying on my bed. Suddenly I felt a surge of optimism arise in my heart; a sense of well-being overcame my fears.

It was difficult breaking the news to my daughters. It reminded me of the morning I told them that Quincy and I were breaking up. I could feel their spirits sink. They were very frightened but bravely tried not to cry. They struggled to focus their attention on my situation, asking pertinent questions and expressing their concern about how I was taking the news. Before I had gotten the test results, I had planned to call Quincy to let him know I was having a routine colonoscopy. I thought we could have good laugh together about the ongoing indignities of old age. Now I was calling him about the results and it was no laughing matter.

"Bear," he said almost immediately, "you have to call Dr. Larry Norton and get on a plane as soon as you can back to New York." Larry Norton was a family friend and the brilliant head of breast cancer oncology at Memorial Sloan-Kettering Cancer Center. Within two days I'd packed up, moved out of my L.A. house, and was on the red-eye flight to Kennedy.

It seemed like things were coming full circle. Quincy was back in my life, being helpful and compassionate, and using his resources and unfailing intuition to get me to the right people. Dr. Norton immediately responded by making sure I received the best medical attention available. For the week before the surgery, I sat with my feelings, remembering that my dad had colon cancer when he was in his late sixties and had fully recovered.

On some very deep level, I had been in denial about my health. Why had it taken so many years to consent to getting this test done? Sometimes a friend or a physician would recommend it, but no one really pressed the issue. Yearly physical checkups were always kind of erratic for me and when I did have them, I always seemed to get an A plus. Like my dad, my attitude about health was positive. I just wasn't in the habit of going into doctor's offices unless I was feeling sick. Now I knew my life was at stake because I had avoided it. I consciously tried to keep my fears and regrets about how negligent I had been to a minimum, trusting it was in God's hands. I knew the old Peggy would have kept this crisis to herself, so my decision to share my situation with the people I loved was a way of opening me up to their love and blessings, which were now my biggest comfort.

A close friend was there with me for every test, picking me up and taking me to each appointment, checking on me several times a day. He put his job on hold, telling the people in his office something important had come up that he needed to take care of. He became my strong and gentle warrior. I began to rely on his strength and generosity.

My GI doctor at Sloan-Kettering was stoic and supremely confident but with a brusque New York manner. I felt vulnerable and almost ashamed of my condition and was hesitant to ask someone that seemingly unsympathetic all the questions that spun through my mind. The ones I was able to get out he answered thoroughly but with professional detachment. He scheduled a colonoscopy to identify the tumor, determine how large it was, and whether it had proliferated on the wall of the colon.

The morning of the procedure, I was wheeled into an operating room in which the walls were green and the lights hung low and bright over the operating table. In Los Angeles, I had been an outpatient in a small doctor's office. I never saw the inside of the procedure room. I was medicated in a comfortable chair and slipped away thinking how routine and safe it was all going to be. Now, two weeks later, I was lying alone on a gurney in a green cap and a green gown. The anesthesiologist began prepping me, strapping me in as the nurses gathered the instruments and laid them out on a tray one by one. I looked up at the ceiling and started crying. Silent tears dripped down my cheeks. My stoic detached GI doctor drifted over to me and took my hand in his.

"What's wrong?" he asked, looking deep into my eyes. He said it so earnestly that it made me laugh. In answer to his question I could have recited a litany of everything that had gone wrong for me in the last two weeks, but instead I squeezed his hand and went off to sleep knowing that my "New York" doctor cared.

On April 8, I went in to have the tumor removed. "I'm going to heaven now," I whispered to my doctor moments before I went under. "Just make sure I come back." I knew my subtle body would lift away from my physical self and I would hover somewhere close so I could see my parents. Strange as it may seem, I knew they would come and guide me through the surgery. Being overjoyed to have them that close, I thought I might get so intoxicated with this reunion that I wouldn't want to return. But I did, and I came back to earth not with a thud but with the realization that I had an uphill battle of will and the faith to get through the recovery.

I underwent chemotherapy to make sure nothing would come back—

not easy but not horrendous, either. My body is surprisingly strong and resilient, and I have God to thank for that. Support for me has been on-going and filled with prayers and blessings from friends, my ex-husband, my children, my doctors, the Siddha Yoga community, and, of course, my teacher Gurumayi Chidvilasananda—a twenty-year student/teacher relationship that has never failed me. Each one of my relationships—whether constructive or painful—has served what I consider a divine purpose: Essentially to know that life is worth living and I'm here to tell you . . . that it is.

82.

Thanksgiving

usually go on long walks as dusk is setting in. This is my favorite time, when the days' thoughts transform themselves into blue shadows. I think about love in all its forms. Love of a man, my children my teacher. Loving myself. There is an element of longing that accompanies me on these walks, a powerful emotion I have felt since I was a child. It's still there. They say longing brings you closer to God and yourself, and for me, it has.

Kidada and Rashida have matured into women whom I respect and admire. They are without a doubt my best friends. They are also grounded and polite and I am in awe of their great beauty—within and without—and giving hearts. Each Thanksgiving and Christmas, the Quincy Jones family comes together. There are his seven children, six grandchildren, a brother, sisters, cousins, plus two ex-wives, one long-time companion, and a handful of special friends. Here in his home there is great cause for celebration. Kidada's husband of two years, Jeffrey, is a gentle being and a good man. He is the best addition I've ever had to my family, as is my brother Bob's wife, Marie. Kenya, Quincy's youngest daughter at twelve years old, is a new light on the family horizon. Self-contained, smart, and generous, she is cherished. On these holidays, we eat, drink, reminisce, and always acknowledge with humor and love how we've all played a part in each other's lives. Snoopy, his wife, two children, and Tina stay close and connected. They will always be special to me. Quincy has reentered my life with his unique soulful way of loving. And there is forgiveness all the way around.

Acknowledgments

To all those with their prayers who have lovingly helped to see me through the last year, I thank you with all my heart: Gurumayi Chidvilasananda, Kidada and Jeffrey Nash, Rashida Leah Jones, Quincy Jones, David and Coco Dalton, Elizabeth Beier and all the staff at St. Martin's Press, Bob and Marie Lipton, Jack C., Dr. Larry Norton, Dr. Eileen O'Reilly, Thea Minello, Dr. Douglas Wong, Dr. Robert Kurtz, Ro Coppala, the staff at Memorial Sloan-Kettering, Lulu, Sasha Premoli, Peter and Uma Hayes, Courtney Ross Holdtz and Nicole Ross, Sarah Smith, Wendy Schecter, Susan Sundholm, Galt Neiderhoffer, Magnolia, Mimi Ercil, Nadia Dajani, Chelsea Field, Scott Bakula, Will and Owen Bakula, "Doc," Ganapati Buga, Panna Hamilton, Jennifer Lipton, Shad, Justine and Bailey Copus, Dr. Leslie Cooper, Ph.D., Sharon Osbourn, Julia Carroll, Janet Humphrey, Aira Mohlmann, Deanna Kleinman, Dr. Saram Khalsa, Don and Kate Bruckner, Allan Warnick and Rex Arrasmith, Billy and Chynna Baldwin, Sandy Jolley, Michael Karlin, Louise C., Aracelly, Ana, Amparo, Luiz, Sally Hershberger, Corey Morris, Marie, Nora Ephron and Nick Pileggi, David Vigliano, Gita Breslin, Donna Bagdesarian, Evelyn Ostin, Joyce Ostin, Nicole and Bernie Katz, Diane Schumacher, Sylvie, Dr. Woodson Merrill, Charm Carlin, Janet Katzen, Belle Zwerling, Bernie Carneol, Ann Jones, Diane Haughton, David, Michael, Nick and Alan, Eric Stamp, Maury De Mauro, Gina Barone, Lynn Von Kersting, Ricky and India Irving, and Sante D'Orazio.